JAWS UNMADE

THE LOST SEQUELS, PREQUELS, REMAKES, AND RIP-OFFS

JAWS UNMADE
THE LOST SEQUELS, PREQUELS, REMAKES, AND RIP-OFFS

By John LeMay
with an essay by
Justin Mullis

BICEP BOOKS

BICEP BOOKS

ISBN- 9798651483501

For Mike Grant,
who loves *Jaws: The Revenge* most of all...

Early poster concept by Roger Kastel.

CONTENTS

Postscript

ACKNOWLEDGMENTS

Thank you first to Michael A. Smith, one of the authors of *Jaws 2: The Making of a Hollywood Sequel*, who was kind enough to assist me with this project. Thank you to actor Billy Van Zandt (Bob in *Jaws 2*) for actually taking the time to discuss his famous death scene with me. Thank you, Joey Palinkas, who accidentally lead me to discover a lost project I hadn't found yet. Thank you, Justin Mullis, for another spectacular essay. And, thank you Kyle Byrd for assisting me with my research and helping me to find some great information!

An early version of the famous *Jaws* poster.

PREFACE

This tome was spawned from a little book I did called *Kong Unmade: The Lost Films of Skull Island*, itself inspired by a similar, earlier book on lost Japanese monster movies. In writing the Japanese monsters book, I did a chapter on an unmade rematch between Kong and Godzilla, which led to an entire book on the big ape. Similarly, while working on *Kong Unmade*, I discovered that in the late 1970s, Dino De Laurentiis wanted to produce a joint sequel to his remake of *King Kong* (1976) and *Orca* (1977). Naturally, it was to be called *King Kong vs. Orca*. Shortly after, I discovered the script for an unproduced *Jaws* sequel, in actuality a spoof, entitled *Jaws 3, People 0*.

For a split second I considered another book on all the unmade sequels and "rip-offs" descended from 1975's *Jaws*. But surely there wasn't enough material for that alone? Or was there? What pushed me over the edge, as usual, was my friend Kyle Byrd who began sharing information with me on various lost projects. My thought process then turned to, "Well, maybe there's enough for a short book?" Now, several hundred pages later, it's no longer what I would call a short book. But, in all fairness, as I did on *Kong Unmade*, I cheated a bit.

To circle back to Kong for a bit, the giant shark (sometimes nicknamed "Jaws") and the giant ape have a lot in common. Naturally, they both had several sequels and also famous rides at Universal Studios, but I'm talking something deeper. The fact of the matter is that most of their fans truly only love one of their movies (the originals in both cases), even though both spawned several films (Kong has been in 9 licensed flicks, while the *Jaws* shark has been in four, plus countless rip-offs like *Cruel Jaws*). Rip-offs are something else that the two franchises have in common. The 1976 Kong remake (itself partially encouraged by the success of *Jaws*) had *A*P*E*, *Queen Kong*, and *Mighty Peking Man* to name a few, while *Jaws* had many more, starting with *Grizzly*. That film was essentially *Jaws* but with a Grizzly bear, though the other rip-offs would usually stick to the water.

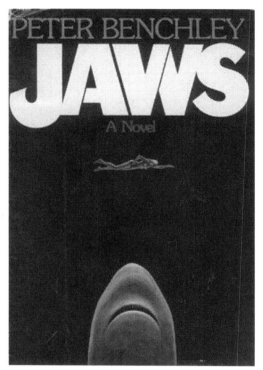

Cover for the original novel by Peter Benchley.

And, just as the Kong imitators were an oft neglected aspect of the big ape's history, so too have the *Jaws* rip-offs been left out in the cold when it comes to serious coverage. So, just as the focus in *Kong Unmade* was lost/unproduced films with detours to knockoffs like *Konga*, it is the same with this book, which will cover quite a few movies that are in no way shape or form "lost." You can find many of them on YouTube or Amazon Prime with a few clicks of your keyboard. But, these rip-offs are an important facet of the history of *Jaws*. Furthermore, these rip-offs occasionally had their own alternate, unproduced versions and unproduced sequels of their own, such as the ludicrous sounding *King Kong vs. Orca*.

Up From the Depths, a Roger Corman produced *Jaws* rip-off, had a similar development to *Jaws 2* and *Jaws 3-D*. Most of the more knowledgeable Jaws fans will remember that *Jaws 2* began shooting with a different director, cast, and shooting script before it was revised. *Jaws 3-D* started as a comedy. While *Up From the Depths* is not a lost film, like *Jaws 2*, there is a lost version of said film that was shot as a comedy spoof like *Jaws 3, People 0*. *Up From the Depths* was shot in the Philippines with a goofy shark monster prop—goofy on purpose just to be clear. Roger Corman disliked the spoof angle, and so had new effects footage shot with a scarier—but still unintentionally goofy—shark monster. So while the film did see release, we will probably never see the alternate comedy version of the film, which initially had a completely different monster on the loose.

Then there are movies that were left uncompleted like *Aatank,* a Bollywood version of *Jaws* that began shooting in the 1980s. Production ceased on the film, and it wasn't completed until the mid-1990s. So while it is no longer a lost film, at one point, it was. The same is now true of a sequel to *Grizzly*, entitled *Grizzly II: The Predator*. I am beyond thrilled to say that after sitting incomplete since the 1980s, it has finally been finished as *Grizzly II: Revenge*.

I suppose the point of this rambling introduction is to say that I hang pretty loose with the terms "unmade" and "lost." And while unproduced or alternate versions of existing movies are the focal point of this book, I hope that you will also appreciate the heretofore neglected histories of many of the red-headed step- children of the *Jaws* lineage, like *Tintorera*, *Tentacles*, and self-proclaimed sequels like *Cruel Jaws*.[1]

I'd also like to state that this book is not about the making of any of the *Jaws* films in and of themselves. Where *Jaws* movies are concerned, this book predominantly covers how they developed on paper, and how mistakes and happy accidents during filming changed the course of the plot at times. So if it seems as though I've left something out in regards to the making of the films, that's not what this book is about. And besides, if you're reading this book, chances are you've already read a book about the making of *Jaws* and its sequels. My goal here is to illuminate lesser-

---

[1] On that note, I'm only covering the pre-2000 era *Jaws* inspired films, there are simply too many post-2000 era CGI shark movies to cover.

known details regarding the plot and development. If you are interested in every production aspect of the films I heartily recommend *The Jaws Log* books for the first and second film, and other superb titles like *Joe Alves: Designing Jaws*; *Jaws 2: The Making of a Hollywood Sequel* and *Just When You Thought It Was Safe: A Jaws Companion.*

Whatever your primary interests may be, I hope you enjoy taking a dive with me into the depths of the history of *Jaws*, its sequels, prequels, rip-offs, and remakes, made and unmade alike...

John LeMay
Summer 2020

STILLNESS IN THE WATER
The Original JAWS

Release Date: June 20, 1975

Alternate Titles: *Stillness in the Water* (Working Title) *The Shark* (Italy) *Jaws: Teeth of the Sea* (Turkey) *The White Shark* (Germany)

Directed by: Steven Spielberg **Special Effects by:** Robert A. Mattey **Screenplay by:** Peter Benchley, Howard Sackler & Carl Gottlieb **Music by:** John Williams **Cast:** Roy Scheider (Chief Martin Brody) Richard Dreyfuss (Matt Hooper) Robert Shaw (Quint) Lorraine Gary (Ellen Brody) Murray Hamilton (Mayor Larry Vaughn) Jeffrey Kramer (Deputy Jeff Hendricks)

Panavision, Technicolor, 124 Minutes

SYNOPSIS On the cusp of the summer swimming season, Amity Island is geared up for their most important time of year. The chief of police, Martin Brody, is troubled over several deaths in the water. Eventually, it is confirmed that a shark is to blame. When hunters kill a shark, the town rejoices and moves on, while Brody knows that they got the wrong shark thanks to Matt Hooper, an ichthyologist. Brody tries to tell the mayor and the city government about this, but they brush his fears under the rug, refusing to close the beaches because they can't afford to. When the beaches open, there is a horrific shark attack, and Brody is proven right. Brody must then set sail with Hooper and a hardened fisherman known only as Quint to kill the shark...

COMMENTARY Picture this. You're sitting in an air-conditioned theater in the hot summer months of 1975. You're watching three men on a boat facedown a gigantic shark. Charlton Heston stars as Chief Brody, who must work with Hooper, played by Jeff Bridges, who had previously been having an affair with his wife. With them is the captain of the boat, Quint, played by tough guy Lee Marvin. Ultimately, Hooper and Quint are killed by the shark. In the film's final moments, the shark launches itself onto the boat staring Brody dead in the eye. And then... it dies in front of him due to wounds inflicted earlier by Quint. No exploding shark. Nothing. And by the way, the movie isn't called *Jaws*. It's known as *Stillness in the Water*.

Now, to be fair, what you read above was a pastiche. There was never a draft of the script where all of that was set to happen with those particular actors playing the characters (but they were all considered at one point). And, though Brody isn't terribly heroic in the original *Jaws* novel by Peter Benchley, which the first script draft allegedly followed closely, there's no way a movie starring Charlton Heston would've ended with him NOT killing the shark. Movies go through a long, arduous development process which is determined not only by the screenwriter and the director, but also the actors playing the characters. As it was, *Jaws* could have turned out very differently from the film we know and love.

Though I have not been able to find copies of Benchley's three script drafts, many sources concur that his first draft was very similar to his novel. And his novel is quite different from the movie. Therefore, a discussion of the book is in order.

What would eventually become *Jaws* began gestating in the mind of Peter Benchley all the way back in 1965, when a 17-foot Great White was caught near Montauk Island, New York. This gave Benchley the idea of a Great

White that begins stalking the waters of a small coastal town and won't go away. The shark then begins to affect the town's economy due to tourism. Benchley didn't take the idea too seriously until he was having lunch with an editor from Doubleday, Thomas Congdon. They had been talking about non-fiction projects until Benchley's fictional shark story came up, which Congdon took to immediately.

As legend has it, Congdon asked Benchley to begin writing, but only liked the opening pages where the shark attacks the swimmer. Benchley feared he was taking the novel too seriously, and so began to angle it towards being a semi-spoof. Congdon disliked this even more and encouraged Benchley to keep it serious. Eventually, the author created a draft of the novel that Congdon liked, and after a few revisions, it was ready for publication.

The last thing decided upon was the book's title. *Stillness in the Water* had been Benchley's original proposed title, along with the more commercial sounding *Leviathan Rising* and *The Jaws of Death*. Benchley and Congdon both liked the aspect of the word "jaws" being in the title, so they decided to call it just that: *Jaws*.

The book was a great success and was one of the most read books of the summer of 1974. However, *Jaws* had been slated for a silver screen adaptation before that. Producers Richard Zanuck and David Brown had read the galleys of *Jaws* before it was published, as it was common practice for publishers to send movie producers novels before they were released. In this case, it was David Brown's wife who saw the book and suggested that he read it.[2] Brown talked with Zanuck, who had also read the book, and the duo knew it would make for an exciting picture and bought the film rights.

Zanuck offered Benchley the chance to write the screenplay because Hollywood was on the verge of a writer's strike. It was Zanuck who instructed Benchley to lose the backstories that didn't relate much to the

---

[2] Brown's wife worked at a magazine where an excerpt of *Jaws* was going to be printed.

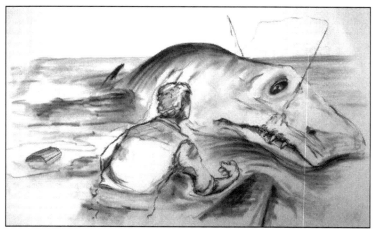

Joe Alves' production sketch based on the book's climax.
© 1975 Universal Pictures

shark, like the affair and the mob connections. "I want this to be an A to Z adventure story, a straight line from beginning to end," Zanuck told Benchley.[3] However, it's unknown just when this advice was offered to Benchley. Since reports claim that the first draft was too close to the novel, presumably Zanuck told Benchley to drop the subplots at the onset of the second draft.

Whatever the case, as stated earlier, there are some notable differences between the movie and the book. Chief among them is an affair between Hooper and Ellen Brody! To delve a little deeper into the differences, Benchley's visualization of Brody is different from Roy Scheider's version of the character as he is a weak-willed, balding, middle-aged man. The fact that Brody is blue-collar while Ellen is from a white-collar family is another backstory within the book that is non-existent in the movie. Hooper is also less likable, and that's putting it mildly. In this version, he is a snobby "white collar" ichthyologist. As it turns out, he and Ellen used to run in the same social circles, and she dated Hooper's brother. While Brody is distracted by the shark, Hooper and Ellen have an affair.[4]

---

[3] http://www.peterbenchley.com/articles/peter-benchley-the-father-jaws-and-other-tales-the-deep

[4] This is not so much as hinted at in the movie, and yet, the novelization for *Jaws: The Revenge* makes mention of Ellen and Hooper having an affair! But, the novels are decidedly their own continuity, even if they were based

Project Development:
STILLNESS IN THE WATER into JAWS

The other dark subplot revealed the reason why Mayor Vaughn was so determined to cover up the shark attack: the town owes money to the mob, and Vaughn is depending on summer tourist dollars to pay it back. It gets darker than that. One of the mob men pays Brody a visit when he makes too much noise about closing the beaches. As an intimidation ploy, the mob man kills the family cat in front of the youngest Brody boy, Sean.

The Ellen-Hooper affair subplot comes to a head just as Brody realizes he will need fisherman Quint and Hooper both to kill the shark. Brody even chokes Hooper out at one point. As a less sympathetic character, it should come as no surprise that Hooper dies in the end. Remember the shark cage scene in the film? As in the book, originally the shark was to break into the cage and eat Hooper until it was changed during shooting. In the book, the shark bites Hooper in half.[5]

The ending isn't too exciting for Brody either, and it is Quint who kills the shark. Specifically, Quint's fate seems to be modeled after Captain Ahab in *Moby Dick*. Quint has stabbed the shark multiple times but becomes entangled in ropes attached to the shark. Quint is then dragged under and drowned. In what turns out to be its death throes, the shark lunges onto the *Orca* to bite at Brody and collapses dead in front of him. In effect, Brody simply survives the encounter and isn't much of a hero.

One of the first directors considered for *Jaws* was Dick Richards, who, during his interview, kept referring to the shark as a whale! For this reason, Richards was let go, and eventually Zanuck and Brown decided to hire Steven Spielberg, who had shot *The Sugarland Express* (1974) with the producing duo.

Spielberg looked at Benchley's script and decided to write his own screenplay for *Jaws*, which Spielberg later

upon the films. In fact, the sequel novelizations were often based upon proto-drafts of the movie scripts.

[5] The original scripts for *Jaws 2* also featured a scene where a character got bitten in half, as well as a subplot where Amity owed money to the mob. This was because when writing *Jaws 2* Howard Sackler intentionally wanted to add in more elements from the novel that he missed the first time around.

SHARK BITES: *THE SUGARLAND EXPRESS*

IN *THE MAKING OF JAWS*, SPIELBERG MENTIONED WANTING TO GIVE A CAMEO TO TWO OF THE CHARACTERS FROM *THE SUGARLAND EXPRESS*. IN THAT FILM, AN ELDERLY COUPLE HAS THEIR CAR STOLEN. SPIELBERG WANTED TO SHOW THE COUPLE IN AMITY GOING FOR A SWIM. THIS WAS ANOTHER OF THE SCENES FROM HIS DISCARDED DRAFT OF THE SCREENPLAY.

described as an "exercise" in preparing for the film. In *The Making of Jaws* documentary, the director revealed that he used a few ideas from his script in the final film, but for the most part, the script was an alternate draft. Among the scenes unique to Spielberg's draft was an alternate introduction to Quint. In Spielberg's early version we would have found Quint in a theater laughing raucously at a screening of *Moby Dick* (1956). His laughter at the effects is so obnoxious that it drives the other patrons from the theater, and the idea was to end the shot on an exterior of the theater where Quint's laughter could still be heard outside. This scene also existed, I presume, to foreshadow what was still Quint's scripted death. Like Ahab, he would become entangled in the ropes attached to the shark and drown, while in the film he is eaten. The sequence was scrapped because Spielberg needed Gregory Peck's approval, and Peck so disliked his performance as Ahab that he wouldn't give Spielberg the rights.

Another scene Spielberg envisioned had the harbor master watching a movie in the foreground, while in the background, the shark swims into the harbor. To illustrate the shark's immense size, we would see a row of boats rising and falling as the shark swam beneath them. The harbormaster would then go outside, lean down close to the water, and empty his coffee pot into the ocean. The shark, unseen, would lunge out of the water just high enough to pull the harbor master into the depths. Spielberg says that this scene was replaced with the scene of the two fishermen trying to catch the shark with a pot roast later.

Speaking of that sequence, based on the comments of the final writer Carl Gottlieb, as well as storyboards, that scene went through quite a few changes too. According to Gottlieb in *The Making of Jaws*, originally one of the fishermen was to have their leg bitten off! The storyboards also paint a totally different picture of the scene. In the film, they try to catch the shark from the safety of a dock. But in the storyboards, they go out on a boat to do it. The shark surfaces in front of the boat and swallows the men whole!

Eventually, Spielberg suggested that playwright Howard Sackler take a stab at Benchley's most recent script. Because the script was basically already written, Sackler asked not to be credited for his revisions. However, it was Carl Gottlieb who turned in the true final draft, which was still being written during shooting it changed so often. From here, tracing the exact evolution of the *Jaws* scripts can be a bit difficult. What is known is that Spielberg added in the element of Brody being a tough New York cop who moves to an island and has a fear of the water. Spielberg knew this would help the audience empathize more with Brody.

Storyboards provide a wealth of information as to different iterations of various scenes. Storyboards have shown that the credits were supposed to display over a POV shot from within the shark's mouth, making the title *Jaws* literal in a visual sense. As in the book, rather than departing from a beachside party, Chrissy Watkins and her lover would emerge from a house on the beach. The man would pass out as Chrissy goes into the ocean to meet her deadly fate. As she does so, it appears that we see the trace of a shark fin. The storyboards imagined the death scene shot from above so that one would not only see Chrissy's naked body, but the shark opening its jaws beneath her. Chrissy would be pulled under and would then resurface, breasts notably visible. Though there is a hint of nudity in the final film, it's still pretty standard for a 'PG' film of the time. Had the film been shot in accordance with the storyboards, the nudity just might have earned it an 'R' rating.

Speaking of 'R' ratings, the shark's big reveal in the lagoon during the 4th of July celebration was originally much more horrific. The sequence, if you'll remember, has Mike Brody and his friends afloat in the lagoon trying to tie a knot. A man comes along to offer the boys some advice when the shark capsizes his boat. The man is pulled under, and we see his severed leg sink to the bottom of the lagoon. An alternate version was filmed where the stuntman was given a blood packet for his mouth. The shark grabs the man, and the man, in turn, grabs Mike![6] As he and Mike sail through the water, the man was to cough up blood on poor Mike, but Spielberg felt it was too much and decided on the version we see in the film.

There was also an alternate death for Alex Kintner. Storyboards showed a more ambitious but less effective scene. There was to be an overhead shot of the shark circling Kintner's raft below the waves. When the shark attacks, its head was to protrude from the water dramatically to eat the boy up. The scene was even shot this way, and photographs have surfaced to prove it (some sources state it's just test footage, though).

Actually, in storyboards, after Alex Kintner is eaten, another man is attacked shortly after and killed as well. And then another, and another. About four people are plucked under by the shark in this iteration.

Alternate version of the lagoon scene. © 1975 Universal Pictures

---

[6] In the script the man is more dignified. Mike reaches out to help him and the man tells him, "It's no good, I'm dead."

Nightmarish test footage from *Jaws*. © 1975 Universal Pictures

Later shooting scripts by Gottlieb only has Kintner getting eaten, but it's still a bit different. Not everyone notices the shark at first. All they know is they've just heard a loud splash. One boy thinks that another boy has splashed him, and so he begins splashing back. Eventually, they notice that the water is pink—they are splashing in watered down blood, which has saturated their hair and now runs down their bodies. About that time, some of the adults finally begin to notice the blood in the water, and the panic starts.

Joe Alves might've directed the shot after Spielberg had already left Martha's Vineyard. It's my assumption that Spielberg shot the scene when the shark wasn't working. Perhaps, when the shark was working, Alves was instructed to get a better take, wherein the mechanical shark, nicknamed Bruce, chomps down on a dummy of actor Jeffrey Voorhees. (An alternate, more likely story says this was unsatisfactory test footage shot early on). As to why it wasn't used, I would assume this was in keeping with not revealing the shark until the 4th of July scene. Other sources say that the shark

SHARK BITES: BEN GARDNER'S BOAT

ONE OF THE MORE ALTERED SCENES IN *JAWS* CONCERNED THE DISCOVERY OF BEN GARDNER'S BOAT. IN THE FINAL FILM, THE DEAD GARDNER'S HEAD POPPING OUT OF THE WRECKAGE PROVIDED THE MOVIE WITH ITS FIRST BIG SCARE. ORIGINALLY, THE SCENE TOOK PLACE DURING THE DAY, AND FEATURED ANOTHER CHARACTER, MEADOWS, ON THE BOAT. MEADOWS, BY THE WAY, WAS PLAYED BY SCREENWRITER HOWARD GOTTLIEB. IT WAS DECIDED THAT THE SCENE WOULD BE MORE EFFECTIVE AT NIGHT, AND SO WAS RESHOT (PARTIALLY IN EDITOR VERNA FIELD'S SWIMMING POOL!). ORIGINALLY, THE HEAD WAS SIMPLY DISCOVERED, BUT IN THE NEW VERSION IT POPPED OUT OF THE BOAT. SPIELBERG GOT HIS WISH AND AUDIENCES SCREAMED AT THE SIGHT OF IT.

was coming up too high out of the water, and looking at the photo, the shark does seem to be unusually high.

The script would also evolve due to some happy accidents that happened during filming—so much so that it would change the manner of death for Quint and Hooper's fate altogether. The famous USS Indianapolis speech by Quint was thought up at the last minute. It was a joint effort between Robert Shaw, Howard Sackler, and John Milius. Supposedly, the scene was thought up to give the crew something to shoot while more repairs were being made on the shark. If you'll remember, Quint recounts the horror of men being eaten alive. Quint then states that he'll never put on a lifejacket again. Or, in other words, he'd rather drown than be eaten. This implication changed Quint's death as it would be more tragic for him to be eaten—his greatest fear realized—than to be drowned.

Hooper's fate was changed for two reasons. One, Spielberg felt it was too much of a downer. And two, some unexpected footage was obtained by shark photographers Ron and Valerie Taylor. The duo was filming a live shark attacking a cage that was specially constructed to a smaller scale to give the real shark an illusion of size. The plan was for the shark to tear into a small dummy representing Hooper. However, the shark's head became trapped in the bars, and in its struggle to free itself, it broke the cage. The footage was spectacular, but there was one problem, the dummy was no longer in the cage. Therefore it was decided that

Hooper escapes the cage, and that way, the wonderful footage of the shark destroying the cage could also be used.

As stated earlier, before this, Hooper was to die in the jaws of the shark as he does in the book. Storyboards confirm this to be true. The shark grabs Hooper in his scuba gear underwater and brings him to the surface in his jaws for everyone to see. Things then proceed similarly to the finished film: Quint is eaten, and Brody shoves a diving tank into the monster's mouth. Brody then climbs the mast as the *Orca* sinks. Rather than rushing at him, the shark raises out of the water below Brody, giving him a very easy shot at the tank, which explodes.[7]

Benchley often said in interviews that he and Spielberg clashed over only one thing: the ending. Benchley knew that in real life an exploding scuba tank would not kill a Great White. "I don't care," Spielberg said. "If I've got the audience hooked for the first two hours, I can do anything I want in the last three minutes and they'll stick with me."[8]

Spielberg was right, and audiences were so enthralled by the movie that no one questioned the ending. Not only that, *Jaws* was such a big hit that it effectively birthed the summer blockbuster as we know it today. It also spawned a multitude of imitators...

SHARK BITES: *JAWS:* THE SERIES?

ACCORDING TO SOME DUBIOUS UNVERIFIED TRIVIA ON IMDB, BEFORE A MOVIE ADAPTATION, THERE WAS TALK OF MAKING *JAWS* INTO A TV SERIES! IF THIS IS EVEN REMOTELY TRUE, PERHAPS WHAT THEY REALLY MEANT TO SAY WAS A TV MOVIE OR MINI SERIES, AS IT'S HARD TO IMAGINE *JAWS* AS AN ONGOING TV SERIES. WHAT WAS THE SHARK GOING TO DO? EAT A NEW GUEST STAR EACH WEEK?

---

[7] Among the trivia listed on IMDB is an envisioned alternate ending where, after defeating the shark, Brody sees several more shark fins coming at him! The 1970s saw a trend of having downbeat endings where the hero is left to die, so this could have been considered, but I have seen no sources for this information outside of IMDB.

[8] http://www.peterbenchley.com/articles/peter-benchley-the-father-jaws-and-other-tales-the-deep

SPECIAL SECTION
CASTING JAWS

Jaws went through a litany of casting decisions, especially for the three main characters of Brody, Hooper, and Quint. Among the front runners for Brody was Charlton Heston. However, it was decided Heston had already been the hero of enough disaster movies like *Earthquake* (1974) and *Airport 1975* (1974). Spielberg felt that the audience would know that the shark didn't stand a chance against Heston. Zanuck and Brown also agreed that a megastar like Heston would distract from the shark. Other alternate choices for Brody included Gene Hackman and Robert Duval, who instead wanted to play Quint (but it was felt he was too young).

Peter Benchley had his own dream cast in mind in the form of Robert Redford, Paul Newman, and Steve McQueen. (It's unknown who he wanted to play who, but I would presume Newman as the oldest would've been Quint, McQueen would've been Brody, and Redford would've been Hooper).

Lee Marvin was Spielberg's first choice for Quint, and though I love Robert Shaw in the part, I have to admit Marvin would've been interesting. Marvin was appreciative of the offer but turned it down and stated that he'd prefer to go fishing! Next up, Sterling Hayden was considered, but he was in deep trouble at the moment with the IRS.

The highest amount of names were bandied for Hooper and included Kevin Kline, Jeff Bridges, Timothy Bottoms, Joel Grey, Jon Voight, and Jan-Michael Vincent.

Ellen Brody, the final piece of the casting puzzle, also had an interesting original choice. Richard Zanuck wanted his wife Linda Harrison to play Ellen. Harrison had been Charlton Heston's love interest, Nova, in *Planet of the Apes*. Had those two been cast, then it would have served as a reunion for the two actors.

Loch Ness Monster on the Loose
NESSIE

Developmental Period: 1975-1979
Intended Release Dates: Summer 1977; December 1978; Summer 1980

Screenplay by: Michael Carreras & Euan Lloyd (Storyline), John Starr (Treatment), Christopher Wicking (First Draft), Bryan Forbes (Third Draft) **Producers:** Michael Carreras, Euan Lloyd, David Frost, Tom Sachs & Tomoyuki Tanaka **Proposed Cast:** Roger Moore, Candice Bergin, Charlton Heston, Julie Christie, Richard Harris, Katherine Ross, Michael Caine, Shirley Lansing, Gregory Peck, Jean-Paul Belmondo, Ryan O'Neal, Richard Burton, Burt Lancaster, Michael York, Cliff Robertson, Richard Chamberlain, Michael Douglas, Ian Ogilvy, Ando, Rosalind Lloyd, Michael Billington **Proposed Creatures:** Nessie, giant shark, monster dog

SYNOPSIS A truck carrying a dangerous chemical compound called Mutane 4 loses a barrel of said compound in Loch Ness. The canister mutates the Loch Ness Monster, which begins growing at an alarming rate and leaves the loch. A series of disasters occur at sea as the monster commences a worldwide tour of destruction...

JAWS UNMADE

COMMENTARY When *Jaws* was released in 1975, it did irrevocable damage to the B-movie monsters of yore. Not coincidentally, even before *Jaws* was released, March of 1975 saw the final Toho Godzilla movie to be released in Japan for some time. *Terror of Mechagodzilla* was Toho's 15th Godzilla film and would be the last one until 1984, when the series was rebooted with an aim towards the realism of movies like *Jaws*.

Around the same time that Toho's flagship monster series was losing steam, Hammer's Frankenstein and Dracula movies were already dead. 1974 had seen the release of their last Gothic horror film, *The Seven Brothers Meet Dracula*. The film didn't even star Christopher Lee, and was a Kung-Fu themed co-production with the Shaw Brothers. In the story, Professor Van Helsing (Peter Cushing) travels to China to fight a vampire cult lead by Dracula, who grew tired of Transylvania and went to Chun King! The film wasn't a failure, but it wasn't a hit either.

Hammer and Toho both saw that the tides of cinema were changing, and it was at this time that the two formed an unlikely alliance. It started with Hammer producer Michael Carreras, who had envisioned a monster movie with Nessie around 1970. However, the studio was still obsessed with making Dracula and Frankenstein films. And, though they had found success with dinosaur pictures like *One Million Years B.C.* (1966) and *When Dinosaurs Ruled the Earth* (1970), stopmotion animation was too time-consuming so far as Hammer was concerned (did you notice the four-year gap between the two films?).

Seeing that Dracula was finally dead, and that *Jaws* was very much alive at the box office, Carreras felt that now was the time to press ahead with his Nessie idea. And it would not be a B-movie. Carreras found an unlikely investor in the form of David Frost (yes, the journalist who interviewed Nixon) and his Paradine Productions. To be more thorough, Frost already had his own Loch Ness Monster-type movie in the works called *Carnivore*, and so he agreed to team up with Hammer.

Jim Danforth animates a plesiosaurus for *When Dinosaurs Ruled the Earth*. Danforth was briefly considered to animate Nessie before Toho got involved.

Though initially he did consider the stopmotion route, Carreras began to think about another company that could handle the effects work.[9] Remembering Toho in Japan, who frequently brought dinosaur monsters to life, he met with Toho president Kukumaru Okuda in 1975. This early meeting date then makes *Nessie* the first unproduced *Jaws* rip-off (that we know of, at least).

A press conference announcing the production was held aboard the ship *Hispaniola* along the Thames on London's Victoria Embankment. "By Easter of next year, Nessie may have traveled through here as well," Frost announced at the conference.[10] At the same event, Michael Carreras announced that bringing Nessie to life would be Toho Studios of Japan, whom Carreras called "the finest experts in the world." He also said that they were currently building a quarter-scale $500,000 model of the monster based off of "existing evidence." Consulting on the project was famed British naturalist and Nessie expert Sir Peter Scott, who Carreras went so

---

[9] Carreras first approached Jim Danforth, but he was already busy on his own soon to be aborted project: Universal's *The Legend of King Kong*. Hammer had also considered Val Guest as a director. Had Guest and Danforth been selected, this would have meant *Nessie* was produced by the same team that made *When Dinosaurs Ruled the Earth*.

[10] Walker, "Nessie: The Loch Ness Monster Part Two," *Dark Terrors* #15.

far as to say was designing the Toho Nessie. Carreras's remarks were naturally more or less hogwash—several artists at Toho designed the monster, not Scott.

The film's proposed director, Bryan Forbes, took a swipe at *Jaws* during this time as well, stating, "Our film will make *Jaws* look like a toothpaste commercial." There were two scenes in *Nessie* that explicitly set out to reference *Jaws*. In the first, *Jaws* is playing on the television set in a luxury yacht that Nessie sinks in the Canary Islands. Two rich scuba divers are frolicking in the depths when they come across the monster. The storyboards for the scene are frightening and depict one of the divers caught in Nessie's jaws as the beast raises its head out of the water. Then there is a scene where a shark as big as the one from *Jaws* comes into contact with Nessie and swims away in fright.

To go more in-depth into the story, Nessie was to start off as a 40-foot Elasmosaurus in Loch Ness, which becomes mutated and enlarged to 200 feet thanks to the radioactive chemical Mutane 4. The story begins with a truck from the Department of Defense Nuclear Research Institute in Scotland, traveling up a winding road near Loch Ness. Due to carelessness, a chemical barrel containing Mutane 4 tumbles into the lake. At the lake at this time is a TV news crew from America, led by the arrogant Mark Stafford (hopefully to be played by Roger Moore),[11] trying to do a story on the legend of Loch Ness. Also, there are serious researchers Dr. White (who Gregory Peck was eyed for)[12] and his colleague Susan (prospectively Candice Bergin), reportedly one of the few sympathetic characters. Also lurking about is a character named Comfort, a scientist turned company man. Eventually, the character becomes an antagonist out to kill Nessie on behalf of the U.S. and British governments.

---

[11] The original lead for *Jaws*, Charlton Heston was also considered.

[12] Forbes had recently seen Moore together with Gregory Peck at a charity dinner in the U.S. and thought the two made a good pair for a disaster film and wanted them both. However, Carreras felt Moore was too light for the role due to his comical portrayals of 007. Furthermore, Moore's agent said the mega-star would require 1 million pounds and a percentage of the film's gross if he were to star.

***Nessie* concept poster by Hammer.** © 1976 Hammer

On a stormy night, a cabin is crushed by a huge creature that has crawled out of the loch. Soon after this, a series of disasters occur at sea: a huge monster attacks an oil rig in the North Sea east of Britain,[13] and a hovercraft sinks in the English Channel. Susan and Mark connect the dots between the creature that left the loch and the current disasters and deduct that it must be Nessie. They research the chemical Mutane 4 and learn that it acts as a steroid. A dog exposed to the chemical in an experiment doubled in size and became violent. Now Susan knows that not only is Nessie growing, but it is now uncharacteristically violent.

Mark and Susan go to ask a famous marine explorer/hunter, Channon, for help in tracking the monster and he agrees. It is thought that Richard Harris of *Orca* (1977) would play this part, and it seems that the character was *Nessie's* equivalent of Quint from *Jaws*.

Having grown to 200 feet, Nessie next sinks a U.S. nuclear submarine near Capetown. Susan pitches an idea to capture the monster in the Sunda Strait luring Nessie with electric stimulus. They would then shoot the beast with a massive tranquilizer and throw a huge net on it. At this point, Channon becomes something of

---

[13] It should be noted that John Sayles' *Sea Dragon of Loch Ness* script also features an attack on a North Sea oil rig.

***Nessie* art by Lee Powers based upon the film's design.**

a double-edged sword as he works to kill Nessie instead of capture her. As the plan goes forth, a tuna net decapitates Channon, the plan fails, and Nessie continues on its way, swimming through some underwater ruins. Nessie was to have gazed at an ancient painting of herself present in the ruins of an underwater city—reinforcing her nature as a rare, mystical beast. Script notes indicate the music was to be underlined with tragedy here, and from this point forwards, the audience sympathy was to be directed towards Nessie à la King Kong.

The monster is on a course for Hong Kong, and Comfort and the military become determined to stop her from landing. An attack is launched on Nessie by the military (and this includes frogmen) in Hong Kong harbor. In the scuffle, an oil tanker is damaged, causing a huge oil spill. The U.S. Air Force takes note of the spill (storyboards show jet fighters in the air) and lights it on fire. The spill becomes inflamed, and as Nessie tragically burns to death, Mark begins a live broadcast where he and Susan would berate the U.S. and British governments and expose the cover-up of Mutane 4.

Making the story a globetrotting affair was supposedly an idea of Toho's. Allegedly an early draft of the script kept the story confined to Scotland, and they suggested Nessie should wreak havoc across Earth's oceans. The ending, where Nessie tragically burned to death, was meant to emulate the ending of Toho's *Rodan* (1956). In that film, a mated pair of monster pterodactyls emerge from a Kyushu mine and are burnt to death in a manmade volcanic eruption. The very last shot of *Nessie* was to be of an egg hatching in the loch—the idea of effects director Teruyoshi Nakano. This may have also come from some Toho higher-ups. Part of the deal with Hammer was that Toho had international rights to their iteration of the Nessie character, meaning they could produce a sequel independent of Hammer if they so desired (*Nessie vs. Godzilla* anyone?).

Toho had since given up on Godzilla for disaster movies, called "Panic Films" in Japan. They had found huge success in the form of *Submersion of Japan* in 1973, which got a theatrical release in the U.S. in 1975 as *Tidal Wave*. Though critics like Roger Ebert found the film guilty by association with the child-friendly Godzilla films, *Submersion of Japan* was a skillfully crafted disaster film that was every bit as good as its American counterparts, which it predated. Around the time that negotiations began on *Nessie*, Toho had just finished another disaster film called *Conflagration*. In that film, terrorists hijack an oil tanker and demand that Tokyo blow up their own Kitayama Oil Fields. If they don't comply, the terrorists will ram the tanker into the oil fields themselves. To dupe the terrorists, special effects technicians are hired to create a miniature of the oil fields and blow them up during a live broadcast meant to fool the terrorists.

Bryan Forbes had seen the sequence and thought it was great. He sent it to Columbia, currently a major backer in the production, as an example of Nakano's work. Columbia was not impressed, but they were also unaware of the context of the scene they were watching. Unbeknownst to them, Nakano had intentionally made some of the miniatures look fake, as they were meant to represent a fake effects scene within a movie. In addition to Columbia's lack of faith in the effects, there were also problems in the scripting department.

Forbes, who had directed *The Slipper and the Rose* (1976) for Paradine, had been brought in to rework the script originally written by Christopher Wicking. He did so under the stipulation that he also be allowed to direct the film. For $10,000 a week for four weeks, Forbes revised the story through three new drafts. Forbes finished work on August 10, 1976, and Carreras then took back the script and secretly reintegrated ideas he fancied from Wicking's version that Forbes had removed. Forbes was very unhappy when he read the revised 135-page script, which was credited to him, and expressed this to Carreras in a letter. Mainly, Forbes was irritated by dull characterization of the leads, as well as having too many disaster movie clichés. Forbes also hated "the more commercial aspect" of the project. According to some sources Forbes left the project after this and was tentatively to be replaced by *Orca* (1977) director Michael Anderson.

And then there were the increasing budget problems. Initially, the budget was set at $4 million but eventually swelled to $7 million. In *A History of Horrors: The Rise and Fall of the House of Hammer* Tom Sachs is quoted as saying, "Paradine had a lot of 'clout' and they managed to come up with quite a bit of cash to get it moving. The problem was that the script wasn't good enough to raise the rest of the cash, and all sorts of people had a go at rewriting it."[14]

Toho, whose job it was to storyboard the project, was also becoming frustrated with the ever-changing script. Reportedly, the studio had also constructed a half-a-million-dollar scale head prop of Nessie! However, this is likely untrue. If Toho had constructed such a pricey prop, photos of it would have surfaced. Toho also would have likely found a way to use the prop in another production to recoup their investment. What is known is that Toho did construct a Nessie maquette. Photos exist of the model, and they are dated July 20, 1976.

At one point, the plan was to start shooting in October of 1976 and finish by January of 1977. The film would then hopefully be out for the summer of 1977. Then came the negative critical reaction to Dino De Laurentiis' *King Kong* remake, released in December of 1976. This gave some of the backers cold feet, which delayed the production start to May of 1977. Then David Begelman, the head of Columbia, was suspended under the charge of financial malpractice, and Columbia dropped the *Nessie* project. Carreras and his group

---

[14] Meikle, *A History of Horrors: The Rise and Fall of the House of Hammer*, pp.221.

would have to seek their financing elsewhere. Adding to their troubles, Twentieth Century Fox soon balked at Hammer's current title, *The Loch Ness Monster*, claiming they had a film in production by that same name! In all likelihood, Twentieth Century Fox too was trying to jump on the *Jaws* bandwagon to produce an aquatic horror thriller. Reportedly not long after this, Toho also became tired of the constant stop and go game and withdrew from the project.

Michael Carreras (left) looks at the script with Christopher Wicking (right).

In an act of desperation, Hammer producer Tom Sachs tweaked the script (cut down to 120 pages with fewer action and effects scenes), now renamed *Nessie: The Loch Ness Monster*, to include possibilities for marketing tie-ins. The script tweaking didn't stop there, and further contributing to different draft versions were Scott Finch, Mort Fine, and Gerald Di Pego from late 1977 into early 1978.[15] Not helping matters was the fact that Anderson was poised to direct with *Orca* star Richard Harris in one of the lead roles. As *Orca* was not

---

[15] Walker, "Nessie: The Loch Ness Monster Part Two," *Dark Terrors* #15.

a big hit at the time, there was a fear that reteaming the men for *Nessie* would be another strike against the film.

By March of 1978, the project was dead when David Frost could see no "light at the end of the tunnel" for the film, then budgeted at $10 million, and liquidated Paradine Productions, Ltd. Carreras and Lloyd were removed from the Hammer board in late April of 1979, yet the duo still tried to find investors for their film, now simply called *Nessie*. Things seemed to be looking up for the production as Carreras made efforts to book the Pinewood 007 stage, and had even secured Katherine Ross as a lead with a co-producing sponsor in the form of Robert Stigwood. It was all too little too late though, Stigwood eventually lost interest, and this time, *Nessie* had finally sunk for good.

Though *Nessie* probably could have been a moderate hit, it was not likely to eclipse *Jaws* as the producers touted. Furthermore, the jabs the prospective film took at *Jaws* would have probably proved embarrassing in hindsight.

On one final note, Nessie did see the light of day in a roundabout way. In 1987, Nessie's proposed effects director Teruyoshi Nakano was poised for retirement. His last film was to be an adaptation of the Japanese folktale *The Bamboo Cutter's Story*. The film adaptation was called *Princess from the Moon* and called for a scene featuring a dragon attacking a sailing ship at sea. Nakano decided to dig up his old Nessie design from ten years ago—not out of laziness; he simply wanted to see the monster realized. And so the "dragon" looks precisely like an Elasmosaurus with humps on its back. In fact, if one compares it to the Toho maquette from the Seventies, this confirms that *Princess from the Moon* does use the *Nessie* design.

JAWS: THE PREQUEL
"Before you knew that it wasn't safe to go in the water..."

Developmental Period: 1975/1977

Idea by: Howard Sackler **Proposed Cast/Characters:** Quint **Proposed Creatures:** Multiple sharks

SYNOPSIS Based on a real-life event, the USS Indianapolis has just successfully delivered materials necessary for the atomic bomb on Tinian Island in the Pacific. They are blasted by torpedoes from a Japanese submarine, and hundreds of men become marooned in the water. A terrifying ordeal occurs where sharks begin picking the survivors off. One of the only survivors is a man named Quint...

COMMENTARY When the first rumblings of a *Jaws* sequel began, an unimaginative member of the public asked how Universal could make a sequel if the shark had been blown up. Producer David Brown had a simple but intelligent reply: "There *are* other Great Whites. They travel alone."[16] This problem had been faced by

---

[16] Loynd, *The Jaws 2 Log*, pp.20.

moviemakers and their monsters before. While creatures like Dracula and Frankenstein were resurrected via supernatural means, when it came to other movie monsters like King Kong and Godzilla, for movie #2 the producers simply created a monster of the same species to take their place. It would be the same here in the form of another shark. The real question was, when and where would it attack next?

The project began gestating before the original *Jaws* had even left theaters (though it had by this time grossed $75 million so far). The first problem faced by the producers was that Peter Benchley had never written a *Jaws 2*—and nor were they going to wait on him to do so.[17] The second problem faced by the producers was the fact that Spielberg didn't want to return, either, due to the harsh filming conditions of the first film.

The first writer that Zanuck and Brown called, Carl Gottlieb, turned the project down. The duo then decided to contact Howard Sackler, who had done an uncredited rewrite on *Jaws*. The duo dialed up Sackler, who was working on a play all the way over in Spain. When they asked him if he would be willing to do a sequel, he first asked the producing duo what they wanted it to be. As the pair had no firm concepts yet, the simple answer was, "Anything you want to write about sharks."

Sackler said yes and may have taken the duo's words to heart more than they anticipated. Rather than a sequel where a new shark turns up, Sackler pitched to them what he called a "pre-sequel"—the term prequel had yet to be invented—focusing on shark hunter Quint. Specifically, the idea was based upon Quint's now-famous monologue in *Jaws* recounting the horrors of the USS Indianapolis when it sunk during WWII. In the words of *The Jaws 2 Log*, "The story would open with the men embarking on the ship and carry through to the bomb that sank it and the mind-numbing finale..."[18] The "mind-numbing finale," of course, was the brutal shark attacks that occurred as the men awaited rescue while stranded in the waters of the Pacific.

---

[17] Benchley was asked for ideas still, of course, just not to the extent that they wanted him to write a whole script or novel for the project.
[18] Loynd, *Jaws 2 Log*, pp.25.

The prequel concept was sunk within one hour of having been pitched to Zanuck and Brown back in 1975. It wasn't the producing duo who shot it down—they liked it—it was MCA President Sid Sheinberg.

"That's a different kind of shirt than we want to wear," Sheinberg said.

"What's the shirt to be, Mr. Sheinberg?" asked Sackler.

Sheinberg's reply was, "The shirt we're already wearing: Amity."[19]

And with that, it was clear that Sheinberg wanted a more traditional sequel, which Sackler relented to and agreed to work on.

The USS Indianapolis c. July 10, 1945.

But that wasn't the end of the story. Sackler's original idea was actually revived after *Jaws 2* had started filming. When the original director, John Hancock, was fired, the producers asked Joe Alves to approach Spielberg again.

He did, and despite having turned it down earlier, Spielberg wanted to help... under certain conditions. Spielberg told the producers that he would only come back to do "Jaws 2" if it was the USS Indianapolis

---

[19] Ibid.

prequel idea.[20] Alves also mentioned that Spielberg wanted $1 million and 10% of the gross. But, unfortunately for *Jaws* fans, Universal wasn't warm to paying Spielberg that much or producing a prequel set during WWII. That, and production on the sequel would have to be pushed back to the spring of 1978. Universal had already slated the picture for the summer of 1978, so that simply wouldn't work.

Because of this, some have mistakenly thought that Spielberg, not Sackler, came up with the idea. In *Just When You Thought It Was Safe*, Jeannot Szwarc (who replaced Hancock as director on *Jaws 2*) is quoted as saying, "That story about Quint's time on the ship was something Spielberg proposed. Steven Spielberg said he would do it if they would wait until after he finished *Close Encounters of the Third Kind*, but they couldn't do that, because they had a solid release date set."[21]

But, how would Sackler's proposed "pre-sequel" have turned out, especially if it was directed by Spielberg? In addition to being a shark movie, it would've also been a WWII feature that could have chronicled one of the greatest naval disasters of all time.[22] In the summer of 1945, the USS Indianapolis had been on a mission to deliver uranium to Tinian Island in the Western Pacific. The uranium was for the atomic bomb that was soon to be dropped on Hiroshima. After successfully completing their mission, on July 30, the Indianapolis was struck by two torpedoes fired from a Japanese submarine. In a matter of only twelve minutes the ship rolled over and the stern rose into the air. 300 of the 1,195 crewmen aboard went down with the ship... the rest would die later.

It was a full three and a half days later by the time that rescue operations found the site of the accident. By that time, around a hundred more men had perished due to the elements and shark attacks. In the words of Quint in *Jaws*, "You know by the end of that first dawn, lost a hundred men. I don't know how many sharks

---

[20] That said, Spielberg is also quoted as saying that he tried to write several new stories featuring Brody and Quint.

[21] Jankiewicz, *Just When You Thought It Was Safe*, pp.185.

[22] Spielberg was interested in WWII pictures as evidenced by his feature *1941*.

there were, maybe a thousand. I do know how many men, they averaged six an hour... I'll never put on a lifejacket again."

In truth, the more commercial *Jaws 2* was probably what audiences really wanted. Had the USS Indianapolis story been told, chances are it would've been a success but probably not to the extent that the crazy "shark vs. teenagers and a helicopter" plot of *Jaws 2* was. The Indianapolis story may have also ended any further *Jaws* sequels.

Though it was never made as a *Jaws* prequel, the harrowing story of the USS Indianapolis was told in other films. Stacey Keach led a TV movie on the subject called *The Mission of the Shark: The Saga of the U.S.S. Indianapolis* in 1991. In 2007, the Discovery Channel produced "Ocean of Fear," a documentary on the incident, as part of their "Shark Week." More recently, in 2016, Nicholas Cage led a big-screen adaptation of the book *In Harm's Way: The Sinking Of The USS Indianapolis and the Extraordinary Story of Its Survivors* by Doug Stanton entitled *USS Indianapolis: Men of Courage.*

JAWS II: "Tentacles"

Developmental Period: 1976

Idea by: Arthur C. Clarke **Proposed Creatures:** Giant Squid, Giant Shark (rumor), Alien Orb (rumor)

SYNOPSIS A giant squid attacks an oil rig, and an alien probe controls a shark... maybe?

COMMENTARY: After the massive success of *Jaws*, many people wanted in on the sequel—except for Spielberg of course, but we've already talked about that. Naturally, Peter Benchley was asked for a concept. His idea: a prehistoric Megalodon shark turns up in Amity (which is actually just the concept for his novel if one is familiar with it). Though I personally find this idea quite exciting, as do other fans, Richard Zanuck and David Brown did not. That, or perhaps they were concerned that they couldn't convincingly bring such a creature to life. After all, Bruce had been a nightmare, and a bigger Bruce likely equaled an even bigger nightmare.

In addition to Benchley, Zanuck and Brown also reached out to legendary sci-fi author Arthur C. Clarke, best known for *2001: A Space Odyssey* (1968). There seem to be conflicting stories as to what Clarke's pitch was about, though. More reliable sources—namely

Clarke himself—state that the pitch centered around a giant squid, not a shark.

However, many sources claim that Clarke fashioned a story that predated Michael Crichton's novel *Sphere*, about an alien object found underwater. Allegedly, this idea was about a mysterious orb found in the Indian Ocean. This object would turn out to be an alien intelligence that is somehow controlling the giant shark![23] In *The Making of Jaws 2*, David Brown mentions the project in passing, recalling that Clarke "had an idea of some great undersea object that was in the Indian Ocean…it was a grandiose idea. We couldn't quite grasp it."

Oddly, Clarke says nothing about alien orbs in an essay he wrote addressing his involvement with *Jaws 2* in his book *Greetings, Carbon-Based Bipeds!: Collected Essays, 1934-1998*, where he predominantly discusses his love of giant squids. According to Clarke, Zanuck and Brown asked him if he'd like to write the screenplay for *Jaws 2*. He replied that "when you've seen one great white shark, you've seen them all," and that he wasn't interested.[24] "If they wanted a real monster, it would be hard to beat the giant squid, Architeuthis. So I promptly sat down and wrote an outline, based partly on a story of mine that *Playboy* had published in 1964."[25] The story was "The Shining Ones," which Wikipedia summarizes as: "Sabotage is suspected at a coastal Soviet base, where a revolutionary thermal electric technology is to be announced to the world within a matter of days."[26] To dig a little deeper into the story, an OTEC project is attacked by a giant squid that can change colors as a way of communicating. The hero of the story considers the squid to be a creature of beauty,

---

[23] Reviewers would have had an absolute field day with that concept if this is true considering that the *New York Times* considered the finished *Jaws 2* to be a stretch as it was. They wrote: "Until great white sharks learn how to fly or use automatic weapons or develop their powers of telekinesis, it would seem that 'Jaws 2' has pretty much exhausted the cinematic possibilities of sharks as man-eating monsters." www.nytimes.com/1978/06/16/archives/film-another-snap-of-jawsthe-great-white-redux.html

[24] Clarke, *Greetings Carbon-Based Bipeds*, pp. 407.

[25] Ibid.

[26] https://en.wikipedia.org/wiki/The_Wind_from_the_Sun

even if it is destructive. It's also possible that Clarke's novel *The Deep Range* (1957) influenced his idea for Zanuck and Brown. In that story, a method is devised to immobilize a giant squid and bring it to the surface for study and captivity by way of chemical anesthesia and electrified fences.

How closely Clarke's "Jaws 2" idea followed these two stories is unknown, but conversely, *Just When You Thought It Was Safe* states that the sequel revolved around the squid attacking an oil rig.

"Anyway, though I had a pleasant telephone discussion with Zanuck and Brown, and later sent them my outline, nothing came of the project," Clarke wrote in the essay. "I was not in the least disappointed, as by then I was much too involved in *2010: Odyssey Two*."[27]

That it was rejected wasn't surprising. It's not that it wasn't a good idea, it's that in actuality, Clarke hadn't really written a *Jaws* sequel. This was evidenced by his proposed title, *Tentacles*, which he admitted that he knew would draw "lewd snickers" from theatergoers. Ironically enough, a giant octopus movie called *Tentacles* was produced in 1977.

In a further twist of irony, Clarke reminisced how he was in Sri Lanka listening to the radio when an interview with Peter Benchley came on. The year was 1991, and Benchley was promoting his new book *Beast*, about a giant squid. Clarke chuckled to himself, knowing that he had the idea first as a *Jaws* follow-up. Ironically, if Benchley had written the book back then it probably would have gotten picked up and produced for theaters. As it was, all it got was a TV miniseries adaptation in 1996.

As for Clarke, eventually he produced the TV series *Arthur C. Clarke's Mysterious World*. One of the episodes centered on finding a giant squid. Remarkably, they did, and a not yet fully grown twenty-foot female was captured on camera.

---

[27] Clarke, *Greetings Carbon-Based Bipeds*, pp. 407.

GRIZZLY
The First "Rip-Off"

Release Date: May 21, 1976
Alternate Titles: *Killer Grizzly* (TV version)

Directed by: William Girdler & David Sheldon **Special Effects by:** Phil Cory & Bob Dawson **Screenplay by:** Harvey Flaxman & David Sheldon **Music by:** Robert O. Ragland **Cast:** Christopher George (Michael Kelly) Andrew Prine (Don Stober) Richard Jaeckel (Arthur Scott) Joan McCall (Allison Corwin) Joe Dorsey (Charley Kittridge) Tom Arcuragi (Tom) **Animal Performers:** Teddy (Grizzly)

Todd-AO 35, Color, 91 Minutes

SYNOPSIS Hikers and campers within a large national park are being slaughtered by a vicious grizzly bear. Head ranger Michael Kelly urges the park superintendent to shut down the park until the bear can be killed, but the superintendent refuses. Kelly teams with helicopter pilot Don Stober and naturalist Arthur Scott to find the bear. Scott determines that the bear is over 15 feet tall and may be a holdover from prehistoric ages...

COMMENTARY *Grizzly* co-writer David Sheldon explained that shortly after the release of *Jaws,* he had met with some friends who had just come back from a camping trip. They told him that while camping in Yellowstone National Park, there had been a bear scare, with a bear supposedly tearing into the tents of campers. "My eyes lit up: that's a movie!" Sheldon joked in an interview years later.[28]

Sheldon's friend, who had just returned from the camping trip, was another fellow writer, Harvey Flaxman, who himself described the project as "*Jaws* on land." The duo agreed to write a movie around the concept, with Flaxman producing and Sheldon directing. Within one week, Sheldon had written a treatment, which Flaxman elaborated into a complete script. Sheldon then took it back and gave it a final polish.[29]

However, even though he was an accomplished director, in the end, Sheldon didn't helm the picture on his own and co-directed it with his partner, William Girdler. Sheldon and Girdler had an arrangement that they would alternate on their films as to who directed. It was Sheldon's turn to direct, only Girdler loved the *Grizzly* script and very much wanted to do the picture himself. When Girdler said he could secure funding for the picture, Sheldon agreed to let him co-direct.

As it was, Sheldon had already secured a deal with Warner Bros to fund and distribute the film (though it hadn't been signed yet). However, because Warner Bros was a big studio, this would also delay production somewhat, and Sheldon and Girdler wanted to ride the *Jaws* wave as quickly as they could. Therefore, though the budget ($750,000) was apparently less through their new distributor, Film Ventures International, they would have the benefit of creative freedom and expediency.[30]

---

[28] "Q & A at New Beverly Hills Screening" with David Sheldon and Andrew Prine.

[29] Flaxman even admitted that his playing the reporter in *Grizzly* was a nod to Peter Benchley playing the reporter in *Jaws.*

[30] Warner Bros was infuriated by this move to begin with, and was even more upset when they saw how well the film did upon release. When the counteroffer occurred, they had even offered to up the film's budget.

SHARK BITES: *GRIZZLY* DELETED SCENES

LIKE ANY FILM, *GRIZZLY* HAD ITS FARE SHARE OF DELETED SCENES. THE FIRST IS SUPPOSEDLY ANOTHER SCENE OF KELLY ASKING THE PARK SUPERINTENDENT TO SHUT DOWN THE PARK. THERE'S ALSO AN ADDITIONAL KILL SCENE, THOUGH THE DETAILS OF WHO IS KILLED AND HOW ARE UNKNOWN. JUST AS HUNTERS KILL A SHARK IN *JAWS* THAT ISN'T THE MAIN SHARK, ONE OF *GRIZZLY'S* CUT SCENES HAD HUNTERS KILL A BLACK BEAR BY ACCIDENT. THE DEATHS OF STOBER AND SCOTT WERE SUPPOSEDLY LONGER AND BLOODIER BUT WERE CUT DOWN FOR THEATRICAL RELEASE.

The film is meant to be set over a hot Labor Day weekend but was filmed in the late stages of autumn in November of 1975 in Clayton, Georgia. The shoot was essentially a race against time to beat the falling of the leaves. Snow proved to be troublesome, and in instances where they could, they would melt the snow to hide the fact that it was really winter. This also caused a few problems with the live on-set bear, Teddy, who was ready to go off and hibernate. Furthermore, Teddy was not really a trained movie bear; he was chosen due to his stature. To get him to do anything, food such as fish were used as bait to get him to move and open his mouth. You see, Teddy never actually roared for anyone. When he "roars," he's really opening his mouth in an attempt to eat whatever they dangled on the pole in front of him. The roars were dubbed in later.

Of course, Teddy was too dangerous to use in many scenes, and other methods had to be devised. At all times, he was kept away from the cast and crew via electrical lines hidden in the foliage. There was also a mechanical bear similar to Bruce the shark on *Jaws*. And by similar to Bruce, I mean there were problems with the mechanical bear. In this case, the mecha-bear (made by a taxidermy company) was left outside one night in the rain, and it ruined the fur! Apparently, the prop was only used in one or two shots, the most notable one being when it attacks the helicopter.

Grizzly was a huge success. In fact, it was the most successful independent film of its time, grossing $39 million. It would hold that record until the release of John Carpenter's *Halloween* in 1978. Though audiences loved *Grizzly*, critics were not so kind, calling it out as a *Jaws* clone. Vincent Canby of the *New York Times* wrote, "*Grizzly*, which opened yesterday at the Rivoli and other theaters, is such a blatant imitation of *Jaws* that one has to admire the depth of the flattery it represents, though not the lack of talent involved."

Grizzly was not only the first major "Jaws rip-off," but it was also one of the best. But make no mistake, despite being a high-quality production and an enjoyable film, it fully deserves its distinction as a *Jaws* rip-off. The similarities between the two pictures goes a lot further than just an animal on the loose.

Richard Jaeckel in Grizzly. © 1976 Film Ventures International

The character types in both stories are similar. Three male leads anchor the film, along with one supporting female character tied to the lead male. Rounding out the rest of the *Jaws*-stereotypes are a deputy, and an authority figure that cares more for tourist dollars than he does public safety. In *Jaws,* we had Sheriff Brody, Hooper, and Quint. Here we have Head Park Ranger Michael Kelly, helicopter pilot Don Stober, and naturalist Arthur Scott. Though Kelly is obviously the Brody-stand-in, it's tougher to say who is supposed to be Hooper and Quint between Stober and Scott. On the one hand, Scott would seem to be Hooper because he's

SHARK BITES: *GRIZZLY* IN JAPAN

ONE PLACE THAT *GRIZZLY* WAS A BIG HIT WAS JAPAN, A LAND FAMOUS FOR GIANT MONSTERS. IT WAS RELEASED THERE IN JULY OF 1976. AS A TESTAMENT OF THE FILM'S POPULARITY, THIS AUTHOR BELIEVES THAT THE GRIZZLY'S POV SHOTS IN THE WOODS WERE COPIED FOR ONE OF THE TITULAR MONSTERS IN *LEGEND OF DINOSAURS AND MONSTER BIRDS* (1977, SEE PP.108). THE JAPANESE LASERDISC EDITION OF *GRIZZLY* BEGINS WITH A SPECIAL MONOLOGUE BEFORE THE CREDITS THAT STATES HOW BEAR ATTACKS ARE BECOMING MORE COMMON.

a naturalist, but he has a lot of Quint's cranky mannerisms and also dresses like him. And yet, despite Scott's similarities to Quint, Stober is still more clearly the Quint equivalent.

This hits home in one scene in particular. You see, for me, *Grizzly* had only one unintentionally funny moment where the *Jaws* element went too far. One of the best scenes in *Jaws* is Quint's speech about the USS Indianapolis. The makers of *Grizzly* do their best to recreate the harrowing speech via Stober, who relates a story around the campfire about a group of Native American hunters being wiped out by a herd of killer grizzlies. If not for the fact that this was the film's most blatant *Jaws* callback, it would be a good scene. But the truth is it's a little too obvious that it was trying to copy *Jaws'* most famous non-shark scene. Actor Andrew Prine even admitted that he "improvised a version of Quint's speech from *Jaws*," though he was referring to a speech from a little later in the film about the Vietnam War, not the grizzlies vs. Native Americans speech.

Overall, the three actors have great chemistry. It should come as no surprise that all three had already done a movie together, the John Wayne western *Chisum* (1970). But, as with any film, there were other actors up for the roles initially. Ben Johnson was the first choice for Stober, and Clint Walker was going to play Kelly but decided to shoot *Snowbeast*, a 1978 Sasquatch thriller, instead. When Prine asked his agent for a script, the agent's response was simply, "It's *Jaws*!" Or, in other words: Take the role, you dummy!

The female lead in *Grizzly* is Kelly's girlfriend, Allison, who is a photographer. Like Ellen Brody, she doesn't do much other than offer moral support to Kelly, who also has a deputy, Tom, similar to Brody's deputy, Hendricks, in *Jaws*. And, of course, the park superintendent takes the place of the mayor of Amity Island. When the grizzly attacks become more frequent, he naturally doesn't want to shut off large sections of the park, as Kelly suggests.

Like the shark in *Jaws*, the bear in *Grizzly* doesn't get a full-on reveal until midway into the movie. Initially, all we see are shots of the bear's claws. Its first victims are a pair of beautiful women out camping. *Grizzly* doesn't mess around with the gore and is bloodier than *Jaws* in many ways, almost qualifying it as an exploitation film. Right off the bat, the bear lops off one of the women's arms.

Mostly we are aware of the Grizzly via POV shots of it walking through the woods, or shots of its huge claws. Naturally, one benefit the producers of *Grizzly* had over the makers of *Jaws* was that, at times, they could utilize a real bear for certain scenes. Lucky for them, Teddy was a staggering 11 feet tall (though the characters claim the bear in the movie is 15-20 feet tall). To explain the bear's immense height, Scott theorizes it is a throwback to the giant bears of the Pleistocene Epoch. Though it isn't mentioned in *Jaws* the movie, in Benchley's book Hooper speculates that the shark they are tracking could be a surviving Megalodon.

The catalyst in *Jaws* is the beach attack on the 4th of July. *Grizzly's* is not as grand as that, but it is more brutal. The incident that finally incites the super-intendent to shut down the park is the maiming of a young boy and his mother (the boy lives but loses a leg while the mother dies).

Unlike in *Jaws*, where only Quint gets it, here Scott and Stober both bite the dust, leaving Kelly as the lone survivor. In the last act, Scott goes out on his own to try and capture the bear, while Stober and Kelly hunt it down in their helicopter. Scott is killed before the two men can get to his location in time... or so we think. Though the bear has been dismembering everyone in the film, somehow Scott gets by with a paw swipe to the face. This is almost unintentionally funny, considering that moments before the bear beheaded Scott's horse, while the same swipe barely harms Scott! Scott falls to the ground with a bloody face but doesn't actually look to have any skin tears.

The bear then buries Scott in the ground to save him to eat for later. A bit later, Scott's eyes flutter. He's alive! Scott shakes the dirt off in a daze and begins to rise. We were only led to believe he was dead. And then, not more than two seconds later, we've been duped again. The bear is watching Scott rise from the ground, and within moments Scott is dead for real. And how does the bear kill him? That's hard to say because the movie cuts away to leave it to our imaginations, but rumors persist a graphic death scene was shot and then cut for some reason.

The film ends with Stober and Kelly being attacked by the bear in their chopper in something of a precursor to the scene from *Jaws 2*. Both men manage to escape the chopper, and the bear chooses to face off with Stober, who unloads his rifle into it to no avail. During the shooting of this scene, THE most dangerous scene for the actors involved, someone forgot to put out the electrical wire. Therefore, a hungover Prine was actually acting against the real bear with his life on the line! And though Prine didn't get eaten in real life, the bear does bear-hug a blood-spewing Stober to death in the movie. Kelly then fires a bazooka at the bear, causing it to explode. Not quite as suspenseful or clever as the finale in *Jaws*, but satisfying none the less.

As already stated, *Grizzly* was a financial success, even if critics drubbed it. And not just in America, but overseas as well.[31] "It broke records in Tokyo and Berlin," said Sheldon. The movie was so successful that another bear on the loose movie was released in 1977 titled *Claws*. In Canada and Mexico, it was falsely retitled *Grizzly II*!

It would be many, many years before a sequel to *Grizzly* was finally completed (see Chapter 29). However, the stars of *Grizzly*, Teddy, Jaeckel, George,

---

[31] Flaxman said the only place it didn't do well initially was the South. To remedy this, they simply changed the poster (originally done by popular comic book artist Neal Adams) to have hunters after the bear rather than the bear attacking a girl.

and director Girdler would return for a spiritual sequel, *Day of the Animals*. That film was released in 1977 and had every forest animal imaginable attack mankind during a strange solar flare.

18 FEET OF TOWERING FURY!

GRIZZLY

THE MOST DANGEROUS JAWS IN THE LAND.

© 1976 Film Ventures International

MAKO:
The Jaws of Death

Release Date: July 1976

Directed by: William Grefé **Screenplay by:** William Grefé & Robert W. Morgan **Music by:** William Loose & Paul Ruhland **Cast:** Richard Jaeckel (Sonny Stein) Jenifer Bishop (Karen) Buffy Dee (Barney) Harold Sakata (Pete)

Color, 91 Minutes

SYNOPSIS Sonny Stein is a salvage diver with a secret living in Key West, Florida. Stein can psychically communicate with sharks thanks to a mystical amulet given to him by a shaman in the Philippines years ago. Against his better nature, Sonny loans one of his sharks to a friend, Karen, a dancer at a nightclub. Specifically, Karen is a swimmer who performs underwater for the patrons (it is thought the shark will make her act more exciting). At the same time, a scientist persuades Sonny to let him study one of his pregnant sharks. Sonny is shocked when the scientist kills and dissects the mother shark, and he learns that the shark he loaned to the club is being mistreated as well. As a hurricane approaches Key West, a storm of another kind brews as Sonny plans his revenge...

COMMENTARY Though it's often lumped in with *Jaws* rip-offs, *Mako: The Jaws of Death* was written before *Jaws* had even been released. The success of *Jaws* then allowed this movie to be produced. So, bottom line, all that this movie really has in common with *Jaws* is that they both have sharks.

In fact, this movie is the opposite of *Jaws* in that the sharks are treated as the victims/heroes in the story... sort of. *Mako* is one of those movies that doesn't really have any sympathetic characters. Richard Jaeckel is always likable, and his character could be someone you could root for if not for his opening scene. Right off the bat, the movie starts with some fishermen catching a shark. While it struggles underwater, Sonny comes along in scuba gear and cuts it loose. He then crawls onto the boat and murders the whole crew! The bodies he tosses overboard for the shark they just caught to feast upon. We don't really know anything about the fisherman other than that they caught a shark. Does this mean they all deserve to die horribly? If the film had told us they were bad people beforehand, then maybe this scene wouldn't be as off-putting, but as it is, it seems as though our hero has murdered some random people.

Richard Jaeckel and Jennifer Bishop, with Buffy Dee in the background. © 1976 The Cannon Group, Inc.

And yet, as the story progresses, Sonny becomes more sympathetic despite what he's done. Throughout the film he's taken advantage of and lied to by pretty much all the other characters. Karen lied to him about the treatment of his shark at the club, and the shark that he gave to the scientist has been dissected in a lab. Unlike the opening scene, when Sonny gets his revenge on these characters, it's handled better all around.

The last 30 minutes of the movie are pretty good. Sonny unleashes his shark on the seedy club owner when he's out for a swim. Sonny intentionally leaves the shark out so that when Karen goes on to perform that night she won't be safe. This makes for one of the film's best scenes. As party-goers arrive at the club for a pre-hurricane celebration, Karen dips into the tank for her nightly performance. When the curtain is pulled up to reveal her underwater act, the patrons are shocked to see her being devoured by a shark!

The movie ends with Sonny getting chased down by the police, and there's an atmospheric scene where Sonny swims in the stormy waters with his sharks and pulls a policeman out of his boat to be devoured. Ultimately, Sonny becomes wrought with guilt over all the killing and mayhem. He removes his protective amulet and jumps into the water to commit suicide (without the amulet, the shark will eat him, and it does).

Mako's shark footage is impressive. As the producers could not afford mechanical sharks as in *Jaws*, real ones were used in their place! Many of them had their teeth removed so that they would be harmless. Some of the sharks were also dead. In one instance, stuntwoman Gay Ingram was to go into the tank with a dead shark that she would wrestle with as if it was alive. Well, it actually was alive and attacked her. So when you see it biting her leg, that's really happening. But, as stated earlier, the shark's teeth had been removed. At other times, sharks had ropes tied to their tales as a way of keeping them from getting too close to the actors.

The film began shooting very soon after *Jaws* was released, in August of 1975. Like many *Jaws* imitators (and later *Jaws 2* itself), it was filmed in Florida, and a few bits were even shot in the Bahamas. When the film was finished, it was picked up by Cannon for U.S. distribution. Excited about the prospect of their *Jaws*-inspired film, they ordered the largest print run in their history up to that time.

Howard Sackler's
JAWS 2

Developmental Period: 1975-1976

Treatments by: Howard Sackler **Proposed Cast/Characters:** Sheriff Brody (Roy Scheider) Len Peterson [land developer] Boyd [owner of "Shark O' Rama Shark Shak"] Mayor Vaughn (Murray Hamilton) Ellen Brody (Lorraine Gary) Mike & Sean Brody **Proposed Creatures:** The Shark

SYNOPSIS As Amity recovers from its recent shark attack, two mysterious newcomers shake up the town on land while a second gigantic shark haunts the waters.

COMMENTARY As related earlier, Howard Sackler's first idea for *Jaws 2* was really a prequel, which Sid Sheinberg shot down immediately in favor of a return to Amity. Sheinberg and the producers were also wise to the fact that teenagers had loved the first *Jaws*. In Richard Zanuck's words, "Kids ate it up...[*Jaws*] was X-rated for anyone over 70."[32]

---

[32] Loynd, *The Jaws 2 Log*, pp.18.

SHARK BITES: *SON OF JAWS?*

WHEN THE STORY BROKE THAT THERE WOULD BE A SEQUEL TO *JAWS*, A REPORTER ASKED A UNIVERSAL SPOKESMAN WHAT IT WOULD BE ABOUT. HIS RESPONSE, "MAYBE THE SHARK WILL HAVE LAID AN EGG OR SOMETHING LIKE THAT." NEVER MIND THAT MOST SHARKS GIVE LIVE BIRTH. SIMILARLY, OTHER NEWSPAPERS IN 1976 JOKED THE NEW MOVIE WOULD BE CALLED "JAWS JR." OR "SON OF JAWS." WHILE THESE WERE JOKEY SUGGESTIONS, IN THE MIND OF DOROTHY TRISTAN, FUTURE WRITER OF *JAWS 2*, THE SHARK IN HER STORY WAS FEMALE AND THE MATE OF THE SHARK IN *JAWS*. AS FOR MORE BAD TITLES, *HOUSE OF HAMMER* #21 CLAIMED THAT ZANUCK WANTED TO CALL THIS MOVIE *MORE JAWS*!

Sheinberg instructed Sackler to write the story around "children in distress." And so he did. Though his script would be heavily revised by Dorothy Tristan and Carl Gottlieb in the future, allegedly it contained all the familiar tropes from the finished *Jaws 2*: the attack on the water skier, shark vs. helicopter, and the group of teenagers attacked at sea.[33]

A notable difference was that the first draft featured a mysterious young man, nicknamed Sideburns, who comes into town.[34] It turns out to be Quint's son, out to collect the reward money his father would have received had he lived through the first film. For some reason, he and Mike Brody team up to try and kill the new shark (this could be a misinterpretation of the actual story, though). Someone didn't take to Quint Jr., and so he was replaced with a mystery man who comes to Amity in an effort to exploit its shark legend in Sackler's second treatment.

To be more specific, the character is named Boyd. In this case, he's not related to Quint, but he has bought

---

[33] Or most sources say this is the case. At least one source acts as though Tristan added the water skier scene, as well as the teenagers at sea, etc. Basically, every book, YouTube video, or "Making of" of *Jaws 2* tells a different story.

[34] The character name of Sideburns carried over into Dorothy Tristan's script as one of the teenagers. The chronology is a bit confusing and uncertain, but even though the Boyd character (which eventually replaced Sideburns in Sackler's second treatment) was dropped from Tristan's screenplay, during the initial shooting of *Jaws 2*, the "Sideburns as Quint's son angle" was revived.

Quint's old business and turned it into the "Shark O' Rama Shark Den"—which more or less exploits the town's tragedy. The Len Peterson character is also present, and Mayor Vaughn is trying secure funds for a new real estate development being pushed by Peterson. A paranoid Sheriff Brody wants to secure funds for a huge underwater fence to be put around the beach instead.

Sackler's version didn't have as many teenagers, and zeroed in on the two Brody brothers, along with Andy and Doug who made the cut into the final film. Teenaged lovers Ed and Tina also appear in this draft, but with smaller roles (and yes, Ed still gets eaten). Brody is even more paranoid in Sackler's treatment than he is in the film. Brody has a nightmare so intense that it teeters on the edge of parody. In the nightmare, Brody sees sharks in every body of water that he looks at, including a swimming pool! Notably, the aborted spoof *Jaws 3, People 0* begins with a shark in Peter Benchley's swimming pool that eats him. One has to wonder if Zanuck and Brown remembered this nightmare scene from Sackler's *Jaws 2* and utilized it in their unproduced parody. Anyhow, Sackler's *Jaws 2* nightmare ends with Brody's dead body washing up in the surf at Ellen's feet.

The killer whale scene is present (considering this treatment was written at some point in late 1975, the theory that the dead Killer Whale scene was a jab at 1977's *Orca* would seem to be unfounded). When Brody sees the whale, he's convinced that a shark is to blame. He takes a police boat out and somehow manages to wreck it in what becomes an embarrassment to the town, and Brody is fired. What's interesting about the firing of Brody is that it would be done away with in the next draft, but the idea was re-instated in the final film.

Sackler's ending is too much of a rehash of *Jaws*. Brody must team up with Boyd and Peterson to hunt the shark on Peterson's boat. In the middle of the action, Boyd falls off the side of the ship after the shark rams them. With Peterson at the wheel, they race to Boyd's location. Brody extends a hand and pulls half of Boyd into the boat—the shark had bitten the lower half off. One has to wonder if Quint's son in the previous iteration shared the same fate?

Brody then gets an idea as the shark continues to batter the boat. Peterson's boat is a twin-engine. If the shark happened to come into contact with the large propellers, it would chop it to pieces. Brody has Peterson raise the twin engines, which he then centers himself in between. Brody kicks his feet into the water, enticing the shark to charge him. At the last possible second, Brody hoists himself back into the boat while Peterson drops the engines. The shark plunges headfirst into the spinning propellers, and a bloody mess is created.

While this ending isn't bad, the one created by Dorothy Tristan in rewrites was much better. And speaking of rewrites, onto the next chapter...

John Hancock's
JAWS 2

Developed: 1976-1977
Partially Shot: 1977

Directed by: John Hancock **Screenplay by:** Dorothy Tristan **Cast:** Roy Scheider (Martin Brody) Lorraine Gary (Ellen Brody) Murray Hamilton (Mayor Vaughn) Richard Herd/Dana Eclar (Len Peterson) Tegan West (Mike Brody) Ricky Schroeder (Sean Brody) Sarah Holcomb (Angela) Gary Springer (Andy) Billy Van Zandt (Sideburns) Lily Knight (Kathy) Karen Corboy (Lucy) David Elliot (Reeves) Lenora May (Laura) Marshall Efron (Deputy Batliner) **Creatures:** Female Shark

SYNOPSIS A downtrodden Amity Island is beset upon by a real estate developer with possible mob ties. At the same time, Chief Martin Brody, suffering a form of PTSD from the recent shark attack, comes to believe that a second Great White is stalking the waters off of Amity. His worst fear is confirmed when the shark attacks his two sons while they are out racing their new sailboat...

COMMENTARY When talk turned to potential directors for *Jaws 2* (Spielberg had already passed), Howard Sackler suggested his friend John Hancock. Zanuck and Brown decided to take a chance on the relatively unknown director, the same as they had done with Spielberg before. Hancock agreed and began working with Sackler on the *Jaws 2* script in early 1976. However, Hancock and his wife, actress Dorothy Tristan, disliked Sackler's screenplay.[35] If you'll remember, Sackler wanted to do the USS Indianapolis scenario. When Sheinberg vetoed that, Sackler apparently just "phoned in" his *Jaws 2* script. Or, this is what Tristan implied in *Just When You Thought It Was Safe*. Tristan was quoted as saying that she felt that Sackler considered the *Jaws 2* script to be "beneath him." According to her, his draft wasn't even typed and was handwritten. "I looked at this and said, 'What is this?! If he's not interested in it, I have some ideas!'"[36]

Though Tristan gets the writing credit on the script, she naturally did a lot brainstorming with her husband. One thing Hancock wanted to do was pick up on the mafia subplot from the *Jaws* novel that didn't make it into the first film. In this case, Peterson and Vaughn have borrowed money from the mob to construct Amity Shores.[37] Tristan pitched her version of the story to Zanuck and Brown, who approved, and so she began rewriting the script. Though Chief Brody's post-traumatic stress disorder was also in Sackler's version, Tristan elaborated on it and also expanded the role of Ellen Brody. It was also she and Hancock's idea to show the negative effects the previous shark attack had on the town. Due to the negative publicity, Amity is struggling economically, hence the subplot about the land developers and Amity Shores (this made its way into the final film too, it's just not implied that Amity is in the middle of a depression). Hancock said, "I wanted

---

[35] This would seem to confirm that Sackler wrote a treatment rather than a script. For starters, one wouldn't write a whole script by hand. Second, it is said in *The Jaws 2 Log* that Tristan added dialogue to Sackler's version. Treatments typically don't have dialogue.

[36] Jankiewicz, *Just When You Thought It Was Safe*, pp.186.

[37] Basically, Vaughn and Peterson are more afraid of the mob if they don't recoup their investment than they are the shark.

the picture to have a different look and feel than the first *Jaws*. Grittier, edgier and more haunted — to show the impact of the first picture on the place and the people."[38]

What Tristan did, essentially, was to add in more characters, inject the teen plot with a bit of romance, and change the ending (where the shark gets chewed up by the boat engines). While Hancock and Tristan were scuba diving to train for underwater filming, they spotted an electrical cable on the seafloor. When they got back to the surface, Tristan pitched the idea that the shark bites it and gets electrocuted. Though Tristan had some wonderful ideas, ultimately, her retooling of the script caused a falling out between her, her husband, and Sackler, who disliked the revisions. This was only the start of the troubles, though, and after a month of filming his version, Hancock would eventually be fired and replaced by a new director.

Fundamentally, Tristan's outline is still the same as the finished *Jaws 2* right from the onset. This version begins with the two scuba-divers being devoured—the main difference is that the sequence is longer and more complex. When the duo discovers the *Orca*, one swims inside to investigate while the other scratches their names on the hull. The other diver then goes inside to search for his friend, and there's a fake scare when his friend begins screaming. But it's a shout of victory rather than fear—he's found an old bottle of Quint's booze.

As the duo swim back to the surface, one of the divers clowns around, pretending to drink it, and so the other snaps a photo with his underwater camera. But then the diver accidentally drops the bottle and has to swim down to get it. He senses another camera flash behind him, and so he turns. The other diver hit the flash by accident because he's being mauled by a giant shark! This could be a gutsy move scripting a full-on reveal for the shark this early on. But, then again, audiences knew what the shark would like anyways, and the script says a cloud of blood partially obscures the shark.

The second diver drops the bottle and pulls out a knife to go rescue his friend. The shark drops its current prey

[38] Jankiewicz, *Just When You Thought It Was Safe*, pp.186.

SHARK BITES: BRUCETTE

THOUGH UNSPOKEN IN THE FILM—AND FRANKLY, HOW WOULD ANYONE EVEN BE ABLE TO TELL?—THE NOVEL BASED UPON TRISTAN'S SCREENPLAY REVEALED THAT NOT ONLY WAS THIS SHARK A FEMALE, BUT IT WAS THE PREGNANT MATE OF THE SHARK FROM THE FIRST MOVIE! TRISTAN CONFIRMED THIS IN AN INTERVIEW, AND SAID SHE GOT THE IDEA FROM PERSONAL EXPERIENCE WHEN SHE KILLED A RATTLESNAKE AND ITS MATE SHOWED UP THE NEXT DAY! IN THE *JAWS 2* NOVEL'S EPILOGUE, IT IS REVEALED THAT AT LEAST ONE OF THE BABY SHARKS SURVIVED. THE FEMALE SHARK FROM *JAWS 2* HAS SINCE GONE ON TO BE NICKNAMED "BRUCETTE" BY FANS.

to seek out its next victim and grabs the oncoming diver. The camera would follow the knife as it sinks down to the ocean bottom, and then the titles would begin to roll from there.

Our first glimpses of Amity reflect the downtrodden atmosphere of the script. The beaches are barren (inhabited only by some stray dogs), and the buildings look neglected and have "For Rent" signs. Brody is going to a promotional event for Amity Shores as in the finished film, but this script notes that he "has the look of a survivor who will never shake off the memory of what he survived."

Here we are introduced to some new characters, like the mayor's son, named Reeves (later changed to Larry Jr.). We are reintroduced to the Brody kids, now older by a few years (Mike is 15 in this script, but in the film, he is 17). Rather than banter with Ellen at the event, Brody talks under his breath during the mayor's speech to a new character named Tom Andrews, a scuba diving instructor (this character appears in the film but only in the scuba diving scene). Brody is already aware of the accident with the scuba divers (though he doesn't know what killed them) and is filling Tom in on the matter.

Though he doesn't know what got them, Brody's suspicions are already on high alert. He asks Tom if his students will be using the new Amity Shores pool, which they are currently sitting around, for training. Tom says that the beginners will, but not the advanced ones, like Mike Brody. This, of course, upsets Brody, who doesn't want anyone near the water in light of recent events. The celebration diffuses the argument, however, and rather than a pretty girl as in the film, the pool is inaugurated by having several Amity officials jump in for a swim race.

The next scene takes us back to the Amity beaches where locals go for a swim, including Harry—as in "That's some bad hat, Harry." In a shark tower above, Sheriff Brody keeps watch. Len Peterson, a real estate developer, pulls up in his Mercedes and asks if Brody can lay off the shark watching as he brings potential investors by. Brody uses this an opportunity to pitch to him buying a massive shark net for the beach as they walk over to Peterson's car. Mayor Vaughn is inside of it and seems to be embarrassed by Brody's suggestion. Once Brody leaves, Vaughn and Peterson have a conversation that illuminates the tedious relationship between Brody and the town politicians.

© UNIVERSAL CITY STUDIOS, Inc.

Roy Scheider filming a scene with David Elliot when the character was still named Reeves rather than Larry Jr. Jaws 2 © 1978 Universal Pictures

This is followed by various other scenes of town life, including Brody giving Reeves a ticket (one of the scenes exclusive to this script that would eventually be shot by Hancock before he was let go). Soon after this we get to the famous water skiing scene. In the finished film, the shark attacks a pair of women, one of which is skiing

SHARK BITES: HOOPER IN *JAWS 2*?

IN THE EARLY STAGES THERE WAS TALK OF WHETHER OR NOT HOOPER COULD RETURN FOR THE SEQUEL. HOWEVER, RICHARD DREYFUSS BEING CAST IN STEVEN SPIELBERG'S *CLOSE ENCOUNTERS OF THE THIRD KIND* MADE HIM UNAVAILABLE. ODDLY ENOUGH, UNIVERSAL CONSIDERED RECASTING INGMAR BERGMAN ALUM ERLAND JOSEPHSON IN THE PART. WHEN UNIVERSAL REACHED OUT TO THE SWEDISH ACTOR HE DECLINED ACCORDING TO *JAWS 2: THE MAKING OF A HOLLYWOOD SEQUEL*. MICHAEL A. SMITH, ONE OF THE BOOK'S AUTHORS, HAS AN INTERESTING OPINION ON THE MATTER. "I REALLY THINK THE SWEDISH ACTOR WAS MORE OF A SMOKESCREEN - THINKING PERHAPS THAT DREYFUSS WOULD RATHER DO THE PART HIMSELF RATHER THAN SEE SOMEONE ELSE DO IT," SMITH SAID. ON IMDB, JOSEPHSON IS QUOTED AS SAYING, "I WOULD RATHER HAVE INTELLECTUAL BATTLES WITH LIV ULLMANN, THAN FIGHTING WITH SOME SHARK." HOWEVER, WHEN HANCOCK'S VERSION OF *JAWS 2* CEASED PRODUCTION, SPIELBERG WAS AGAIN APPROACHED ABOUT *JAWS 2*. IT WAS UNIVERSAL'S HOPE THAT DREYFUSS WOULD FOLLOW SPIELBERG TO THE PROJECT IF THE DIRECTOR RETURNED. AND INDEED, WHEN SPIELBERG SAT DOWN TO WRITE UP HIS OWN SCENARIO, BY HIS OWN ADMISSION, HE INCLUDED HOOPER AND BRODY IN THE STORY. ACCORDING TO A DUBIOUS REPORT IN *HOUSE OF HAMMER* #21, IT WAS REPORTED THAT DREYFUSS EVENTUALLY RELENTED TO DO A *JAWS 2* CAMEO BUT WAS TURNED DOWN!

while the other pilots the boat. In this proto-version of the scene, there are a pair of couples water skiing. In other words, two water skiers and two people in the boat for the shark to torment. In this case, the victims see the shark before it strikes, whereas in the film, it sneaks up on its victim. It all ends the same way though, with a woman trying to pour gasoline on the attacking shark and the boat exploding.

Hancock, in particular, lamented the loss of this scene, which was Tristan's idea and not Sackler's, according to him. "...the sequence was much darker than it wound up being," Hancock said in *Just When You Thought It Was Safe*. "It was bloody and grim — and it would have been a good sequence. I really missed getting to shoot that. I tried to talk Zanuck into being the male water skier, but he said 'Oh, that's all I need!'"[39]

---

[39] Ibid, pp.187.

The Marvel Comics adaptation of *Jaws 2* used the original script by Dorothy Tristan, not the revised version. Jaws 2 © 1978 Universal Pictures

Brody investigates the incident, talking to an older woman who witnessed it, but the pair of teenaged lovers (Ed and Tina) had yet to be added into the scene. Also, Brody knew one of the dead couples. When Brody pulls up to his home, the sailboat subplot is introduced as he finds Mike, his friend Andy, and his youngest, Sean, shining a new sailboat that Mike bought off a friend. The kids express their excitement about taking it out on the water, which naturally stresses Brody out further.

The original actor to play Mike Brody, Tegan West (left), walks with Gary Springer (right), who played Andy in both versions of the movie. Jaws 2 © 1978 Universal Pictures

Next, a scene plays out in the Brody kitchen, where it is learned that Andy will be moving away. His mother can't find work anymore in Amity, which is brought up to remind the prospective audience of the tough times that have befallen the town.

That night Martin tosses and turns in bed and eventually gets up to go into his office (Sackler's over the top nightmare had been removed). There we would have seen a photo of he and Hooper together shaking hands along with a plaque that read "Martin Brody, Amity Man of the Year, 1975." The plaque, complete with a tiny pair of shark jaws, would make it into the finished film, but not the photo with Hooper.[40] At his desk, Brody makes the sodium pentothal bullets—a scene that occurs a little later in the finished film. Also, Ellen catches him coating the bullets and becomes upset. This instigates a conversation about the recent boating accident, which Brody correctly believes to be a shark attack.

---

[40] In the final film, Brody misses a call on Hooper's behalf, who is on a research vessel called the Aurora.

After this, Brody goes for a walk along the beach and finds the driftwood in the surf. It's the one that has the dead body from the boating accident attached to it. Again, this is another scene present in the final film that occurs later on. This is followed by a sequence at the coroner's office where it's clear that the body has been lacerated in addition to being burned. Brody and the coroner can't conclusively prove whether the lacerations were caused by metal fragments from the explosion or a shark's teeth. There is talk of closing the beaches down, but Brody can't bring himself to do it without proof.

Next, we check back in with the Brody children and Andy, working on the sailboat at the harbor. Two attractive girls, Angela and Brook, walk by, and the older boys strike up a conversation with them. The boys take the girls sailing all the way to the old lighthouse. There, along with Ed and Tina (the happy couple that's constantly making out in the finished film), they find a dead killer whale floating in the water (in the film, it's washed up on the beach). Brody is alerted and comes to investigate.

Rather than having a marine biologist examine it on the beach (which is the case in the film), here the scene between Brody and Dr. Elkins takes place within a laboratory and is also a bit longer. The doctor confirms rather quickly that the whale died of a Great White. There's no argument or debate between her and Brody about this. There's also a good deal of exposition on the travel patterns of Great Whites, which reinforces Brody's suspicion that one is lurking in the waters off Amity again. The scene is quite lengthy, and Dr. Elkins explains the different types of stimuli that sharks respond to, with sound at the top of the list... a rather crucial detail for the climax.

Many will remember an exchange in the finished *Jaws 2* where Brody asks if sharks can send signals to one another from a long distance. In this iteration, the scene is spelled out a little more explicitly.

BRODY
See, I've read how dolphins send out whole messages -- I just wondered if a shark --(pauses, embarrassed) I mean, that one I killed...how do we

know it didn't communicate with other sharks before it died. Maybe it had a mate or something. Maybe I left a trace in the water, a smell -- or maybe they just sense me in some way you don't know about yet. They never go for revenge or anything like that, do they?

> DR. ELKINS
> (slightly amused)
> Sharks, Mr. Brody, never take anything personally.

The prospective audience could have interpreted this exchange one of two ways. Either Brody is so paranoid that he really believes a shark is stalking him, or, if you personally like that idea and want to believe it, then Brody is being stalked by the shark. Brody's line about the shark having a mate was Tristan's nod to her unspoken backstory for the shark, that it was the larger female mate of the first film's shark. That all said, the end line about sharks not taking anything personally does appear in the finished film. As one last aside before we move on, Zanuck wanted the part of Dr. Elkins to go to his wife, Linda Harrison (who Zanuck also wanted to play Ellen Brody in *Jaws*). Supposedly Sheinberg shot it down.

Next up is a variation of the scene where Brody shoots at a school of Blue Fish. In this case, Brody is arguing with the mayor about the dead whale (and what it could mean) when he spots a black shape in the water and goes chasing after it. This version of the scene is less dramatic. Brody never fires on the school of fish; he just yells at everyone to get out of the water with his gun drawn. At the last second, a lifeguard manages to convince him that it's really just a school of fish. An embarrassed Brody puts his gun away but spills some of his special bullets. In the film, Sean helps him pick up his shell casings, but here the mayor gets down to help Brody pick up the bullets. When Brody tells him what they are, the mayor places a sympathetic hand on his shoulder, afraid that Brody is about to crack. Vaughn then suggests that Brody take some time off before the summer gets into full swing. All in all, Tristan offered a more sympathetic version of Vaughn than what we'd see in the film.

That night, Brody and Ellen take a walk on the beach and their conversation has shades of *Jaws: The Revenge*, with Martin talking about his intense fear of the shark returning and his suspicion that it wants revenge. This far out train of thought, which Ellen herself would embrace in the fourth film, causes her to begin crying due to Brody's troubled state of mind. The scene ends with Brody yelling at the shark in the ocean.

The next scene continues this script's more sympathetic portrayal of Mayor Vaughn. While all the other town politicians debate firing Brody, Vaughn defends him, holding out hope that within a few weeks Brody will be "back to normal" while the others aren't so sure. Unlike in the film, Brody retains his job and is never fired (though he was fired in Sackler's earlier version).

While the adult Brody and Vaughn have a civil relationship, the same cannot be said for their sons Mike and Reeves, who have quite the rivalry going. In the following scene, as the boys ready their boats in the harbor, they get into a fight, and Reeves pushes Mike into the water. When Sean begins taunting Reeves, he then picks Sean up and tosses him into the water, calling him shark bait! Andy and Mike rescue Sean from the water as Reeves and his friend walk away. This scene was filmed with the original choice for Sean, Ricky Schroeder, when Hancock was still shooting the picture. However, in the finished film, Reeves/Larry Jr. is not as much of an antagonist.

The story progresses similarly to the finished film, with Brody asking Mike not to take his sailboat out in light of everything that's happened. However, Angela entices Mike to take it out anyways so that they can be alone. As Mike gets his sailing gear, Sean manages to blackmail his way onto the trip by threatening "to tell" as all young siblings do. As in the film, Sean doesn't sail with Mike. Two other female characters, one of whom is an ex-fling of Mike's named Laura, invite Sean to come with them on their boat instead. As an aside, the actress who played Laura, Lenora May, remembered in *Jaws 2: The Making of a Hollywood Sequel* that she filmed a

SHARK BITES: QUINT JR.

ACTOR BILLY VAN ZANDT CONFIRMED THAT DURING SHOOTING HE ACTUALLY WAS PLAYING QUINT'S SON. SIDEBURNS' FIRST SCENE WOULD'VE CLUED US IN TO THIS FACT, AS HE ENTERS THE STORY WHISTLING QUINT'S "FAIR SPANISH LADIES" SONG. HOWEVER, THE CHARACTER BEING QUINT'S SON HAD NO REAL BEARING ON THE STORY AND NONE OF THE OTHER CHARACTERS EVER LEARN OF HIS PARENTAGE. LIKE BOB BURNSIDES, IT WAS PLANNED FOR SIDEBURNS/QUINT JR. TO GET BITTEN IN HALF. LIKE FATHER LIKE SON.

scene where she cried over Mike going on a date with another girl.

The scuba diving scene, where the divers in training encounter the shark occurs here too. The only real difference is, in this version of the script, we know the diving instructor better because of his conversation with Brody earlier in the script. In the film, he has the same character name, Tom Andrews, but isn't very prominent outside of this one scene. Actually, in this case, it is Andrews himself who encounters the shark and surfaces too fast.

After that scene, the teenage sailboat race commences as in the final film. The only difference here is that so far, we only have a firm grasp on a handful of characters outside of the Brody boys, and this portion of the script introduces quite a few more.

As the main group races off, Ed and Tina's boat lags behind. Unlike the film, we don't see Ed's death. The action cuts away after he accidentally falls in the water. On the mainland, Brody is talking to a lifeguard over the radio, asking if he's seen Mike's boat. The lifeguard tells him the other boats are too far out to see, even with binoculars. But then, he notices Ed and Tina's sailboat in distress. We cut back to the sailboat race for a bit, and then to Brody in the police boat investigating Tina's sailboat. Notably, in this version, Ellen is not with him as in the final film (that would become a point of contention for Hancock when Sheinberg insisted on the change).

Another significant deviation occurs in the helicopter scene. In the film, the chopper first appears after the shark has attacked the teenaged sailing troupe. In this script, the helicopter is sent to direct them back to shore as a result of Tina's testimony about the shark—which the other teens know nothing about. When the helicopter informs them to return to shore, they assume it is simply to ruin their fun. Ironically, in this case, it is the chopper's reverberations that attract the shark to the area.

The shark reveals itself as Doug, one of the nerdier teenagers, is trying to re-inflate part of his sailboat. The shark bursts from the water and bites into it, "shaking it like a terrier." Doug is thrown into the water and manages to swim to Mike's boat before the shark can get him. Mike and Andy pull Doug in, then to warn the other boats about the shark (they are ahead and so didn't see what happened) Mike blows his whistle to get their attention. But it's the shark's attention he draws. She head-butts the bottom of the boat and sends all three teenagers sailing through the air. As in the film, Mike receives a bad bump to the head and is unconscious.

Mike is rescued by one of the teens named Polo, while Angela and Andy climb aboard another boat. As in the film, some of the sailboats run into each other in the chaos and become entangled while the sailboat containing the injured Mike is able to get away. The shark relentlessly attacks the tangled mass of sailboats and eventually grabs an unnamed red-headed girl. At one point, Reeves uses one of the masts as though it is a lance to try and pierce the shark's skin, but he is unsuccessful in doing so. Next, Andy takes a turn with the mast, but he doesn't fare any better. Andy tries a second time, and the shark bites the pole in half.

Brody meets up with Polo's boat and Mike (now conscious). Mike informs him that Sean is on the boat still and asks to go with him. Brody more or less tells him he will function better knowing that Mike is safe and makes him stay. Unfortunately, Brody's boat runs aground. The boys set to helping Brody get himself unstuck. If this sounds boring, it's because Tristan needed something to slow Brody down as the helicopter scene was coming up.

In this case, the helicopter scene takes place near sundown rather than during broad daylight (filming any major sequence during a sunset with natural outdoor lighting is a nightmare, so it's no surprise this was rewritten). In this iteration, rather than one pilot, there is a pilot and a spotter aboard the chopper. The helicopter intends to throw the kids a tow line from above, but the buffeting air gusts from the rotors are too harsh on the sail barge. For that reason, the chopper lands nearby. As the spotter tosses them a line, the shark charges the craft. The pilot lifts off, but it's too late, the shark grabs onto the landing gear as it takes off and pulls the chopper into the water.

Just when you thought it was safe to go back in the water...

JAWS 2

Coming to theatres everywhere June 16th.

This teaser poster, set at sunset, may have been influenced by John Hancock's version of *Jaws 2*, which would have featured the shark attacking the raft at dusk at one point. Jaws 2 © 1978 Universal Pictures

The pilot is trapped within the chopper as it sinks, while the spotter swims towards the raft. The shark wounds the spotter badly enough that he can no longer swim, and then doubles back to the sinking chopper. In an eerie scene, as the helicopter fills with water, the pilot watches the shark swim towards him. But, it doesn't eat him, and the shark merely watches as he drowns through the glass of the cockpit. Andy has jumped in to help the spotter, but there's another problem: the helicopter has leaked fuel into the water. After the chopper explodes, it lights a trail of fire along the spilled fuel that reaches the raft and catches it on fire. The kids can no longer stay on and must jump into the water with the shark. But, lucky for them, the shark is afraid of the flames (due to being set on fire itself earlier), and the flames also enable Brody to spot the sail barge from a distance.

Andy and Doug manage to swim through the wreckage and find a fire extinguisher, which they use to put out the flames so that they can get back on the raft. We cut back to Brody on his boat, which has since been knocked loose from the rocks, and it is now night (Polo's boat, with Mike, has gone back to Amity). Brody comes across the remains of Doug's boat and fishes it out of the sea with a boathook to have a look. As he does so, he observes several smaller sharks in the water. But, they begin to scatter, and Brody knows in his gut it's because the big one is coming. In a spooky scene, Brody waits for the shark, but all he hears is silence, and he can see nothing in the black waves. Brody begins to tap the water with the boat hook in hopes of making enough noise to attract the shark. But nothing happens. Brody decides he's wasting time and needs to find the kids. As he restarts the motor, his spotlight catches the big one's fin slicing through the water. Brody fires his poison-tipped bullets at it, and it disappears beneath the waves.

The spooky scene, set within a fog, is terrifying:

> Brody pursues the ghostly form through the fog. It glides before him like a reflection of the moon racing across the water, leading him as much as fleeing, a dark mirage that he follows with a strange elation, curving after it first one way, then another, never quite getting a shot...becoming hopelessly turned around.

Later, as Brody is now literally lost within the fog, the shark butts the bottom of the boat, knocking the bow into the air momentarily and causing Brody to drop his gun into the water. The poison-laced bullets will not be what kills the shark, but if you've seen *Jaws 2*, you already knew that...

When all hope of finding the kids seems lost, Brody hears a police whistle. It is Andy, who spotted the lights on Brody's boat, and is sending out a call for help. Brody pinpoints the sound and heads towards them. Brody makes contact with Sean and the frightened teenagers and makes arrangements for them to board the boat. However, so as not to unbalance the precarious raft they've created out of the wreckage, they must do so two at a time. Reeves and another character named "Sideburns" inch their way towards Brody's boat when the charred head of the shark bursts up from the wreckage to snap at them. The shark doesn't get the boys, but Brody has to circle around again. The shark divides its attention between Brody's boat and the raft equally, as if trying to keep Brody from accomplishing his goal.

Brody has to throw the kids a towline, and a tense scene occurs where Sideburns and Andy have to fish it out of the water before the shark can grab it. They do so, and Brody attempts to tow them towards a sandbar. The line snaps 25 yards from the sandbar and the raft, stressed from being pulled, begins to come apart. In a desperate measure, Brody begins to splash his legs into the water to attract the shark so that the kids can swim to the sandbar (this idea was a remnant of Sackler's story, where Brody entices the shark into the boat propellers). The shark darts in Brody's direction, and Brody pulls himself back into the boat just as it rams it. The shark then turns its attention to the swimming teenagers—Angela, Doug, and Laura (the others were too timid)—and races after them. Without a moment to spare, they make it to the sandbar.

Brody repeats the maneuver to distract the shark, and seeing that the first round worked, five more teenagers swim for the island. But the shark won't be fooled twice, and it goes for the kids. It catches up to them and begins toying with its prey, brushing against them and pressing its nose against Reeves's body. But Brody is quick enough to come to their rescue, ramming the shark with his boat.

Now eight of the kids are safe, but Sean, Sideburns, and Andy remain on the raft, being ravaged by the shark. It knocks them into the water, but Brody is close enough to snag Sean before any harm can come to him while Andy makes it to the sandbar. Sideburns then suffers what would have been the most gruesome scene in the entire franchise had it been shot. Sideburns swims for the boat and Brody tosses him a lifeline. But, Sideburns is suddenly propelled out of the water, the shark has got him. Brody pulls and Sideburns makes it to the boat—or his upper half does. The poor teen has been bitten in half below the waist to Brody's horror (a similar scene would be featured in *The Last Shark*). The severed torso pours blood into the water, attracting the shark.

The shark bursts from the water in front of Brody's face. Brody grabs the hook attached to the boat's towline and jams it right in the monster's eye. This is great except for one thing, the line is now connected to the shark, and as it retreats, it begins to pull the boat under. In the chaos, as the ship is dragged by the shark, a rubber raft accidentally inflates at the same time that Sean falls overboard. Sean climbs into the raft as the towline disgorges itself from the shark's eye. The towline, as luck would have it, attaches itself to an underwater electrical line (this idea didn't come from nowhere; as in the finished film, this script had a scene where it was accidentally discovered by Hendricks earlier). Brody is trying to get the boat moving again and must pull the line up first as it's stuck to something. Brody tows the line back up with the wench but finds it stuck to the electrical cable. The shark then lunges itself onto the boat, trying to do to Brody what the previous shark did to Quint. Brody hops overboard and jumps into the raft with Sean while the shark dislodges itself and slips back into the sea. As the shark rockets towards them, Brody positions the raft behind the electrical line. Inspiration strikes Brody, and the scene plays out as in the finished film, with Brody coaxing the shark to bite the cable. As Sean is with him in the raft (and has no clue why his father is encouraging the shark to come at them) there's an added layer of suspense. As in the film, the shark bites into the line and fries itself—a visual that might have been more exciting at night, with the electricity coursing through the shark. The script also inserts a curious shot of a shooting star as the dead shark sinks beneath the waves.

The script has a wonderful endnote that not only made it into the finished film but also one-upped the ending exchange between Brody and Hooper from the first film. As Brody embraces Sean in the life raft, he says, "Finally got your brother to take you sailing, didn't you?"

"They made me come," Sean responds, and the end credits were to begin rolling as Brody rows the raft back to the sandbar where the stranded teenagers are.

Before he began shooting, Hancock had lunch with Spielberg, who gave him some advice for working with the mechanical shark and also a few ideas, namely the shot of the shark swimming through Amity harbor early on. In fact, this sequence would end up being one of only a few scenes that were shot by Hancock that made its way into the final film.

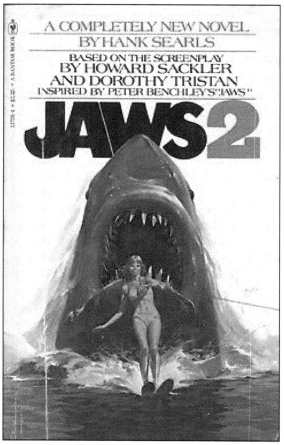

The *Jaws 2* novelization based on Tristan's screenplay.
Jaws 2 © 1978 Universal Pictures

The original Brody boys: Ricky Schroeder (left) and Tegan West (right) shooting a scene for John Hancock.
Jaws 2 © 1978 Universal Pictures

Hancock then began shooting the picture based off of a newer version of the script we just reviewed. Among the most notable changes was that the Sideburns character had reverted back to being Quint's son! On that note, many of the teens in Hancock's version were played by different actors, notably Mike, Sean, and Angela (who would be renamed Tina in the new version).[41] As already stated, Ricky Schroeder (later to become famous on *NYPD Blue*) was playing Sean Brody.[42] Among the actors who would stay were the ones cast for Andy, Sideburns/Quint Jr., and Reeves

---

[41] The actors were also allowed some creative control over their characters via the props department. Billy Van Zandt remembers, "Keith [Gordon] and I raced to the props department. He beat me to the glasses so I grabbed the hat."

[42] To better explain, Hancock had lobbied for Schroeder for Sean Brody. It was his main casting caveat. When he was let go, Schroeder was fired, more or less, out of spite for Hancock. Or at least that was Hancock's slant on it. Marc Gilpin, who was recast as Sean Brody, implied that Schroeder couldn't cry on cue and that's why he was let go. Actress Karen Corboy, who played Lucy when Schroeder shot his scenes, also recalled that the young boy had trouble hitting his marks.

(though the latter two's names would change to Bob and Larry Jr., respectively).

All of the Hancock footage was shot at Martha's Vineyard. Hancock was at one point quite frustrated by the sunny weather, which wasn't conducive to the downbeat look he was going for. For one exterior shot, he had firetrucks spray the street so it would be wet, and then brought in fog generators. Filters were then used to give the outdoor lighting a darker look.[43] Also making things difficult was the fact that shop owners on Martha's Vineyard naturally didn't want to comply with Hancock's boarded-up look. "Only one drugstore let us board up the windows," Hancock lamented.[44]

Hancock's obsession with the depressing atmosphere didn't stop there. Extras and bit-part actors were supposedly sent to the dressing room to change into darker clothes if they showed up in bright colors. The sails on the sailboats were reported to be black, and so on. Filming didn't only occur within Martha's Vineyard; some of the sailboat footage was filmed out at sea as well, according to actors interviewed in *Jaws 2: The Making of a Hollywood Sequel*.

Trouble arose for Hancock in part because Sheinberg and Zanuck had a strained relationship. This strained relationship began when both men wanted their wives cast as Mrs. Brody in the first *Jaws*. Sheinberg, as we all know, was married to Lorraine Gary. Zanuck was married to Linda Harrison, whom he had met when he was producing *Planet of the Apes* in 1968 (Harrison played Nova).

Zanuck had asked Hancock and Tristan to write in a role for Harrison. This was how the Dr. Eckler character was created, even though Harrison ironically didn't play the part in the finished film. The problems arose when Sheinberg and Gary invited Hancock and Tristan over for dinner. While there, they pitched them the idea that Ellen Brody go on the final boat rescue with her husband. Hancock wasn't keen on tweaking the script

---

[43] When this scene was reshot later under new director Jeannot Szwarc, the opposite problem occurred. As the reshoot happened in the fall, Martha's Vineyard no longer had that summertime air about it.
[44] Loynd, *Jaws 2 Log*, pp.64.

during shooting for this, and when Zanuck found out about it, his response was, "Over my dead body!"

Hancock was now caught in between two powerful men. But, because it was Zanuck who brought him onto the picture, Hancock decided he should side with him. This proved to be a mistake. When Sheinberg saw the newest draft of the script, which didn't include Ellen in the boat rescue scene, he began to give Hancock the cold shoulder.

However, Hancock's eventual firing wasn't entirely due to the issues regarding Sheinberg and Zanuck. Hancock's picky demands with the look and color pallet on the film were expensive. As they say, time is money, and when Hancock would change his mind on details at the last minute, it was costly. Actress Lenora May, who played Laura in Hancock's version, remembered in *Jaws 2: The Making of a Hollywood Sequel* that "John was vacillating so much, he was never sure of his shots. He would set up something and say, 'No we don't need a crane' and then an hour later he would ask for the crane. Things like that. I heard he was costing them a lot of money. He just wasn't efficient."[45]

Right as shooting concluded in Martha's Vineyard, and production was set to move onto Florida, Hancock and Tristan were let go. According to *The Jaws 2 Log*, Hancock had shot for 18 days, and his last day was particularly troubling. Hancock had become very frustrated trying to film extras departing a ferry and blew up on his assistant director, Scott Maitland. This, in addition to not tweaking the script to Sheinberg's liking, was possibly the straw that broke the camel's back. Even before the final day of shooting, many a person involved on *Jaws 2* in interviews would later recount Hancock's odd camera angles that they saw in the dailies, and many agreed that what Hancock was doing wasn't working. Producer Verna Fields, in particular, didn't like Hancock's direction.

Though Hancock was fired, he and Tristan's storyline ended up being told after all, just not in the medium of film. As it was, Marvel Comics had already begun producing their licensed adaptation of the film.

---

[45] Smith and Pisano, *Jaws 2: The Making of a Hollywood Sequel* (Kindle Edition).

Naturally, the Tristan script was what had been given to them at the time. The same was true of the novel by Hank Searls. So, if you want to experience the Hancock version of *Jaws 2*, happily, you can do so through those two adaptations.[46]

Jaws 2 © 1978 Universal Pictures

---

[46] Because of the creation of the Richard Donner Cut of *Superman II* in recent years, some have asked why the same thing can't be done with Hancock's version of *Jaws 2*. The sad truth is simply that not enough footage was shot to do so (again, Hancock only shot for 18 days which doesn't equal a lot of footage in Hollywood terms). Nor could Hancock's sequences be plugged into the existing *Jaws 2* because many of the characters were played by different actors.

TENTACLES

Release Date: February 25, 1977 (Italy); June 15, 1977 (U.S.)
Alternate Titles: *The Beast with the Deadly Arms* (Germany)

Directed by: Ovidio G. Assonitis (as Oliver Hellman) **Special Effects by:** Gianfranco Maioletti **Screenplay by:** Jerome Max, Tito Carpi & Steven W. Carabatsos **Music by:** Stelvio Cipriani **Cast:** John Huston (Ned Turner) Shelley Winters (Tillie Turner) Bo Hopkins (Will Gleason) Henry Fonda (Mr. Whitehead) Delia Boccardo (Vicky Gleason) Cesare Danova (John Corey) Claude Akins (Sheriff Robards)

Technovision, Technicolor, 102 Minutes

SYNOPSIS Radio signals used during construction of an underwater tunnel near Solana Beach agitates a giant octopus that begins killing locals. Though local law enforcement doesn't know what to think of the disappearances, reporter Ned Turner and killer whale trainer Will Gleason suspect a giant octopus is to blame. Turner's nephew has a near-death experience with the octopus during a sailboat race, and after that, Gleason sets out to kill it...

COMMENTARY On the surface, *Tentacles* seems like a no-brainer. After all, if a movie about a huge shark proved to be a hit, then why not a giant octopus? Sadly, compared to *Jaws*, *Tentacles* is something of a non-event. Partly to blame for this fact is that the movie's "original star" died—in a manner of speaking—before the movie got off the ground. As it was, the producers supposedly spent $1 million on a life-sized, scale octopus prop.[47] Said prop sunk to the bottom of the ocean the moment the cameras started rolling and never resurfaced. Or at least, that's the truth as best that I can piece it together. There are a few snippets here and there of a scale octopus head and tentacles, but most of the time, the monster is brought to life via shots of a real octopus... which obviously isn't very big.

Considering that this film was out to ride the success of *Jaws*—the same narrator, Percy Rodrigues, even did the *Tentacles* trailer!—perhaps it's a bit ironic that its mechanical monster malfunctioned even worse than Bruce the shark. But, even if the octopus had worked, it's debatable just how much better the film would've been. It absolutely wastes the roles given to megastars John Huston, Shelley Winters, and Henry Fonda. Notably, Huston and Winters both disappear from the film a little over an hour into it, and Fonda's role was little more than a cameo to begin with.[48]

It should also be noted that *Tentacles* was an Italian production which was filmed in California. Ultimately, nobody loved to rip off *Jaws* more than the Italians! *Tentacles* was the first of several to be followed by *The Last Shark*, *Cruel Jaws*, and others.

Whereas *Jaws* presented the fear of things unseen in the water beneath your feet, *Tentacles* presents a monster with long appendages that can yank you from off the land and into the water. This is illustrated very early on in the film, right after the credits roll. And,

---

[47] This doesn't entirely add up, as the budget was reportedly $750,000. But, perhaps that was what was leftover after the Octopus prop sank?

[48] John Houseman was part of the original cast but dropped out before filming. Yul Brynner also had to drop out due to scheduling conflicts.

during the credits, you can tell just where the film is going when the camera stops to focus on a billboard advertising an upcoming yacht race. Automatically we all know that this will take the place of the 4th of July celebration in *Jaws*.

Tentacles' first kill almost makes me wonder if it's trying to one-up the Alex Kintner scene in *Jaws*. In *Tentacles,* the first victim is a baby! You read that right. A woman is sitting with her infant overlooking the beach when she gets up to go talk with a friend who has pulled over on the side of the road. POV shots from under the water—along with some bad Italian music comparable to *The Last Shark*—lets us know that something is lurking in the waves. The women converse as passing cars occasionally obscure the baby. After a school bus passes, we see that the infant is gone! The mother runs to the overhang and looks down into the water, seeing her child's stroller in the ocean.

The film also apes the scene in *Jaws* where Hooper gets frightened by a dead body—but *Tentacles* does it incredibly well to its credit. We've been watching a young couple out fishing via POV shots from the water for a while, implying the octopus is stalking them. As the tension mounts, the young man drops his fishing pole in the water. When he goes to grab it something suddenly bursts from the ocean. Though we all think it's going to be a tentacle, it's a corpse. Then comes another tip of the hat to *Jaws* when the body is examined, but nobody wants to pin it on a monster (then again, who would suspect a giant octopus?) and suggests an accident related to the construction of a seafront tunnel.

SHELLEY WINTERS   HENRY FONDA   JOHN HUSTON

TENTÁCULOS
TENTACLES

It's around this point that we're introduced to John Huston's character, and overall the actor seems too old to be playing a go-getter reporter. Huston basically phones his performance in—not that there was anything particularly interesting to do with the role to begin with. Speaking of phoning it in, we are first introduced to Henry Fonda's character while he's on the phone, and he doesn't fare much better than Huston. His second scene is also on the phone, this time with Huston, and is very unlike Fonda. But, in Fonda's defense, he was recovering from a recent operation—he had a pacemaker installed. Furthermore, all his scenes were shot in only one day.

We get our first glimpse of the tentacles 23 minutes in when two scuba divers come across the monster. As stated earlier, the creature is presented via footage of a real octopus. It then exudes a mass of black ink, which one of the divers is pulled into by an unseen tentacle.[49] The other diver makes it back to his bathysphere and crawls inside. He radios the ship above to pull him up ASAP. The scene is suspenseful enough, and there's a good scare when the bathysphere's progress suddenly halts, and the diver turns to look out the window and sees a massive eye staring back at him. Needless to say, he doesn't make it to the surface.

The next attack scene has a husband and wife and their swimming instructor out on a boat. The two men go for a swim while the wife suns herself. Again, we see a real-life tiny octopus trying to portray the giant cephalopod crawling across the seafloor. Next, we see some sort of head prop pop out of the water briefly, plus some sort of full-body prop from a distance which attacks the boat. There are also a few scale tentacles that encircle the wife in the water, which are well done.

Another boat goes out looking for that one in the darkness of night, which makes for a spooky scene. The octopus sinks that ship too, and the miniature boat used isn't terribly good (though at least it's glimpsed fleetingly). A woman jumps overboard as the octopus's tentacles, barely visible, pull the ship under. She swims through the pitch-black water in terror. Like Chrissy Watkins in *Jaws*, she swims towards a buoy. The growling octopus then surfaces but is again represented by a real octopus pretending to be big. The prop tentacles then ensnare the woman and lift her into the air in what might be the movie's best scene up to this point.

Taking the place of *Jaws'* 4th of July celebration is a sailboat race, which as the viewer, you know is going to end badly. And, having watched the shoddy effects up to this point, one has to wonder just how they're going

---

[49] One has to ponder if this is how the scene was written, or if this was how the scene was tweaked considering the octopus prop didn't work?

The octopus prop from *Tentacles*. © 1977 AIP

to pull it off. The scene wasn't as bad as I thought it would be, but it still reeks of compromise in light of the broken octopus prop. There are a few shots of the octopus prop head peeking out of the water, and it looks pretty good. But mostly, we see the scene from the monster's POV (as a way of not showing the monster) with people screaming at it and falling out of their sailboats in terror. The best shots are of the head prop approaching the sailboat belonging to Ned's nephew, ten-year-old Tommy. But don't worry, Tommy doesn't end up being the next Alex Kintner, that honor befalls his friend Jaimie who gets dragged under the water on the sailboat. This is the only person the octopus actually kills during the entire scene, and once it's over, you can't help but feel that something far more exciting was written but couldn't be shot. The musical composition, "Too Risky a Day For a Regatta," actually ends up stealing the scene, and the composition has gone on to become a quasi-classic in its own right.[50] That said, though it has an excellent sense of momentum, it sounds more like something Thomas Crowne would steal a priceless painting to.

The death of the young boy sets up the showdown between man and monster. And no, in this case, the man is not John Huston's character. After the sailboat scene is over, John Huston, Shelly Winters, and Henry Fonda all disappear—their characters receiving no proper exit. All in all, it cements the fact that there was really nothing to the characters to begin with. From this point forward, the story becomes more of a bromance

---

[50] The film's composer would go on to do other creature features like *The Great Alligator* and *Piranha II*.

between Will Gleason, the whale trainer, and a scuba diver, John Corey.

The plan is for Will to use his trained killer whales to slay the octopus, and a long nighttime conversation between he and John in the cabin of his boat seems to be this film's version of the Quint speech in *Jaws*. Or, that is to say, it has the same mood about it due to the lighting and camera work. Whereas Quint told a horror story, Will talks of his deep love for killer whales and how misunderstood he feels that they are.

The way the two men set out to kill the beast on a boat in the ocean is also similar to the climax of *Jaws*. They are towing the whales behind them in a special container to unleash them when they find the octopus, but an accident occurs, and the whales get out. So the duo decides to don scuba gear and hunt the octopus themselves with spear guns. The giant cephalopod comes along and confronts them (this is done by unleashing the real octopus on miniature figurines of the men). Just when it appears Will is about to be eaten, his whales show up to save him. The killer whales vs. octopus fight is brought to life via killer whale puppets biting the tentacles of the real octopus (the octopus may be real, but it was dead before the scene was shot). Though the idea looked great on paper, its execution on screen gives *Tentacles* more in common with a Japanese monster movie than it does a summer blockbuster like *Jaws*. But the musical score for the fight is good at least and instills the scene with an excellent sense of excitement and momentum.

However, watching the whales fight the octopus while John rescues Will can only be entertaining for so long. It's also at this point that the viewer realizes the giant octopus thing is never actually going to pay off. As it is, a normal-sized, real octopus passed off as a giant one the entire movie is ultimately all you get. This might have flown in a B-Movie ten years earlier, but those days were past. In all other respects *Tentacles* has the sheen of a summer blockbuster which makes the effects all the more disappointing.

Upon release, critics were not kind to the film, nor should they have been. However, whether the film cost over a million or under a million, the final gross was $3 million, so presumably it made some kind of profit.

TINTORERA:
Killer Shark

Release Date: April 7, 1977 (Mexico); September 15, 1978 (U.S.)
Alternate Titles: *Tintorera: Killer Shark* (U.S.) *Tintorera! Sea Monsters Are Attacking* (Germany)

Directed by: René Cardona Jr. **Special Effects by:** Miguel Vázquez **Screenplay by:** René Cardona Jr., Christina Schuch & Ramón Bravo (novel) **Music by:** Basil Poledouris **Cast:** Susan George (Gabriella) Hugo Stiglitz (Steven) Andrés García (Miguel) Fiona Lewis (Patricia) Eleazar García (Crique)

1.85 : 1, Color, 126 Minutes

SYNOPSIS Steven, a U.S. born man of Mexican descent, returns to a Mexican coastal village where he takes up the occupation of shark hunting. He has a torrid affair with an Englishwoman, Patricia, but the two part ways when Steven can't confess his love for her. Patricia finds solace in the arms of handsome swimming instructor Miguel, whom Steven is jealous of. One morning while out on a swim, Patricia is killed by a 19-foot tiger shark. Steven goes to confront Miguel to ask where she went.

Miguel, not knowing her fate, assumes she has gone back home. An unlikely friendship develops between Steven and Miguel, who go into the shark hunting business together. The two even willingly enter into a relationship with the same woman, Gabriella. Things take a tragic turn when Miguel is killed by the tiger shark. Gabriella leaves, and Steven vows revenge...

COMMENTARY By 1977, there had already been quite a few variations on *Jaws*. *Jaws* with an octopus? Check. With a Killer Whale? Check. With a Grizzly? Check. With psychic sharks? Check, again. But... *Jaws* in the form of what amounts to a softcore porn film???[51]

Enter *Tintorera*, which is essentially an exploitation film to showcase bodies in and out of their swimsuits more than anything else. This is apparent right off the bat, as one of the main characters, Miguel, is essentially a gigolo. In between romance scenes we'll occasionally get a few shots of the shark swimming—maybe chomping a few fishes—to remind us that it's still in the movie.

In terms of the plot structure, the film isn't terribly similar to *Jaws*, but it does have a few of the obligatory *Jaws*-type scenes. *Jaws* began with Chrissy Watkins swimming nude in the ocean before being attacked by the shark. As it was dark, there was no explicit nudity. *Tintorera* is the polar opposite. During the first shark attack (35 minutes in), Patricia goes skinny dipping in broad daylight, leaving nothing to the imagination in the shark's POV shots.

The shark kills Patricia via stock-footage of a real shark eating bloody chunks of meat. Though the stock footage is more "real" (and bloody), it's less fun than *Jaws*. Also, in real life, the shark was only about seven feet long, while in the film, it's portrayed as being 19 feet long.

You would think Patricia's death would serve as the film's dramatic lynchpin with her two lovers perhaps vowing revenge on the shark, right? Instead, Steven and Miguel never even find out that the shark ate her! Maybe it's all meant to be a bizarre coincidence?

---

[51] Or a telenovela if you're watching the cut version which removed the nude scenes.

The scene where the shark bites Miguel in half is well done. In one of the few scenes to use actual special effects (rather than just archival footage of sharks eating something bloody in the water), Miguel's bottom half sinks to the ocean floor. For another shot, a real shark was given a prop of Miguel's severed head to carry in its jaws.

After Miguel's death it would seem the movie finally has the dramatic lynchpin that it needs to give it some buildup to the climax. However, it never really takes advantage of the momentum, and the movie plods along for another 30 minutes, picking up a subplot from earlier about two sisters vacationing in Mexico. Steven goes for a swim with the girls, and one of them gets grabbed right out of Steven's arms by the shark in an excellent shot. Compared to future *Jaws* rip-offs like *Cruel Jaws* or *Deep Blood*, which sported horrid, choppy editing, this scene is clear and concise by comparison. I'm not even sure how it was accomplished since all of the shark footage looks to be a real shark!

The ending is artful, but not very exciting. Steven ventures into the ocean during a spooky night-time dive to kill the shark. He uses a dead manta ray as bait, and when the shark comes sniffing around as planned, Steven shoots the shark, and then the shark grabs Steven. Steven's flashlight sinks to the seafloor, and the screen tints itself a red color (the blood of Steven and the shark). We then fade into a picture of the trio of lovers (Steven, Gabriella, and Miguel), a love ballad plays, and the credits roll.

Tintorera was a joint British-Mexican production shot in Mexico. Like *Jaws*, it too was based on a novel. Interestingly, it was written by an actual shark expert, Ramon Bravo, who had studied a real 19-foot shark called Tintorera. Bravo had discovered the sleeping sharks of Isla Mujeres and helped with this film's underwater photography, which it has to be admitted, is impressive.

Due to censorship in Mexico at the time, *Tintorera* could only play in a heavily edited version in its country of origin, though most European countries saw it uncut. Among the film's fans are Quentin Tarantino, who showed it at the 8th Morelia International Film Festival.

JAW MAN:
The Lost AIP Spoof

Developmental Period: 1977

Screenplay by: John Brosnan **Proposed Cast/ Creatures/Characters:** Jaw Man (John Cleese)

SYNOPSIS A scientist trying to find a cure for cancer begins injecting himself with shark antibodies. Gradually, he begins turning into a Sharkman himself. His first episode occurs at a seafood restaurant where he flips out. Next, he starts attacking people out at sea, then public swimming pools, until, ultimately, his reign of terror even extends to private home bathtubs! His killing spree is almost brought to an end when he is harpooned. He is then netted and strung up on a seaside pier, but he slips back into the water and escapes. Sometime later, a shark is caught and killed by local fishermen. While the body dangles from a peer, it slowly reverts to the form of a man.

COMMENTARY Today, the late author John Brosnan is best remembered as the creator of *Carnosaur* (1984), under the pen name of Harry Adam Knight. Brosnan is one of the unsung heroes of science fiction who occasionally had a million-dollar idea that never took off. Case in point, *Carnosaur* predated *Jurassic Park* by six years and had the exact same concept: genetic engineering bringing dinosaurs back to life. All poor Brosnan got out of his book was a Roger Corman adaptation, while Michael Crichton's novel was filmed by Steven Spielberg.

Back in 1977, Brosnan had another interesting idea, though I wouldn't say it was a million-dollar one. Due to the success of *Jaws*, Brosnan envisioned a Jekyll and Hyde-like spoof on the concept, wherein a scientist injecting himself with shark DNA in an attempt to cure cancer becomes a man shark! Notably, the man shark concept pre-dated Peter Benchley's own man shark ideas that came to fruition in the form of 1994's *White Shark* novel. However, I'd say Brosnan had the right idea in making the story a comedy.

Brosnan reminisced that, "It occurred to me, like it occurred to countless other exploitation-minded people that one might be able to cash in on [*Jaws*]."[52] Brosnan mentioned his man shark idea to the husband of his literary agent, whom he referred to only as Peter, who liked it very much. Peter and Brosnan teamed up to write a script based on the idea. Peter first approached Sir John Terry of the National Film Finance Board about the project.

"To my amazement," Brosnan remembered, "Sir John liked our script and offered to put up half the total budget, providing we found a distributor and the other half of the money."[53] The next step was finding the distributor, and Peter approached his old friend Mike Deeley, then the head of British Lion (a now-defunct U.K. distributor). Deeley loved the script as it turned out, his only caveat was that he wanted John Cleese for the part. Now, you wouldn't think that a high profile actor like Cleese would be unwanted for the part, but Brosnan and Peter had some good reasons for not wanting the actor. As it was, John Cleese had a habit of rewriting scripts to his liking, and Brosnan and Peter wanted to keep their script the way that it was. They

[52] Brosnan, "A Different Set of Jaws," *You Only Live Once* (2007). https://efanzines.com/YOLO/YouOnlyLiveOnce.pdf.
[53] Ibid.

also may have felt that an overly comic actor in the part might have been too much. Plus, they also felt it was unlikely Cleese would even take the role. And so the duo parted ways with Deeley.

That discouragement aside, the duo sought out a producer and found one in the form of Norman "Spike" Priggin. Previously Priggin had served as the producer of Joe Losey's films of the 1970s, but had recently made the switch to horror films. "Spike" liked the script, but like all producers, wanted to change it. Brosnan recalled that, "When I met Spike at our first script conference it immediately occurred to me that he would, if he'd been a few years younger, have been perfect for the role of the shark-man himself, as he had the sort of jutting jaw that looked as if it could slice through two inch armour plate with ease."[54]

Furthermore, Peter had warned Brosnan beforehand that Spike could "be pretty ferocious." Plenty of palavering occurred between the three men as they read over the script, with Brosnan humorously recounting that,

> At first I was hesitant to cross swords with him in case he leapt up and bit me in the leg, but soon I was putting up a strong battle to protect my golden words: "But that's a very funny line. The funniest in the whole script! And it's important too! It's a plot point!" "No, it's not," Spike would say. "It's weak, schoolboy humour. Cut it!" I cut. And cut, and cut. But I must admit that by the time Spike had hacked his way through the whole script it was much improved.[55]

The polished script was submitted to Rank, currently under the management of Sir Frank Poole. Ironically, while Rank distributed a lot of exploitation type films, they became very "moral" as Brosnan put it about what they would produce themselves. As it was, Poole's wife had seen the script and considered it to be in poor taste! So the duo next took the script to EMI. However, they were uninterested in the script because of the earlier

[54] Ibid.
[55] Ibid.

disagreement between Brosnan, Peter, and Mike Deeley. British Lion, which Deeley headed, was possibly about to merge with EMI. Therefore EMI didn't want to greenlight a project that Deeley had more or less rejected.

But then fortune seemed to finally smile upon the prospective film. Peter had a friend named Ian Shand, who had recently come into a small fortune and wanted to get into the movie business. He then offered to produce the film. And so Spike was out, and Shand was in. Things got even better when Shand met the English representative for American International Pictures (AIP), which was the leading producer and distributor of genre/exploitation films in the States. The rep, Steve Previn, absolutely loved the idea. "I'm sending this to the States right away with a recommendation that we do it! They always follow my advice, so you can count on shooting this in October without fail!" he told Brosnan.[56]

After this, an art director was hired for the project, studio space was booked, and location scouting began. Many scenes would take place within an old seaside aquarium that had been converted into a laboratory. The centerpiece of the set was to be a large glass tank containing a ten-foot-long tiger shark. Inquiries were made into what it would take to rent a shark, and the producers discovered that would be a tall order. So, instead, they decided rear projection could be used for those scenes. Now they just needed shark footage. As their bad luck would have it, no sharks were available in any English aquariums!

Peter then began making arrangements to go to an aquarium in the U.S. when they got more discouraging news. As Peter was talking to a technician at Pinewood, the tech told him how the crew of The Spy Who Loved Me had just gone to the U.S. to do the same thing! In the Bond film, the villain had an underwater lair codenamed Atlantis that also contained a shark aquarium. His henchman was even famously named Jaws (the steel-toothed giant played by Richard Kiel). When Peter found out about the shark inspired henchman, he and Brosnan both felt a bit disappointed,

---

56 Ibid.

as they felt that James Bond was beating them to the punch with their own shark man. Part of the disappointment came from the character's name being Jaws, as AIP had decided to title Brosnan's man-shark movie *Jaw Man*.

Peter and Brosnan then made it their goal to beat *The Spy Who Loved Me* to theaters as preparations continued. Designs were made for the main set, actors (specifically in regard to their swimming skills) were being tested, and *Jaw Man* was even announced in a few movie magazines like *Castle of Frankenstein*. But, AIP turned fickle on the men. Suddenly, and seemingly without warning, they decided not to produce the film two weeks before shooting was to begin!

Jaw Man was dead before it even got into the water. AIP felt the silly plot was too close to the old monster movies they used to produce back in the 1950s. "Apparently no one had told the AIP mob that it was a spoof," Brosnan remembered.[57] The other reason, oddly enough, was that the film was too "cheap." B-Movies were out thanks to *Star Wars*, and now movies needed to be pricey "event" films to matter. AIP may have done better with *Jaw Man* than they did with their ill-received (and expensive) *Jaws*-rip-off *Tentacles* had they went on with production.

Brosnan ended his original piece on the experience, written in 1977, by stating, "Shand is trying to interest some Arab friends in the idea and Peter is thinking seriously of going back to Deeley and saying that he's changed his mind about John Cleese."[58]

---

[57] Ibid.
[58] Ibid.

THE BLACK PEARL

Release Date: August 1977
Alternate Titles: *Manta Ray* (Mexico) *The Secret Cave* (Canada)

Directed by: Saul Swimmer **Screenplay by:** Victor Miller, Tony Recoder, Rodney Sheldon & Scott O'Dell (novel) **Music by:** Eumir Deodato **Cast:** Mario Custodio (Ramon Salazar) Carlos Estrada (Blas) Perla Cristal (Mrs. Salazar) Carl Anderson (Moro) Emilio Rodríguez (Padre Gallardo)

Color, 95 Minutes

SYNOPSIS When Ramon Salazar, the son of a village patriarch who dreams of becoming a pearl diver, ventures into a forbidden cave, he finds a gigantic black pearl. However, the cave is also the den of the mythical Manta Diablo, which turns out to be a very real giant Manta Ray. The Manta Diablo sinks a boat carrying Ramon's father at sea, and so Ramon takes to the ocean to kill the beast.

COMMENTARY "You've seen giant sharks. You've seen giant octopi. Now, from William Cash-Saul Swimmer Productions comes *The Black Pearl*, the story of a giant manta ray." This ad, accompanied by some splendid artwork in *House of Hammer* magazine, was my introduction to *The Black Pearl*. Though the ad would have you believe that this film was possibly another *Jaws* rip-off like *Tentacles*, the film was based upon a 1967 novel by Scott O'Dell.[59] However, *Jaws'* success most likely did result in the novel being optioned for a movie. The film is so obscure today that I thought it was an uncompleted project for a time, but it did see release in late summer of 1977.

You've seen giant sharks. You've seen giant octopi. Now, from William Cash-Saul Swimmer Productions comes **The Black Pearl**, the story of a giant manta ray.

Very little is known about the early stages of the production, outside of an entry in Jim Danforth's book *Dinosaurs, Dragons & Drama*. Danforth presented what

---

[59] This project shouldn't be confused with the 1934 Polish production called *The Black Pearl*, which apparently involved a giant octopus in some capacity that was later recycled for one of the *Flash Gordon* or *Buck Rodgers* serials.

could have been a very different version of *The Black Pearl* on a technical level had he been involved. Danforth definitely had the skills to pull off the impressive scenes glimpsed in pre-production artwork.

Danforth was in the middle of trying to get an adaptation of Edgar Rice Boroughs' *At the Earth's Core*[60] off the ground when he was approached by Saul Swimmer about doing some effects work on *The Black Pearl*. At the time, rather than a large prop or animatronic, Swimmer was considering using stop-motion effects more akin to monster movies of the past—the same type of films that *Jaws* had more or less made irrelevant.[61]

Danforth was asked by Don Weed (presumably one of the film's early producers) to construct a plastic model of the Manta Ray. However, they weren't approaching Danforth to be the special effects director of the whole film, just one or two sequences. Specifically, they were eyeing Danforth to create and direct the effects portions of the scene where the manta attacks a small fishing boat. Danforth got as far as storyboarding a few scenes, including one where the manta ray leapt out of the ocean in the moonlight. In his memoirs, Danforth revealed that the manta might have been a simple black silhouette in these shots, so had it been filmed, traditional animation could have been used. When this storyboard proved to be a hit, the producers also asked Danforth to storyboard a scene showing the manta ray getting harpooned as it leaps over a boat. Danforth recalled that this intimidated him because the great Mentor Huebner was also doing preproduction art for *The Black Pearl*. "I liked Mentor, and we got along very well. However, I knew that my storyboard work couldn't compare to his, and I told him so."[62]

For whatever reason, possibly budget woes, Danforth's stopmotion method was eventually abandoned in favor of a quicker method: a giant manta

---

[60] Danforth would be beaten to the punch by Amicus's adaptation, released in 1976.

[61] I mean to say in the eyes of audiences at the time they were now irrelevant, I absolutely love the old style monster movies, as I'm sure many of you do as well.

[62] Danforth, *Dinosaurs, Dragons & Drama*, pp.108.

ray prop. However, this prop was in no way shape or form capable of the movement Danforth could have afforded it had he worked on the project. Had he done so, it's possible *The Black Pearl* would not have faded into obscurity.

Scene from the climax of *The Black Pearl*.

Even Danforth was unaware that the project was completed for many years. He remembered, "At the time, I heard that some production filming for *The Black Pearl* was being done in Spain. For many years, I had the impression that the film had not been completed, but sites on the internet state that it was released in 1977."[63]

After playing in theaters, the film secured a VHS release in the early 1980s, but to the best of my knowledge has never been put on DVD. Therefore, *The Black Pearl* is something of a lost film today. Clips from the VHS posted to YouTube (courtesy of a video review by SCHLOCKMEISTERS) seem to imply that not much of the monster manta was shown.

What is shown is what appears to be real footage of a manta ray intercut with a good-looking scale prop of the monster. The editing is a bit choppy to compensate for the limited ability of the prop, but we do see it leap out of the water and capsize a fishing boat early on. Its next significant scene comes when Ramon returns the pearl

---

[63] Ibid.

to the sea, and the Manta leaps out of the water to terrorize him and another fisherman. The other fisherman harpoons the manta diablo, which then begins pulling their boat. The man then jumps onto the back of the ray and begins to stab it. The ray pulls the man under and doesn't surface again, and that's it apparently. Ramon keeps the pearl and sells it to help his village.

It's a shame that there is no DVD release of *The Black Pearl*, as it looks to be a quality production.

Developing
LEGEND OF DINOSAURS

Release Date: April 29, 1977 (Japan)
Alternate Titles: *Legend of Dinosaurs and Monster Birds* (Japan) *The "Legend of Dinosaurs"* (U.S.) *Giants of the Past* (Germany) *The Monsters of Prehistory* (France) *Magnitude 10 Earthquake* (Italy) *Legend of Dinosaurs* (Russia)

Directed by: Junji Kurata **Special Effects by:** Fuminori Obayashi **Screenplay by:** Isao Matsumoto & Ichiro Otsu **Music by:** Masao Yagi **Cast:** Tsunehiko Watase (Ashizawa) Nobiko Sawa (Akiko) Tomoko Kiyoshima (Junko) Shotako Hayashi (Akira) Fuyukichi Maki (Muku)

Toeiscope, Color, 92 Minutes

SYNOPSIS An ice cave full of prehistoric eggs is rumored to lie beneath the forests of Mt. Fuji which brings Tokyo geologist Ashizawa to the area. During his investigation, Ashizawa meets an old flame, Akiko, a photographer scuba diving in Lake Sai with her friend Junko. It becomes apparent that something is lurking in the waters after several mysterious deaths occur including Junko's. Soon Lake Sai is besieged by scientific equipment and investigators who have no luck in finding the monster, alleged to be a Plesiosaurus. In the ice cave, one of the eggs hatches a Rhamphorynchus that kills two spelunkers. Determined to see the dinosaur in the lake for himself, Ashizawa and Akiko go scuba diving. With no luck finding the monster, they travel up an underwater passage into the ice cave where they find the broken egg and the grizzly remains of the two victims. Back on the surface, the newly-hatched Rhamphorynchus kills several of the town's populace and then returns to the forest. Making their way outside the cave, Ashizawa and Akiko are shocked to see the Plesiosaur roaming the woods. Soon it battles the returning Rhamphorynchus as Mt. Fuji begins to erupt. The Plesiosaurus is killed when it falls into a fissure caused by the massive eruption. Ashizawa and Akiko's fate is unclear, though they are at least together.

COMMENTARY Ever wonder what the Japanese reaction to *Jaws* was?[64] As much as Japan loved giant monster movies, surely they'd have a response? Well, they did, and many consider this to be one of the worst monster movies ever made. Trumpeted as the highest budgeted Japanese movie ever produced by powerhouse Toei Studios, *Legend of Dinosaurs and Monster Birds* was also a flop when released in Japan.

The roots of this project are many-faceted, and reach back not only to *Jaws*, but also the looming Dino De Laurentiis *King Kong* remake. Toei Studios was renowned in Japan for their Yakuza movies, and let Toho and Daiei churn out the giant monsters. But, with all the hype generated by the Japanese release of *Jaws* and the impending Kong remake, Toei finally wanted in on the game.

Rather than copying *Jaws*, they first tried to ape Kong. To do so, they teamed with Amicus Productions of England to produce the obnoxiously titled *Kongorilla*.

---

[64] It was released in Japan in December of 1975, and like everywhere else, was a huge hit.

Legend of Dinosaurs © 1977 Toei

When Amicus went belly-up, they turned their attention to a giant Devil Ray from outer space in *Devil Manta*. When they could find no backers for that, they decided to do an aquatic monster movie similar to *Jaws*. Only, instead of sharks, they wanted to use dinosaurs. The idea was that of Toei president Shigeru Okada, who specifically wanted to do a movie similar to *Jaws* that they could hopefully export to other territories.

The initial story draft was much closer to *Jaws* than the resultant film (set in an inland lake). The story pitch was set on Kisogashima in the Satsunan Islands, where an unspecified aquatic dinosaur[65] was to munch on beachgoers. It would also fight an Archaeopteryx, a ludicrous idea considering these prehistoric birds/reptiles were not very large at all.

Possibly for the sake of cutting the budget, the location was changed to Lake Sai, a body of water at the foot of Mt. Fuji. Despite being set in an inland lake, the film still has plenty of callbacks to *Jaws*. As in that film, the monster kills several people before we actually see it. First, a couple on a paddleboat are capsized by an unseen object. Next, a headless horse is found in the woods (in the trees no less!).[66]

Before we get a full-on reveal of the monster, we are teased in the form of a hoax. You will no doubt remember in *Jaws* there is a scene of two boys staging a prank with a shark fin right before the real shark appears. That happens here as well, shark fin and all (even though the Lake Sai monster is known to the locals as a dragon or dinosaur and not a shark).

During the middle of a country music festival on the lake, two scuba divers operate a large, black shark fin in the distance. Their friend, on shore, makes sure to point it out to everyone. Panic ensues for a while, until the female lead, a photographer, uses the zoom lens on her camera to confirm that it's a fake.

As the two pranksters swim to shore to meet their friend at a remote location on the other side of the lake, the real monster rises from the water and eats them while their friend watches in horror. The friend runs to the local government offices to tell them that the real monster has appeared. The mayor just chides him for not doing a better job of the hoax earlier and doesn't believe him at all.

---

[65] It's possible their initial idea was for a Kronosaur which was more shark-like than a plesiosaur. It's possible that they chose the plesiosaur to stick it to Toho, who was still struggling to bring their *Nessie* movie to life.

[66] This is a good spot to note that there are several scenes of the plesiosaur on land. Usually, these scenes are accomplished via the plesiosaur's POV as it walks through the woods. The shots are quite similar to *Grizzly's* POV shots from the bear's perspective. Considering that *Grizzly* was popular in Japan, this could have been the inspiration.

SHARK BITES: *TERREMOTO 10 GRADO*

IN ITALY, *LEGEND OF DINOSAURS* WAS RE-EDITED INTO MORE OF A DISASTER MOVIE CALLED *MAGNITUDE 10 EARTHQUAKE*. IT COMPLETELY REMOVED THE ORIGINAL SCORE AND REPLACED IT WITH MUSIC TRACKS BY JOHN BARRY FROM *THE DEEP*! ARGUABLY, IN MANY INSTANCES, BARRY'S SCORE IMPROVED THE FILM, EVEN IF THE SCORE WAS PROBABLY USED ILLEGALLY...

The Italian edit, *Terremoto 10 Grado*, was guilty of some false advertising where *Legend of the Dinosaurs* was concerned.

You see, there's just a hint that the local village either paid the boys to perpetrate the hoax or were complicit in it somehow. As in *Jaws*, the theme of a village in need of tourist dollars is front and center. Actually, this film is an interesting inverse to *Jaws* in that the locals promote their monster, which they think to be mythical, as their main tourist draw. (Ironically, this is somewhat similar to an idea that was discarded from Howard Sackler's original *Jaws 2* story wherein a promoter begins exploiting the shark attack.) Once the monster rears its ugly head for real and people start dying, there is both fear and rejoicing on the part of the village. Now more people than ever have been drawn to the village, even if no one is allowed to go into the water.

The film's most famous scene involves the plesiosaur stalking a girl in a raft. Though its effects are inferior to

Jaws, the scares generated by the staging of the scene are top-notch. Perhaps it's because the lake is so foggy and isolated. The girl is waiting on her friend, Akiko, who is scuba diving in the lake's depths (why the dinosaur doesn't eat her, we do not know). The girl, named Junko, innocently dips her feet into the water from the raft and begins to kick them. Out pops the head of the plesiosaur from under her feet. It grabs her by the foot and lifts her high into the air, and then drops her. The animal is deliberately and cruelly toying with its food. It submerges, watching Junko from a distance as she tries desperately to swim to shore. It surfaces underneath her, lifting her up on its slimy head. Junko screams and falls back into the water. Curiously, the dinosaur watches Junko panic and struggle in the water, and we fade out, not actually seeing her get eaten.

Akiko then returns to the raft, curious as to where Junko has gone. Shouting for her, a hand suddenly emerges from the water and grips the raft, still alive. "There you are," Akiko says, relieved. She grabs Junko's hand, and in quite the jump scare, the half-eaten torso plops into the raft! Of course, Junko could not possibly still be alive to move her arms at this point, but it's a good scare nonetheless and manages to make this film even gorier than *Jaws*.

Still from the famous raft scene in *Legend of the Dinosaurs*.

U.S. VHS release.

Years later, Richard Matheson would pitch a *Jaws* sequel where a great white swims upriver and becomes trapped in an inland lake. There, it naturally eats the locals, who have no idea that a great white is in the lake. The spooky raft scene from *Legend of Dinosaurs* makes me think we missed out on Matheson's treatment in some ways. *Legend of Dinosaurs* raft scene would have worked great with the shark from *Jaws*, stalking its unsuspecting victim in the fog.

One of the bigger nods to *Jaws* in *Legend of Dinosaurs* comes during a village meeting discussing the monster. You'll remember that during the meeting scene in *Jaws* an official draws a shark on a chalkboard. Here, they have drawn a plesiosaur on their chalkboard. Ben Gardner's head gets a nod too, as does the floating leg in the lagoon. As Ashizawa and Akiko scuba dive in the lake, a severed head floats in front of them (predating a similar scene from *Jaws 3-D*). But it's more of a shock factor than a scare factor. Soon after that, they swim up a tunnel that leads them into a cave where the Rhamphorynchus has hatched. Akiko grabs for something that turns out to be a severed leg (this predates a similar scene from *Jurassic Park* involving Samuel L. Jackson's dismembered arm).

The ending is nothing like *Jaws*, though, and goes completely off the rails due to the limited mobility of the two dinosaur props as they are pitted against each other. It looks a bit like two museum exhibits banging into each other. To add some excitement, Mt. Fuji erupts, and the lava swallows the two beasts up.

As stated earlier, Toei had allegedly pumped a great deal of money into the film (though it doesn't look it), making it their highest budgeted feature ever. Again, this was largely done because they had high hopes that it would be a profitable release overseas. It wasn't.[67] In the U.S., the most coveted market of all, the film was released straight to video. To add insult to injury, it was picked up by the company currently releasing all the kid-friendly Gamera movies to home video. As such, a film that was actually gorier than *Jaws* was mistakenly put under the company's "Just For Kids" label! Thanks to this mistaken moniker, I saw this film long before I would ever see *Jaws*. So, for me, this was the first movie to make me afraid to go into the water...

---

[67] Well, it was in the Soviet Union oddly enough. It was one of the highest grossing Japanese films ever released there! In fact, when 1993's *Godzilla vs. Mechagodzilla* was exported to Russia they renamed it *Legend of Dinosaurs 2*!

115

Is anything
worth the terror of

THE DEEP

A Columbia/EMI Presentation · The Casablanca Filmworks Production · A Peter Yates Film
ROBERT SHAW · JACQUELINE BISSET · NICK NOLTE
"THE DEEP" · LOUIS GOSSETT and ELI WALLACH
Based on the novel by Peter Benchley · Screenplay by Peter Benchley and Tracy Keenan Wynn
Produced by Peter Guber · Directed by Peter Yates · Music by John Barry

Developing
THE DEEP

Release Date: June 17, 1977

Directed by: Peter Yates **Special Effects by:** Ira Anderson Jr. **Screenplay by:** Peter Benchley & Tracy Keenan Wynn **Music by:** John Barry **Cast:** Robert Shaw (Romer Treece) Jacqueline Bisset (Gail Berke) Nick Nolte (David Sanders) Louis Gossett Jr. (Henri 'Cloche' Bondurant) Eli Wallach (Adam Coffin) Dick Anthony Williams (Slake) Earl Maynard (Ronald) Bob Minor (Wiley)

Panavision, Metrocolor, 123 Minutes

SYNOPSIS A vacationing couple, David Sanders and Gail Berke, discover what appears to be a gold medallion while scuba diving in Bermuda. Along with the medallion is a strange vial of liquid. They take their finds to experienced diver Romer Treece, who theorizes that the gold could have come from a Spanish galleon. The vial turns out to be morphine from another wreck, the *Goliath*, a U.S. military ship that sunk during WWII. A local crime lord, Cloche, catches wind of the finds. Using voodoo as an intimidation ploy, he forces

Sanders, Berke, and Treece to recover the morphine for him. Instead, Treece plans to recover the Spanish treasure and place explosives on the *Goliath*, so that the morphine will be forever out of Cloche's reach...

COMMENTARY In the early 1970s, back when he was a writer for *National Geographic*, the magazine offered Peter Benchley a choice between two assignments. Option number one was poisonous sea snakes in the Coral Sea. Option number two was the history of shipwrecks in Bermuda. Benchley took option two and went to Bermuda, where he met Teddy Tucker, a legend in the world of deep-sea diving. Benchley and Tucker became friends, and the trip begat another ocean-themed story in Benchley's mind, but this one wouldn't be focused on a monster. Its focus would be the deep itself. Furthermore, one of the main characters in the story was inspired by Tucker. In 1976, after *Jaws* was already a monumental hit, *The Deep* was published and soared to the top of bestseller lists.

As was the case with *Jaws*, *The Deep* was optioned for film rights before it was published. Producer Peter Gruber read it when it was still in its galleys (or page proofs). As Zanuck and Brown did with *Jaws*, he read it in one day and immediately optioned the rights on November 5, 1975, for $500,000.

Benchley recalled once again writing three drafts of the script, which were in turn rewritten by others.[68] However, *The Deep* screenplay ended up being much more faithful to the novel than the *Jaws* screenplay was. Benchley also went to Bermuda for much of the shoot, and as in *Jaws*, shot a cameo.[69] Shooting began in July of 1976 and utilized the real wreck of the *RMS Rhone* in the British Virgin Islands.

Though *The Deep* certainly stands on its own, the fact that it came from the same man who wrote *Jaws* didn't hurt it. One could just almost argue that some audience members did look at it as a quasi-sequel to *Jaws*. The casting of Robert Shaw also connected it to *Jaws*. In fact, though based on Teddy Tucker, his character is

---

[68] How the drafts differ is unknown, but in the novel Treece dies in the end.
[69] This cameo was for extra footage intended for the extended TV version, however.

inevitably still reminiscent of Quint, just dressed in different clothes and sans Quint's mustache. He's also a bit more refined than Quint, but only slightly.

Marvel Comics adaptation.

Still, some members of the production naturally wanted it to be known that this was not a *Jaws* sequel. In newspapers of the time, Gruber said, "Neither [Shaw] nor I was concerned about prior associations. He's too damn good an actor to repeat himself, and besides, the roles are entirely different. This is 'The Deep' not 'Jaws II'."

All that said, the producers initially eyed Steven Spielberg to direct, but he was already tied up with another film. Furthermore, the release poster was a callback to *Jaws* but without a monster. In fact, it was ingenious in its simplicity. The poster features Jacqueline Bisset in a wet t-shirt struggling to make it to the surface. She is positioned where the shark was in the poster for *Jaws*. Had the producers truly been shameless about evoking *Jaws*, they might have had the giant eel chasing her.

Though *The Deep* is in no way shape or form focused on a monster, it does still have one in the form of a large eel. It is teased in the very first scene. As Gail pokes a pole into various holes, an unseen menace grabs ahold of it and pulls her hand into the void. As the pole is attached to her wrist via bracelet, she becomes stuck and must struggle to get away in a tense scene. Eventually, she pulls free, and we are left to wonder what grabbed her. The eel reveals itself 47 minutes into the movie to Treece and Sanders as they dive within the sunken *Goliath*. And it's a pretty grand entrance too, with the eel biting the head off of a fish right in front of the camera. Sander's scuba gear becomes hooked in

JAWS UNMADE

SHARK BITES: CASTING *THE DEEP*

AS WAS TYPICAL, MANY ACTORS WERE CONSIDERED FOR *THE DEEP* BEFORE FINAL DECISIONS WERE MADE. FOR GAIL, CANDICE BERGEN, KATHARINE ROSS, AND CHARLOTTE RAMPLING (FROM *ORCA*) WERE CONSIDERED. FOR TREECE, SEAN CONNERY, ROBERT MITCHUM, BURT LANCASTER, AND CHARLTON HESTON WERE EYED. AND FINALLY, FOR DAVID SANDERS, JEFF BRIDGES AND RYAN O'NEAL WERE PURSUED.

Nick Nolte, Robert Shaw, and Jacqueline Bisset in *The Deep*.
© 1977 Columbia Pictures

some wreckage as the massive eel strikes at him, but lucky for him, his camera flash goes off accidentally, scaring it away.

The eel makes one last appearance in the climax. As the trio of heroes dives into the *Goliath* one more time, Cloche's goons come calling, and a fight erupts between the various scuba divers. As Treece struggles with an underwater attacker, he catches a glimpse of the eel's hole within the ship and gets an idea. He navigates the fight to the opening and manages to get the man's head into the entrance of the eel's abode. It promptly sticks its head out and bites the man, crushing his skull into a bloody pulp in his jaws. To create this scene, a mechanical eel had to be created. Like Bruce the shark, it was nicknamed "Perry." Marvel Comics, in their adaptation, prominently featured the eel on the cover— almost making it seem as though this was another Benchley water monster thriller.

Jacqueline Bisset in *The Deep*. © 1977 Columbia Pictures

The Deep ends happily, with the bad guys defeated and the Goliath sinking so deep into the depths so that the morphine will be lost to the ages. Treece also manages to grab another bit of treasure before he races to the

SHARK BITES: *THE DEEP II*

IN THE EARLY 1980S THERE WERE PLANS FOR *THE DEEP II*, AS EVIDENCED BY PAPERS IN THE PETER BENCHLEY COLLECTION AT BOSTON UNIVERSITY. THOUGH I HAVE NO IDEA WHAT THE STORY IS ABOUT (THE UNIVERSITY DOES NOT ALLOW COPYING OF CERTAIN DOCUMENTS, ONLY IN PERSON VIEWINGS) I CAN AT LEAST PIN DOWN THE DATES. THE ARCHIVES LISTS THERE BEING CORRESPONDENCE BETWEEN BENCHLEY, ICM, AND COLUMBIA PICTURES REGARDING *THE DEEP II* FROM OCTOBER 1, 1982, INTO THE NEXT YEAR ON NOVEMBER 17, 1983. STORY NOTES ON THE SEQUEL WERE COMPLETED EVEN BEFORE THAT, AND WERE DATED SEPTEMBER 24, 1982. AS TO WHY PRODUCTION NEVER COMMENCED, THAT IS UNKNOWN.

surface. The final shots are of him breaking the water's surface, holding the artifact in his hands (even though he dies in the book).

It's no wonder *The Deep* was well-liked by moviegoers. For starters, its underwater sequences were unparalleled. And, perhaps thanks to James Bond composer John Barry, has a 007-like feel to it at times. Additionally, *The Deep* has some action scenes in it that are on par with set-pieces from the Bond series. A fight in an outdoor elevator shaft is excellently executed and would've been right at home in a Bond adventure. Another scene has the heroes trapped in the deep when the villains chum the waters above and attract sharks to the surface. Therefore, they can't swim back to their boat and have to remain on the ocean floor. The Bond producers likely took note of *The Deep*'s popularity, as one of the next Bond films, *For Your Eyes Only* (1981), would feature extensive underwater scenes.[70]

The Deep was another hit for Benchley at the box office, going on to become the 8th highest-grossing movie of 1977. *The Deep* was such a hit that it supposedly saved Columbia from financial ruin at the time, according to Benchley.

---

[70] The very next Bond movie was *Moonraker* (1979), which was inspired by the success of *Star Wars* (1977), but I still hold to the idea that *The Deep* inspired the underwater portions of *For Your Eyes Only*.

Developing
ORCA

Release Date: July 22, 1977
Alternate Titles: *Vengeance of the Deep* (Finland) *Orca - The Avenger of the Deep* (Sweden)

Directed by: Michael Anderson **Special Effects by:** Giuseppe Carozza, Jim Hole, Alex Weldon & Basilio Cortijo **Screenplay by:** Luciano Vincenzoni & Sergio Donati **Music by:** Ennio Morricone **Cast:** Captain Nolan (Richard Harris) Rachel Bedford (Charlotte Rampling) Umilak (Will Sampson) Annie (Bo Derek) Novak (Keenan Wynn) **Animal Performers:** Yaka & Nepo (the Orca)

Panavision, Color, 92 Minutes

SYNOPSIS Captain Nolan and his crew endeavor to catch a live killer whale in hopes of selling it to an aquarium. During the attempt, a pregnant female whale and her unborn child are killed in a horrific accident. The female's vengeful mate then makes it his mission to kill Nolan and begins stalking him within the waters of a local fishing village. When the whale causes trouble for the townspeople, they ostracize Nolan and force him onto the high seas. With Nolan is a beautiful whale biologist, Rachel Bedford, who turns out to be the lone survivor in the conflict with the Killer Whale...

COMMENTARY In the middle of the night, Luciano Vincenzoni, a producer for Dino De Laurentiis, got a phone call from his boss. An excited Dino had just seen *Jaws* and wanted to jump on the bandwagon. He told Vincenzoni to find "a fish tougher and more terrible than the great white." It's uncertain what kind of creatures Vincenzoni considered before the Killer Whale, but eventually he was directed to just that by his brother, Adriano, who had an interest in zoology.

Actually, just like *Jaws*, *Orca* is based on a book. I'm assuming what happened was that after Vincenzoni decided upon a Killer Whale, he learned about the book and decided to look into it for copyright reasons. Perhaps liking what he saw, a screenplay was then written based off of the book. Oddly, author Arthur Herzog, who also wrote *The Swarm*,[71] goes uncredited on the film. This might be understandable if the *Orca* film deviated significantly from the book, but it really doesn't aside from the lead character having a different name. While he's Captain Nolan in the movie, in the novel, his name is Captain Jack Campbell.

The book itself has nods to *Jaws* within the first few pages, with Campbell quipping that the film didn't scare him, and he fell asleep during it! Furthermore, when he goes to inspect a 25 foot Great White that has been mounted on display, it doesn't even phase him. In the novel, we learn that Annie, the character played by Bo Derek in the film, is his sister. In the movie, this could be the case, but it's never confirmed. Nor does Nolan's excellent backstory from the film descend from the book, where Campbell reveals his wife divorced him and left. The film's backstory is much better, as Nolan's wife was killed by a drunk driver while she was pregnant. This creates a connection between Nolan and the whale, with Nolan stating that he's the whale's "drunk driver." In the book, Nolan's psychological trauma comes from a complicated relationship with his father.

---

[71] *The Swarm* was also adapted into a film in 1978.

Another difference between the book and the film is that Campbell and Rachel have more of a love story in the novel. As for another minor subplot, Campbell has a pet dog, named "Dog," who is killed by the whale. Other notable scenes had the villagers firing a canon at the whale! A prominent subplot that may have been cut from the movie because of either time or budgetary constraints was a scheme to catch the whale by the villagers. Two fishing schooners place a net between themselves and ensnare the whale in it. The whale is so strong that it dives down and manages to smash the two boats into each other.

Still from the ending of *Orca*. © 1977 Dino De Laurentiis Company

The final act of the book has a few differences. On the *Bumpo,* to help hunt the orca is a French Canadian character named Robichaud. This character dies in the same manner as Rachel's assistant, getting plucked from the boat by the whale. There are also some scuffles with the whale before they reach the icy waters. In one, Campbell shoots at it with a rifle. In another, he throws a grenade at it.

Initially, the ending of the book seems similar to the film. Everyone is dead but Campbell and Rachel, who have escaped their sinking ship and are running across the ice while the whale follows beneath them. The whale creates a crack in the ice, which separates them.

Campbell becomes trapped on a makeshift island of floating ice, which the whale has tipped upwards. Campbell grips the top with a rifle in his hands, as Rachel begs him to shoot the orca. But Campbell is enticed by the creature's eyes and finds himself wanting to die and end his misery. He lets himself slip towards the gaping jaws. The orca curiously veers away and dives into the water. The animal doesn't kill Campbell and does a victory leap into the air as a rescue chopper comes near. Presumably, Campbell survives, and one could interpret the ending to mean the whale wants Campbell to live on in misery after he's beaten him. In the film, the same exact scene plays out up until the point that the whale kills Nolan.

Luciano Vincenzoni and Sergio Donati adapted the book into screenplay form, and Robert Towne did some uncredited rewrites on it. Filming then commenced with the village scenes being shot in Newfoundland while the climax was shot in Malta. Richard Harris was very much enamored with the role of Nolan and rightfully became incensed whenever people called the film a *Jaws* knock-off. Charlotte Rampling was also committed to her role and studied whales before production.

Speaking of whales, for all the hate the movie received as a *Jaws* "rip-off," the animatronic killer whales in the film were much better executed than the mechanical shark in *Jaws*. Between the real Killer Whale footage and the fake animatronics, it's tough to spot the difference.[72]

Orca is a different animal than *Jaws* in that it doesn't necessarily make you afraid to go into the water. Because, Orca isn't after you; he's after Captain Nolan and his crew. In fact, before the bad blood, Orca saves a minor character, named Ken, from a killer shark. Incidentally, Orca also kills Ken later too. As Nolan sets out on the high seas, Rachel and Ken accompany him. Orca leaps out of the water and pulls Ken under (presumably, Orca doesn't eat his victims, he just bites them to death). The next to expire is Annie's boyfriend,

---

[72] In *Jaws'* defense, it's a bit easier to make a real-looking killer whale because of their sleek, shiny skin texture. Sharks are a bit more difficult due to their skin texture.

Paul, who dies by the same method more or less. Orca knocks him out of a lifeboat and into the water where he bites him and drags him under (a moment later his body floats to the surface to reiterate that Orca is killing these people out of spite, not hunger). Even Umiak, a Native American character sympathetic to the whale, dies when Orca pushes an iceberg into the boat, which crushes it into an icy cliff (Umiak dies in the ensuing avalanche).

Though at first the climax might seem similar to *Jaws*—being that a boat crew goes out onto the ocean to battle the monster—they're still fairly different. As stated earlier, after the ship sinks, Nolan and Rachel must run across the ice sheets, while Orca swims underneath. Wondering where he will burst from next generates some good suspense. As in the novel, eventually he pushes Nolan on an ice sheet into the water away from Rachel. What he does next recalls a scene from *Jaws*, specifically the one where Quint dies. Orca jumps onto the ice sheet, tipping it into the air, causing Nolan to roll down towards his mouth. But Orca doesn't bite Nolan, which is somewhat anticlimactic (maybe the producers feared the death scene would be too close to Quint's?). Instead, Orca torments Nolan by swimming around him in circles. Finally, he beats him to death with his tale and flicks him back onto the shore.

Another way that *Orca* differentiates itself from the other *Jaws* rip-offs, like *Grizzly*, is that humanity never triumphs over the whale. That said, it's debatable whether or not Orca lives, some speculate the final shots of him swimming under the ice are meant to imply he's committing suicide by suffocation. Whatever the whale's fate, man doesn't kill him. Furthermore, for a while, one can almost root for Orca. True, he kills Keenan Wynn's character, Novak, early in the film, but Orca's mate had just died, and Novak was party to that. However, Orca's biting off of Annie's leg makes him much less likable. Annie had even objected to the whole whale capture plot and only went along with it reluctantly.

Ken is another of Orca's victims that didn't deserve it. Ken wasn't even there when the female whale died, and he would have objected to it if he was. Orca also

SHARK BITES: THE LEG SCENE

THE STANDOUT SEQUENCE FOR MANY IS WHEN ORCA DISMANTLES THE SUPPORTS UNDER NOLAN'S WATERFRONT HOME, CAUSING IT TO TUMBLE INTO THE WATER. BECAUSE BO DEREK'S CHARACTER IS SYMPATHETIC, IT'S QUITE SUSPENSEFUL. IN ONE OF THE FILM'S MOST SHOCKING SCENES, ORCA BITES HER LEG CLEAN OFF! IN THE BOOK, THE WHALE CRUSHES HER LEG WITHIN THE CAST AND IT HAS TO BE AMPUTATED, SO THE FILM VERSION DEFINITELY IMPROVES UPON THE SCENE. *STARLOG* #9 OFFERED SOME FASCINATING BEHIND THE SCENES INFORMATION ON THE SCENE REGARDING THE REAL WHALE CARRYING OFF THE LEG. *STARLOG* REPORTED THAT, "TRY AS THEY MIGHT, THE REAL WHALE WOULD NOT TAKE THE FABRICATED LEG IN ITS MOUTH. FINALLY A SPECIAL TRAINER WAS BROUGHT IN, THE WHALE WAS MADE TO ACCEPT THE APPENDAGE AND THE SHOT WAS COMPLETED. THE NEXT DAY, WHEN THE NEXT SCENE WAS BEING SET UP, THE TRAINER GOT IN THE TANK WITH THE WHALE AND IT WENT FOR HIS LEG. IT ALSO WENT FOR THE LEG OF ANYONE ELSE WHO GOT NEAR IT. AND, TRY AS THEY MIGHT, THEY COULDN'T UNTRAIN IT." [*STARLOG* #9,PP.10]

causes an electrical fire that results in a power plant exploding within the fishing village. Presumably other innocents died then too. So while it's tempting to call Orca a hero, he kills and maims too many innocents along the way for that.

Orca was reported to cost $6 million and made $14 million, so it was profitable, but it was not a *Jaws* level mega-hit like Dino had hoped for. *The Hollywood Reporter*, however, listed *Orca's* budget at $12 million. If that's true, then the film barely broke even. Nor were many critics kind to the film. The *Los Angeles Times* said, "A lousier movie may get made one of these days or years, but it will have to wrest the trophy from the dead and icy grasp of *Orca*." And yet, none of these factors dissuaded Dino from considering a sequel...

Orca © 1977 Dino De Laurentiis Company

KING KONG VS. ORCA

Developmental Period: 1977-1978

Idea by: Dino De Laurentiis **Proposed Creatures:** King Kong, Orca

SYNOPSIS A revived King Kong battles Orca the Killer Whale.

COMMENTARY Despite its lukewarm reception, it would seem Dino De Laurentiis was determined to make a sequel to *Orca*. He was also determined to make a sequel to his 1976 *King Kong* remake, in part to reuse the expensive props created for the movie. So, it would seem, Dino decided to kill two birds with one stone: *King Kong vs. Orca*.

Of course, what Dino probably really wanted to do was "King Kong vs. Jaws," but as he didn't own the giant shark, his killer whale would have to do. As it turned out, due to complicated legal matters, Dino would actually need Universal's permission to produce *King Kong vs. Orca*. And why was this?

Well, that's a long story that could be a book in of itself. The short version is, in the late 1970s, a battle

Left: The cover of *Famous Monsters* #146 which depicted a more ambitious version of the scene from *A*P*E*. Right: Ad for a *King Kong* and *Orca* double bill.

was raging as to who owned Kong: RKO or the heirs of Merian C. Cooper? The courts ruled in favor of the Cooper Estate, who almost immediately sold film rights for King Kong to Universal, who had tried and failed to beat De Laurentiis at remaking *King Kong* in 1976.

As Universal no doubt hated *Orca*, they would most certainly not allow Dino to make a Kong film where he fights the sea beast. Actually, I wonder why Universal didn't take the idea and make a "King Kong vs. Jaws" themselves? It's a little silly, of course, but still an undeniably fun idea.

"King Kong vs. Jaws" was certainly in the mind of other filmmakers, notably Paul Leder, who shot the Kong rip-off *A*P*E* in Korea. The notoriously bad film opens with an ape being transported to Disney World via ocean liner. It escapes into the water, where it immediately begins battling a great white shark! Don't get too excited, though. What you essentially get is a man in a bad ape suit wrestling what appears to be a dead shark and throwing it around. The scene was famously hyped on a cover for *Famous Monsters*, and in my opinion, illustrated just how cool such a scene could have been with better effects.

This ad for *Jaws* was touting the shark as the box -office victor over the *King Kong* remake of 1976.

"King Kong vs. Jaws" aside, due to *Orca's* more intelligent nature (the shark in *Jaws* was, after all, a mindless eating machine), he may have made for a better opponent against King Kong. No actual story details have ever surfaced, and truthfully it was probably little more than a title. However...

Recently a fan on Deviant Art made a mock-up DVD cover for *King Kong vs. Orca*. On the back of the mock slipcase, they list a synopsis. I have no idea if this is their own conjecture, or if they're repeating information that they heard about the project. If it's their own conjecture, I would say that it's actually spot on (coming up with an excuse for Orca to fight King Kong is a little difficult).

First, a little background on Dino's various "King Kong 2" pitches. Though a sequel wasn't made until 1986 in the form of *King Kong Lives*, where the ape is revived via science, this was the plan from day one. Aside from *King Kong vs. Orca*, Dino had three other potential Kong titles floating around: *King Kong in*

Lost Project: KING KONG VS. ORCA

Africa, King Kong in Moscow, and *Bionic Kong.* All three had the same premise, that being Kong is resurrected through science and technology, and the Russians are out to get him for nefarious purposes (probably to use as a weapon).

The presumably fan-made plot outline for *King Kong vs. Orca* has a similar premise. Kong is revived by a team of doctors through science. Among them is Charlotte Rampling's character from *Orca,* Dr. Rachel Bedford. Though she was a marine biologist in *Orca,* in the world of giant monster movies, I suppose it's not too much of a stretch to believe that she would be part of a team to examine a giant, intelligent creature like Kong. In the hands of a smooth screenwriter, the idea could be passable.

Once Kong is revived, it's decided to transport him back to Skull Island. This is where Orca comes in. Even though Orca had no beef with Bedford in the first movie, he's apparently changed his mind and is out to get her now. As Bedford is on the boat with Kong, Orca attacks the ship. As Kong has developed an attachment to Bedford, he wants to defend her. And with that, our conflict is established!

This storyline is reminiscent of an aborted King Kong movie from Merian C. Cooper called *The New Adventures of King Kong.* The unmade film would have presented the untold story of Kong's journey to New York, where the ship carrying him is attacked by sea monsters. The crew lets Kong loose to defend them.

Actually, there was yet another unmade film this one resembles. It was called *Baboon: A Tale About a Yeti* and was penned by effects genius Willis O'Brien. That story climaxed with the Yeti on a boat being transported to civilization when it is attacked by Killer Whales. The Yeti battles them in the water and dies.

But, just one more time for you speed readers and folks who don't pay close attention: the *King Kong vs. Orca* outline I just presented is presumably fan-made.

Moving along, had *King Kong vs. Orca* been shot, just how silly would it have been? Probably pretty silly. In fact, Willis O'Brien probably could have created the ape vs. killer whales battle more realistically through stopmotion in his 1961 Yeti movie. As it was, ape suits look terrible when wet. Just look at the abomination from *A*P*E** and Toho's two suitmation King Kongs when they're in the water.[73] There was even a deleted scene from Dino's *King Kong* where the ape walks on land after having been in the water, and the suit doesn't look great. So, a movie where the climax depended upon a wet monkey suit battling a fake killer whale was a bad idea, hands down. Then there was also an issue of size. In the 1976 movie, Kong is depicted as 42 feet tall on Skull Island but bumps up to 55 feet in New York![74] Orca was said to be 25-30 feet long in the movie. So, either the fish needed to grow or Kong needed to shrink for the conflict to work.

As to why Dino would want to even do a sequel to *Orca*, which basically only broke even, I would assume it was similar to the reason he wanted to knock out a *King Kong 2*: he wanted to reuse the expensive Orca props made for the first movie.

Though the *Orca* sequel never came to be, the Kong sequel did in 1986's notorious *King Kong Lives*, in which the ape falls in love with another of his species named Lady Kong. It was easily one of the most lambasted movies of the late 1980s... until one year later when *Jaws: The Revenge* came out. Ironically, that film more or less borrowed the plot of *Orca*, itself a *Jaws* imitator, with the Great White singling out members of the Brody family for revenge.

But, even when Dino let go of *King Kong vs. Orca*, that didn't mean he was done with the big whale just yet...

---

[73] These two films are *King Kong vs. Godzilla* (1962) and *King Kong Escapes* (1967). Both have scenes of Kong in the water and the suit looks terrible.

[74] The same thing happens in the original film, by the way. They did the Skull Island sequences first. But when they came to the New York scenes they realized that Kong was too small and bumped his size up. So, it was a tradition in a sense.

JAWS 2
Rated R

Release Date: June 16, 1978
Alternate Titles: *Teeth of the Sea II* (France/Canada)

Directed by: Jeannot Szwarc **Special Effects by:** Robert A. Mattey & Roy Arbogast **Screenplay by:** Carl Gottlieb & Howard Sackler **Music by:** John Williams **Cast:** Roy Scheider (Chief Martin Brody) Lorraine Gary (Ellen Brody) Murray Hamilton (Mayor Larry Vaughn) Joseph Mascolo (Len Peterson) Jeffrey Kramer (Deputy Jeff Hendricks) Mark Gruner (Mike Brody) Marc Gilpin (Sean Brody) Ann Dusenberry (Tina) Barry Coe (Tom Andrews) Gary Springer (Andy) Donna Wilkes (Jackie) Gary Dubin (Eddie) Billy Van Zandt (Bob Burnside) John Dukakis (Polo) G. Thomas Dunlop (Timmy) David Elliott (Larry Vaughn Jr.) Keith Gordon (Doug) Cynthia Grover (Lucy) Ben Marley (Patrick) Martha Swatek (Marge)

Panavision, Technicolor, 116 Minutes

Jaws 2 © 1978 Universal Pictures

SYNOPSIS Things are looking up for Amity Island, which is on the cusp of a massive real estate development called Amity Shores. Casting a shadow on the town's bright future is Chief Brody's suspicions that another Great White shark is lurking in the island's waters. After an incident on the beach where Brody mistakes a large school of fish for the shark and creates a panic, he is fired. Soon after, Brody receives word of a shark attack after his two sons set off as part of a teenaged sailing party. Brody commandeers a patrol boat to rescue them...

COMMENTARY After shooting on *Jaws 2* was shut down in mid-1977, a number of directors were suggested to replace the fired John Hancock, including Steven Spielberg himself. In *The Jaws 2 Log*, Spielberg claimed that when Universal called him in a panic, he told them that he'd spend the 4th of July weekend "trying to find the solution to a sequel." Spielberg went on to say that that if he could write it, and if Zanuck and Brown would delay the production to the spring of '78, he'd do it. "I spent three days at the typewriter and wrote seven or eight schematic breakdowns. I kept the Dreyfuss and Scheider characters in it,"[75] Spielberg said, but he eventually gave up on the concept, feeling that it would've been redundant overall. However, he did like Howard Sackler's Quint prequel, and Joe Alves claimed Spielberg said he would do that version and not a sequel. Whatever new scenario Spielberg envisioned— be it a sequel with Brody and Hooper or a prequel with Quint—Universal could not wait on the director, who wouldn't be free until Spring of 1978.

Other potential directors discussed were the first film's editor Verna Fields (editors usually make excellent directors) and production designer/producer Joe Alves. However, legalities within the industry forbade this. With no Spielberg, and it being illegal to use Fields and Alves, there was even talk of canceling the production altogether. Rather than a lost version of *Jaws 2*, it almost became a lost film entirely. Thankfully, Alves suggested Jeannot Szwarc, a TV

---

[75] Loynd, *Jaws 2 Log*, pp.74.

Still from Jaws 2. © 1978 Universal Pictures

director whom Alves knew from his work on Rod Serling's *Night Gallery*.

After some discussion, Szwarc was brought onto the production. He reviewed Hancock's existing footage and agreed with Fields and the others that it wouldn't work for him. Not only did Szwarc strike all of Hancock's footage (except for the shark fin gliding through the harbor), he also decided to recast many of the teenaged actors. But that still wasn't the end of the film's changes. Carl Gottlieb was asked to tweak the script— he couldn't rewrite it altogether as too much preproduction had been done on the existing ideas.

In interviews, Gottlieb acts as though the studio was thinking of throwing out the teenaged sailor subplot altogether, but he fought for them to keep it. "They had all these kids they hired and I said, 'Don't junk the kids, they're good actors and if the kids are in jeopardy, it takes it off of Scheider — he's not gonna get in the same shark jeopardy twice."[76] Someone else who offered suggestions on the rewrites was Lorraine Gary, who suggested that Ellen be working with Len Peterson. Therefore, the Peterson character was made to have a romantic attraction to Ellen (though the two do not have

---

[76] Jankiewicz, *Just When You Thought It Was Safe*, pp.142.

an affair as she and Hooper did in the novel).[77] For this reason, the character was recast to be more youthful and attractive in the form of Joseph Mascolo (before that Peterson was played by Dana Eclar).

Another change that came along with Szwarc was the return of actor Jeffrey Kramer as Deputy Hendricks from the first film. Actually, Kramer had been filming under Hancock but had gotten fed up and left. The reason was, Dorothy Tristan wrote in a new deputy character named Batliner. The new character received all the important bits, while the Hendricks character more or less just cracks a few jokes. So, Kramer quit. When Szwarc came on board, he asked where the Hendricks character was, as he had enjoyed him in the first film. He was informed of what had happened, and so he called Kramer. Szwarc offered to do away with the Batliner character and give all the dialogue and action meant for that character to Kramer.[78]

Szwarc utilized some ingenious strategy to restart the production before the script was rewritten by Gottlieb. Szwarc was smart enough to know that many of the set-pieces, or the shark attack scenes, would be kept. He argued that since the water skiing scene would be time consuming to film that they should shoot it while Gottlieb did his work. And why this scene as opposed to... let's say the helicopter scene? The chopper scene would have required the teenage cast, whom Szwarc was in the process of recasting. The water skiing scene didn't require any important casting decisions.

The water skiing scene is a good example of how even though the movie was on its final trajectory, there were still to be many changes made along the way. As written at the time, the water skier was to see the shark fin and mistake it for a dolphin. She was to smile and wave at it, then call for her friend to look too. The water skier's death was visualized differently, too. Storyboards showed the skier unaware of the shark after she's been capsized. As she speaks with her friend, the shark

---

[77] Before this development, Gary herself came up with a backstory that Ellen was having an affair with a man in a nearby village.

[78] It's possible Szwarc gave him even more scenes, because in the new shooting script by Gottlieb, Hendricks is not waiting for Brody at his home when Brody gets fired, while in the film he's a significant part of the scene.

sneaks up on her and can be seen opening its mouth under the water. A version of the scene was even shot this way but was deemed unsatisfactory and reshot later.

The water skier, Christine Freeman, recalled this iteration of the scene too. She said she remembered that scuba divers were waiting beneath her feet to yank her under to simulate the shark. However, the shark would freeze in mid-lunge, and eventually they gave up on the idea.[79]

The sequence of events for the fire was scripted differently as well. In the then-current script, the driver doesn't pour gasoline on the shark when it attacks. Instead, the shark severs a fuel line to the engine. All the woman does after that is fire a flare at the shark. The actress who played the driver was a stuntwoman named Jeannie Coulter. She remembered that her death was toned down in this scene. "They did film a scene of me dying but they told me it was just too morbid. You know I'm in the boat and I'm on fire and I just lay there and die," she said in *Jaws 2: The Making of a Hollywood Sequel*.

This brings up a rather important question that was asked in the final phases of *Jaws 2*'s development: Should it be 'R' rated or not? *Jaws 2* had the highest budget of any Universal feature up to that time. An 'R' rating would severely limit the audience, and therefore the profits. This caused a great deal of debate as to the number of people that could be killed and how. The original body count for *Jaws 2* was at or close to a dozen people. According to actor Marc Gilpin, there was even talk of the shark eating his character: Sean Brody!

After reviewing the script, Sid Sheinberg felt that only Ed should die, the rest of the teens should live. However, arguments still carried on about the deaths of Marge and Bob (previously named Sideburns). In terms of Bob, Brown suggested filming two different versions of the scene to choose from.

Bob's death had been a long time coming—ever since Sackler's second draft. In that version, a proto version of Bob, called Boyd, is bitten in half. If you'll remember,

[79] Smith and Pisano, *Jaws 2: The Making of a Hollywood Sequel* (Kindle Edition).

Boyd was a retooled version of Quint's son. Boyd evolved into Sideburns, a normal teen for a while who reverted back to being Quint Jr. thanks to Dorothy Tristan. This idea of Sideburns being Quint's son was done away with, and though the actor playing Quint Jr./Sideburns was retained, he was now renamed Bob Burnside. Burnside was a play on Sideburns, and Bob... well, his corpse was going to bob in the water, get it? Eventually, Bob's death would be toned down and then eliminated altogether.

Second perhaps only to Bob's death was the death of Marge, the girl who rescues Sean only to be plucked into oblivion by the shark. The scene is similar to what plays out on film except the script had blood in the water after she is pulled under in Gottlieb's version from September 1, 1977. The revised script from September 19th revealed Marge was pulled under the water by the chopper pilot! He had escaped the confines of the chopper and gone to rescue her. He then swims Marge back to the upside-down chopper, which has an air bubble in the cockpit. Jerry M. Baxter, the actor playing the pilot, remembers filming the scene.

The *Jaws 2* helicopter scene. Jaws 2 © 1978 Universal Pictures

Marge's rescue was done for a very specific reason. Sheinberg didn't want Marge to die for rating reasons, but Brown felt that the teenaged sailors needed to see one of their own perish. Therefore, a compromise was created wherein the kids see Marge get pulled under and assume she's dead—but the audience would see that the pilot had rescued her. Eventually, it was decided in post-production that Marge had indeed died.

Then there is the urban legend of an alternate death scene for Marge, where she is seen screaming in the jaws of the shark. Supposedly this scene was included in the film's Swedish version. The actress who played Marge, Martha Swatek, more or less confirmed that no such scene was shot. She did specify that there were four takes of the scene, two with blood and two without blood. She speculated that perhaps the Swedish version used the blood take, but there was certainly no take of her in the shark's mouth.[80] Billy Van Zandt also confirmed this statement and told me, "I read on a fan site that there was an alternate, bloodier take of Marge's death, but that's not true, we only shot it the one way."

The biggest ado was made of Van Zandt's character's death. In the "final draft" by Tristan from November of 1976, Bob was to be bitten in half and his torso pulled up by Brody, leaving a trail of blood in the water that the shark would follow to Brody. It is implied in *The Jaws 2 Log* that a June 1977 revision toned the scene down a bit, but still has a passage reading, "[Bob's] torso, severed at the waist, pours blood into the water."[81] By September of 1977, the scene was toned down again, and Brody would not fish him out of the water. Instead, the way in which his dead body floated would imply that his bottom half was gone: "His body floating unnaturally high in the water, the life vest holding what's left of his upper torso afloat. The current takes it away."[82] Though still severed at the waist, apparently there would have been less blood in this version.

---

[80] The Marge death scene is part of a long line of unseen sequences, like the "Spider Pit" scene in *King Kong* (1933). It's agreed upon that the *King Kong* scene was shot but excised from theatrical screenings, and yet people like Ray Bradbury claim that they saw it. I can relate. I too believed Marge's death scene was more violent. Before I had even read of the rumored alternate take of Marge's death, when I had re-watched *Jaws 2* on Blu-Ray for the first time in many years, I too thought the scene was odd, and remembered it being bloodier than the bloodless scene I saw.

[81] Loynd, *Jaws 2 Log*, pp.41.

[82] Ibid.

Still of one of Van Zandt's unused death scenes.
Jaws 2 © 1978 Universal Pictures

Van Zandt recalled that the next evolution in the death of Bob was to have him on a pontoon boat kicking his way to shore. The shark would then just bite his legs off. "I think they made a cast of my legs for that scene," Van Zandt said.[83] When that was considered too violent, it changed to having the shark drag Bob and the pontoon down at the same time. This scene was eventually shot with Van Zandt performing his own stunts. "They had a stuntman who looked nothing like me so I asked to do it. David Brown told me I could, but it would have to be the last thing we shot in Florida. I asked him why and he said, 'In case you die.'"[84]

However, just to be safe, they also shot a take where Bob does make it to shore. When I asked Van Zandt if he would have preferred it if his character had died, he responded, "Of course!" Van Zandt also remembered talking to Verna Fields about it (Fields was among those fighting to kill Bob). "I mentioned [to her] how I had seen a John Wayne movie recently where half the town got gunned down, and it wasn't rated R. Her response was, 'Yeah, but we didn't know who they were.'" In other words, because the victims were personalized in *Jaws 2*, the deaths were more impactful. And again, Fields was just echoing the sentiments of the higher-ups, as she was among those who felt the film had more of an impact by retaining Bob's death. Szwarc was horrified

---

[83] Interview with Van Zandt by the author.
[84] Ibid.

when he learned Universal wanted to tone down the violence. "The worst thing we can do is to censor ourselves," he said.[85] Ultimately it was decided to let Bob live, lest one more death give the movie an 'R' rating.

This was probably the right call for the franchise, as an 'R' rating would have severely cut the profits—and the profits were fantastic. Though *Jaws 2* didn't outperform the original, it made a bundle for Universal. Before the movie was even released, Sheinberg said, "I'm planning ideas right now for Jaws 3."[86] Peter Benchley even foresaw a *Jaws 3* as *Jaws 2* was shooting. In an article about his upcoming adaptation of *The Deep* (1977), Benchley mentioned that although a sequel to *Jaws* was Universal's right, a third movie meant they'd have to negotiate something with him. "But if they ever decide to do a third Jaws film, then they'll have to come talk to me again," Benchley said.[87] And indeed, there would be a third Jaws film. Supposedly, as *Jaws 2* was winding down production, David Brown was thinking of making *Jaws 3* a spoof, but that's a story for another chapter.

[85] Loynd, *Jaws 2 Log*, pp.84.

[86] Ibid, pp.213.

[87] Kleiner, "Benchley Finds 'Deep' Satisfaction."
https://newspaperarchive.com/galesburg-register-mail-aug-09-1977-p-5/

SPECIAL SECTION

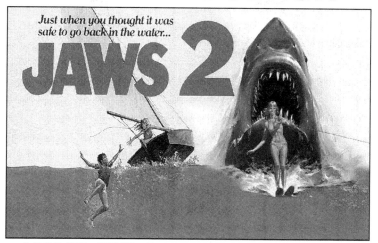

Just when you thought it was safe to go back in the water...

JAWS 2

JAWS 2'S DELETED SCENES

Sequences of violence and gore were not the only scenes cut from *Jaws 2*. Some were of a more mundane nature. Billy Van Zandt recalled two of his earliest scenes were removed. The first one he remembered filming was of he and David Elliot riding bikes through Amity past a pair of girls (this scene was likely removed because it was footage shot by Hancock). Van Zandt's first scene in the Szwarc version of the film would have better set the tone of his character as a snob. "My introduction was walking into the Holiday Inn with twin girls and a case of beer."

Most of the deleted scenes concerned the rivalry between Brody and Peterson, who asks if he can cut in on he and Ellen's dance at the opening ball (there's also a deleted scene of Ellen spiking the punch there). In retaliation, Brody later gives Len a parking ticket. There's also an extended version of the scene where the townspeople are in Brody's office complaining about relatively minute things. More impactful to the story was a cut scene where the city council votes on whether or not to fire Brody, and Mayor Vaughn is the only one who votes not to. Because of this deletion, for all the audience knows, Vaughn was ready to get rid of Brody just like the others.

As to scenes pertaining to the shark plot, there are a couple that got cut. One had Deputy Hendricks taking Tom Andrews out to the site of the *Orca* to search for the missing divers. Andrews is shown recovering the camera as well. This scene actually made its way into Brazilian TV broadcasts in the 1980s. This is odd because some of the deleted scenes mentioned previously (the Amity Shores gala, Brody's office, etc.) occasionally were included in U.S. TV broadcasts, but the scuba diving scene never was.

A scene of the shark approaching the sinking helicopter was also included in U.S. TV broadcasts, as well as the Brazilian one. It's curious as to why it was cut at all as it only lasts 25 seconds and therefore doesn't impede the momentum of the surface scenes too much. It's also quite terrifying, as the shark eyes the pilot trapped within the glass cockpit. One reason why the scene may have gotten removed was that we didn't see the pilot die, which might have distracted some viewers when the action returned to the surface as they pondered his fate.

This publicity still from an unused scene in the movie led some to believe that Mayor Vaughn was comforting Ellen Brody after Martin died in an alternate ending! There was never an alternate ending featuring Martin Brody's death, though.
Jaws 2 © 1978 Universal Pictures

Developing
PIRANHA

Release Date: August 3, 1978

Directed by: Joe Dante **Special Effects by:** Jon Berg & Phil Tippett **Screenplay by:** John Sayles **Music by:** Pino Donaggio **Cast:** Bradford Dillman (Paul Grogan) Heather Menzies (Maggie McKeown) Kevin McCarthy (Dr. Robert Hoak) Keenan Wynn (Jack) Barbara Steele (Dr. Mengers) Dick Miller (Buck Gardner) Belinda Balaski (Betsy)

Spherical, Metrocolor, 94 Minutes

SYNOPSIS When two teenagers go missing in the vicinity of Lost River Lake, a private investigator, Maggie McKeown, is sent to find them. She enlists the help of Paul Grogan, a backwoods native who knows the area well. They find some of the couples' belongings at an abandoned government facility, in the center of which is a large pool. Thinking the teenagers might have drowned, they drain the pool into Lost River. Unbeknownst to them, they have just unleashed a mutated swarm of piranhas into the river...

COMMENTARY Roger Corman had begun his career as a B-movie king back in the 1950s. In the 1970s he was still going as strong as ever as the head of New World Pictures. Corman took note of *Jaws'* success and wanted to do something similar right away. However, he didn't secure the funding for his "tribute to Jaws" until three years later—after *Jaws 2* had come out no less!

But, *Piranha* doesn't really start with Corman, it wasn't his idea. It was the brainchild of another B-movie producer Jeff Schechtman (and, if Corman is the B-movie king, then Schechtman is regarded as the prince). Backing Schechtman was Japanese actress turned producer Chako Van Leeuwen (real name Hisako Tsukuba), who still owns the rights to the *Piranha* franchise to this day.

Schechtman says he got the idea for a killer fish movie from the title of an article. You see, back in 1975, Earl Gottschalk wrote an article predicting the *Jaws* rip-offs to come. His piece was titled "In the Shark's Wake, Watch for Piranhas, Gators, More Sharks. A Reign of Terror by Animals is Projected by Hollywood in Bid to Ride 'Jaws' Tide." Schechtman zeroed in on the word piranha and decided to make Gottschalk's prophecy come true. He then had a script written by Richard Robinson (*Kingdom of the Spiders*). Next Schechtman connected with Japanese producer Leeuwen, who put up some money, and the two then went to Roger Corman and New World Pictures.

From left to right are stars Bradford Dillman, Heather Menzies, Director Joe Dante, and actor Kevin McCarthy, on the set of *Piranha*. © 1978 New World Pictures

Going off of Corman's biography, *How I Made a Hundred Movies in Hollywood*, the film wasn't always called *Piranha* (he doesn't mention the initial title). To helm the film, Corman hired an editor from his trailer department, Joe Dante, for the job. Dante saw the script before it was rewritten and described it as "underwhelming." Dante told EW that, "The author hadn't figured out exactly what to do after people found out there were piranhas in the water."[88] According to Dante, a bear would chase people into the water and some of them would get eaten by the fish. Once the bear goes away they get back on land and then a forest fire starts, so back in the water they go! "We should rewrite this," Dante told Corman.

To rewrite the script, John Sayles, then trying to break into Hollywood, was brought on board by Corman. "Roger and Frances gave me Robinson's script, and said: 'Forget this. Just keep the title and the idea of piranha in North American waters.' I had to start the screenplay over again," Sayles recalled in *Starlog*.[89] Sayles wrote two drafts of the script[90] and then Corman officially greenlit the production.

The film was notable for being a first for New World, as they co-produced the film with United Artists. Both companies contributed to the $1 million budget, and UA would get international distribution rights while New World would get domestic rights in the U.S.[91]

Shooting began in late February of 1978, and filming locations included Los Angeles, California, and San Marcos, Texas. Predominantly the film was shot in Texas, though. One of the locations necessitated some script doctoring. Originally, Sayles envisioned a rather grand water park being attacked by the fish, but it had to be scaled down to match the less luxurious location. To help with the script, Dante cast Sayles as a soldier, necessitating his being on location to tweak the script as needed.

---

[88] Collis, "Fishy Business."
 https://ew.com/article/2010/08/18/cameron-piranha-3d-dante/
[89] Swires, "John Sayles," *Starlog* #94 (May 1985), pp.44.
[90] In order to secure military cooperation for filming, Sayles wrote a dummy draft where the military ends up being the heroes of the story (when, in fact, they were always meant to be portrayed as villains).
[91] However, as always, there are conflicting stories as to this. Corman revealed that as soon as Dante shot his test footage (reportedly the very first scene of the movie) that he decided it was already over budget at $750,000. He insisted that the budget be cut by $100,000 until one of his producers reminded him that they were negotiating with UA, which would likely pump more money into the production, and so Corman agreed to forgo the cuts.

There were numerous casting changes both before and after shooting began. For the first few days of filming, Eric Braeden (*Escape from the Planet of the Apes*) played the scientist who created the piranha. Braeden shot some footage in the water before he quit to work on another project. Reportedly, he was a bit appalled at the primitive shooting conditions and all the fake blood that was pumped into the water. Dante says that Braeden was very polite when making his exit though, and the part was recast with Kevin McCarthy.

As for other differences in casting, Barbara Steele's part was originally written with a man in mind until she came along. Peter Fonda was offered the lead role and turned it down. Coincidentally, Eric Braeden's nemesis from *Escape from the Planet of the Apes*, Bradford Dillman, took the lead role, which would have made the movie a reunion of sorts if Braeden had stayed on.

Piranha, which pre-dates 1980's *Friday the 13th*, starts off like a slasher movie with the old sex equals death cliché. Two runaway teenagers decide to go skinny-dipping in what is unbeknownst to them a pool containing mutated piranhas. The film plays it cool like the opening of *Jaws*, not exactly letting us see what's eating the two onscreen victims. Their death precedes the title sequence, and following that, the first thing we see is a *Jaws* video game. The film is basically letting us know right away that it has no qualms about being a *Jaws* sendup. However, *Piranha* easily blows other rip-offs like *Tentacles* and *The Last Shark* out of the water with its originality. Really, the only nods to *Jaws* are the numerous, underwater POV shots of fluttering feet before the fish attack. *Piranha* also has the "big event that can't be canceled" angle present in so many of these films. In this case, it's a big party to launch a new real estate development along Lost River Lake.

Those two things aside, *Piranha* is its own animal entirely apart from *Jaws*. In fact, though Universal wanted to sue New World for spoofing *Jaws*, when Steven Spielberg saw the film he loved it. Once Universal found this out, they backed off. Spielberg even went so far as to dub it "the best of the *Jaws* rip-offs."

Whereas in that film one big fish is out to get you, in this one it's a swarm of little fish. The composer, Pino Donaggio, wisely doesn't try to give the fish a theme song that tries to match John Williams' *Jaws* theme. Instead, an unsettling sound effect accompanies their killings. If anything, I'd compare it to the shower scene in *Psycho*, (Joe Dante has said that the noise is a dental drill, which makes sense). The piranhas' kill scenes are quite effective, and one of their first real victims is Keenan Wynn, also the Killer Whale's first victim in *Orca* the previous year. Wynn is fishing on the dock, his feet dangling in the water. The fish begin to attack him, and we cut away. When we find Wynn later, he's crawled onto land, his legs eaten down to the bone!

A big plot point in *Piranha* is stopping the fish before they can reach a children's summer camp along the river. And the film doesn't pull any punches when it gets there either. The kids do get attacked by the piranha, but none of them die (a few might have lost fingers and toes though...). According to comments made by Dante in *Starlog*, the summer camp scene served as the ending action scene at one point. Corman knew he couldn't massacre a river full of children, and so added in a "second" ending where the piranha attack adults swimming in the river.[92] "Roger wanted a *Jaws* scene," Dante told *Starlog*. "But he didn't want to lose the summer camp bit because there was a possibility of having people eaten there, too."[93]

The scenes of carnage are quite spectacular. And, whereas the same year's *Jaws 2* cut its gore down to get a 'PG' rating, *Piranha* went for the hard 'R.' That's probably part of the reason it was so successful; it showed what *Jaws* wouldn't. For what they are (piranha puppets on sticks that the crew are jiggling), the fish effects are quite good. "We tried using rubber fish that Phil [Tippett] came up with but that didn't work," Dante told *Starlog*. "It was frustrating. Finally, Jon [Berg] came

---

[92] On the note of the child characters, there were apparently some reshoots with one of the actors. The final cut has a scene where a boy loses his father to the fish in the river in the middle of the movie. He is rescued by the main characters unharmed. Apparently an alternate version was shot where the boy had numerous lacerations from the fish, though.

[93] Naha, "Piranha," *Starlog* #18, pp.61.

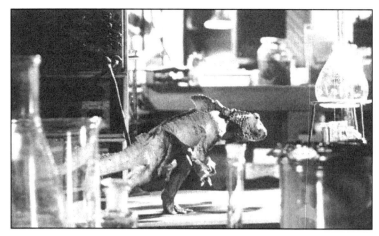

This stopmotion mutant piranha was originally intended to have a much bigger role... © 1978 New World Pictures

up with a fish on a rod that was controlled by hand off-camera. We shot it at eight frames per second and it looked pretty good on screen."[94]

For a while, Dante toyed with making the piranhas stop motion. Dante said in *Starlog #18* that, "Initially, we wanted to use all stop-motion. When we approached Jon Berg, who worked on *Star Wars*, with the idea, he was horrified. We had to throw that idea out, although we did have Phil Tippett do some little stop-motion guys for Kevin McCarthy's lab. We just wanted to have them in there." Indeed, the lab features an odd bipedal piranha mutation that walks across the screen a few times.[95] If the inclusion seems oddly random, it was the last vestiges of another idea. Originally, Dante wanted the little monster to grow larger and larger until, at the end of the movie, it attacks a pier. But, the budget wasn't big enough to allow any such scene, and it was dropped.

Though the 1970s had begun with eco-friendly, pro-environment genre movies like *Godzilla vs. the Smog Monster* and *Frogs*, this movie's heroes kill the deadly piranha by intentionally polluting the river! Dillman's character must brave the piranha-infested waters to

---

[94] Ibid, pp.60.
[95] Phil Tippett would late use the creature for screen tests for the Tontons on Hoth for *Empire Strikes Back*. Photos exist to prove it.

turn an underwater valve that will release dangerous chemicals into Lost River. He is connected to the heroine's speedboat via rope so that when about a minute and a half has passed, she can speedily pull him out. The scene is quite suspenseful and exciting, with Dillman getting yanked out as the piranha are feeding on him (he does survive, by the way).

The film's final shots are spectacular. A newscaster is asking Barbara Steele's character if it's possible that some of the piranhas escaped and found their way into the ocean. She says that the fish weren't bred to survive in those conditions and that there's no reason to worry. Cue a final shot of the ocean to some ominous music, and the screen begins to tint to a deep red color as the credits start to roll.[96]

And indeed, as *Piranha* was a big hit, it would eventually spawn *Piranha II: The Spawning*. After only three weeks in release, *Piranha* had recouped its $1 million budget, grossing over $2 million by that time. Ultimately it made 14 times its original budget with $14 million in grosses. Ironically, when editing the picture, Joe Dante was worried that it was one of the worst films ever made. Instead, it launched his career. Before moving onto bigger fish like 1984's *Gremlins*, the success of *Piranha* would manage to entangle Dante in not one, but two unmade sequels about aquatic menaces...

Still from a *Piranha* lobby card. © 1978 New World Pictures

---

[96] Corman asked Sayles to write in an ending that could produce a sequel.

ORCA PART II

Developmental Period: 1978/1979

Idea by: Dino De Laurentiis **Proposed Director:** Joe Dante **Proposed Creatures:** Orca

SYNOPSIS Orca takes his revenge to the next level, stalking his prey not only in the water, but also on land...

COMMENTARY It would seem that even after *King Kong vs. Orca* was dropped that Dino De Laurentiis wanted an *Orca Part II*. Though I had heard of *King Kong vs. Orca*, word of a sequel without Kong was news to me. I discovered this via a quote from Joe Dante in the wonderful book *Just When You Thought It Was Safe: A Jaws Companion*. Dante stated that, "*Piranha* had gotten me a picture at Dino DeLaurentiis' that I didn't make called 'Orca 2,' about the killer whale — they actually wanted to make a sequel to that! Luckily, it didn't happen, so when it died, I was hired to do 'JAWS 3, PEOPLE 0' instead!"[97]

---

[97] Jankiewicz, *Just When You Thought It Was Safe*, pp.193.

Unfortunately, information on *Orca Part II* was scarce. For a while, I was worried that was all I would have to go on. But, thankfully, Dante talked about the project on Gilbert Gottfried's Amazing Colossal Podcast on February 8, 2016. The portion of the interview where he talks about *Orca Part II* is, in a word, hilarious. "After I did *Piranha,* I got a lot of offers for aquatic movies...I worked with Dino De Laurentiis briefly on *Orca 2,*" Dante began the conversation. And then he started to imitate the Italian producer. "And Dino says, 'Orca is a crazy he's a gonna kill everybody!'"[98] This caused Gottfried to laugh uncontrollably at Dante's spot on Dino impression.

Dante continued on that, "Orca was going to go on land and kill people and leave seaweed at the crime scene." Again raucous laughter from Gottfried and his co-host. "This actually didn't strike me as a particularly viable idea. I managed to talk him out of it."[99]

Considering that the first *Orca* was a revenge movie about avenging a dead mate, one could compare it to *Death Wish,* which De Laurentiis also produced. So I have to wonder, did Dino want to make Orca the Charles Bronson of the seas? Who, or what, was Orca going to avenge next? I wouldn't have been terribly surprised if the idea was that Orca was going to attack all humankind either for ecological reasons (animals attacking mankind for polluting the earth was a common staple of animals attack films) or if he singled out mankind for hunting whales. Or, maybe the grief-stricken whale had cracked since the last movie? Or, crazier still, maybe he got a new mate who was also killed by a whaler? (Hey, Charles Bronson's new girlfriends were always getting whacked in the *Death Wish* sequels!)

Like *Jaws, Orca* was not a film that needed a sequel. In fact, many people believe that the final shots of *Orca,* of the titular character swimming under the ice sheets, were meant to imply that Orca was committing suicide now that his mission had been finished. So not only was Orca supposed to be dead according to some, but

---

[98] https://www.gilbertpodcast.com/1494-2/

[99] Ibid.

bringing the whale back for more revenge would have undercut the original film badly.

And then there was Dino's way of going about it. To go back to Dante's comment ("Orca was going to go on land and kill people and leave seaweed at the crime scene."), it's no wonder Gottfried burst out laughing. I take the original *Orca* pretty seriously and yet even I get visions of Orca sneaking onto land in a trench coat and murdering someone in a dark alley. As dumb as it sounds, I think I get what Dino was going for, though. He desperately wanted to one-up *Jaws*. His thought process was probably that with Orca you weren't safe in the water or on the land. I'm sure that had the film gotten made, there would have been a play on *Jaws'* "Just when you thought it was safe to go in the water..." tagline.

Actually, though rare, some killer whales do come onto land to catch their prey. According to an article by Damian Wroclavsky on Science News, there is only one pod of killer whales in the world that hunt this way, and they hail from off the coast of Patagonia.[100] These whales essentially swim full bore towards the beach at sea lion pups reclining on the shore. The speed propels them to slide onto land, capturing the pup in its jaws. The orca will then wiggle itself back near the water in hopes of catching a wave that will help propel it back into the sea.

In all earnestness, if this was Dino's idea, it's quite terrifying. I can see it now. Some unsuspecting soul walking towards the water's edge, letting the tide run across their feet when—Bam!—Orca shoots out of the water to grip them in his jaws. It actually could have worked. And that would have given the franchise a one up on scares compared to *Jaws*, where the shark most certainly would not come up to the beach.

I also have to wonder just how far on land Dino intended the whale to get? Dante mentions that finding seaweed at the crime scenes would be a plot point. If Orca had merely waddled up onto a beach and bit someone in half, the seaweed probably wouldn't be that

---

[100] Wroclavsky, "Killer whales bring the hunt onto land," *Science News*. https://www.reuters.com/article/us-argentina-orcas-feature/killer-whales-bring-the-hunt-onto-land-idUSMAR71901420080417

big of a deal. You expect to find seaweed on a beach. I also would not have put it past Dino to set the movie some place where there are lots of canals. Places within a city that Orca could potentially swim and grab unsuspecting locals and tourists... Venice, perhaps?

There is one other angle to consider about Dino's idea. Though myself and others take *Orca* seriously, there are quite a few people that consider the film to be high camp. Dino may have realized this and decided to just run with it, hence his hiring of the self-aware director of *Piranha*, who quickly acknowledged in his own film that yes, it was a quasi-parody of *Jaws*.

As stated earlier, Dante moved on from *Orca Part II* to do a parody of *Jaws* itself, which we will cover in a future chapter.

Bert I. Gordon's
DEVIL FISH

Developmental Period: 1978

Screenplay by: Bert I. Gordon & Alan Caillou **Proposed Director:** Bert I. Gordon **Proposed Creatures:** Giant Devil Fish, giant sharks

SYNOPSIS A giant devil fish gets mixed up in a plot involving government intrigue.

COMMENTARY Not to be confused with *Devilfish*, the completed 1984 film, also known as *Monster Shark*, *Devil Fish* was an aborted film from Bert I. Gordon. If that name sounds familiar, Gordon produced a bevy of B-movies like *Beginning of the End* (1957). In that film, live grasshoppers were turned loose on photo blowups of Chicago to create some of the effect shots. He was still using the same tricks in the late 1970s with movies like *Empire of the Ants* (1978). Though a few scale giant ant props were used, many shots simply composited in real ants with the actors.

Gordon holding the *Devil Fish* model.

Despite being a b-movie maestro, Gordon had high hopes for his *Jaws*-inspired *Devil Fish*. "It's like an underwater *Star Wars*. It's sort of a James Bond-*The Deep-Jaws* adventure," he told *Starlog* #20 in 1978. Unfortunately, not much is known about the plot, other than a giant devil fish figured into it. All Gordon offered on the story was that, "There won't be any giant, atomic mutations in this film. The story features government intrigue, oil interest, action...everything."[101] The first comment was probably Gordon's attempt to distance himself from his older sci-fi pictures where atomic radiation created monsters, like the giant grasshoppers in *The Beginning of the End*. Gordon wanted the devilfish to be real, and said, "It's a 30-foot swordfish. When it attacks, it moves its sword back and forth like a scythe and then leisurely eats the pieces. I'll be using a live devil fish in this movie as well as giant sharks."[102] From that last comment, one might assume perhaps the story had the devil fish fight a "giant shark" as a swipe at *Jaws*, but that's just conjecture.

In a separate interview, Gordon elaborated on the sizes of the monsters again, stating that the sharks would be 50 feet long and that the Devilfish would be 30-feet long! This is much bigger than the 30-foot shark in *Jaws*. "No phony shots," Gordon assured the

---

[101] "The Bite of the Devil Fish," *Star Log* #20 (March 1979), pp.16.
[102] Ibid.

SHARK BITES: *DEVIL MANTA*

MONSTER MANTA RAYS WERE ON THE MINDS OF SEVERAL PRODUCERS IN THE LATE 1970S. TOEI OF JAPAN, PRODUCER OF *LEGEND OF DINOSAURS AND MONSTER BIRDS*, HAD ALSO TOYED WITH THE NOTION OF A DISASTER MOVIE ABOUT A GIANT MANTA RAY FROM SPACE! *DEVIL MANTA*, AS IT WAS TITLED, MIGHT HAVE BEEN CONSIDERED BEFORE THE DINOSAUR FILM AND MIGHT HAVE BEEN REVIVED AFTER IT. STUDIO LORE STATES THAT TOEI WAS THINKING ABOUT THE PRODUCTION UNTIL *STAR WARS* CAME OUT, AT WHICH POINT THEY DITCHED THE SPACE MANTA FOR SPACESHIPS IN THEIR 1978 OPUS *MESSAGE FROM SPACE*. IMAGES © 1977 TOEI

reporter. "And the fish are real fish. Using the methods I developed to create illusions on the screen…They won't be mechanical models like the ones they used in *Jaws*."[103]

When Gordon mentioned using a live devilfish the reporter pointed out a devilfish model on his desk. "This is a pretty crude model," Gordon admitted. "We wanted to test out its motor action," he continued. "You see, at one point in the script we have to blow up some fish. We're going to use large mechanical miniatures. We wouldn't actually explode live fish."[104] This comment probably also reveals the climax of the story, where, like Bruce in *Jaws*, the titular Devil Fish would be blown up.

---

[103] Naha, "Bert Gordon's Creature Features," *Starlog* #16 (September 1978), pp.33.
[104] "The Bite of the Devil Fish," *Star Log* #20, pp.16.

Gordon even learned to dive to helm the picture and apparently scouted some of the underwater locations himself. Though Gordon supposedly scouted locations "around the whole world," the main filming locale was apparently to be some "eerie scenery near the Bahamas, Key West, Florida and the California coast" which had unique lava formations. "It will give the movie a look that is unreal," Gordon said.[105]

Gordon scuba diving to scout locations. This image was also used to create an advance poster seen in *Variety*.

Gordon announced the project at the 1978 Cannes Film Festival, which included a poster, apparently modeled after one of Gordon's own dives. In addition to the poster, concept paintings also existed, though unfortunately none have surfaced so far (not that I can find at least). A *Starlog* reporter was lucky enough to see some of the paintings and described one as "portraying a team of divers swimming through what seems to be an underwater zoo/science lab." Gordon told the reporter, "We're story boarding like crazy. Every single camera angle is being painted."[106]

Gordon seemed to also be doing his best to compete with *The Deep*, which had an extensive amount of underwater photography. According to Gordon, over 50 percent of *Devil Fish* would take place underwater. Gordon said that he planned to laminate all the storyboards and have them on location. "Before a scene, I'll give direction above water and then take the painting down below during the actual filming of the scene. It will remind everyone of just what I need," Gordon said.[107]

[105] Ibid.
[106] Ibid.
[107] Ibid.

Gordon planned to shoot 125 feet down, which he claimed had as of yet not been done before. The picture was budgeted at $5 million, and the plan was to do a year's worth of principal photography, followed by six months' work on special effects. "I've devised a method of visual effects that has never been used underwater before—a traveling matte process, with multi-mattes. Some underwater shots will involve five and six separate pieces of film," Gordon said.[108]

Sadly, the production company, First Artists, went belly-up and that was the end of *Devil Fish*. Before this happened though, Gordon optimistically told Starlog that, "I'd like to pick up a copy of *Variety* and read the headlines: 'Devil Fish Outgrosses Star Wars!'"[109]

---

[108] Ibid.
[109] Naha, "Bert Gordon's Creature Features," *Starlog* #16 (September 1978), pp.33.

BARRACUDA

Release Date: January 1979
Alternate Titles: *Barracuda: The Sea Horror* (Australia)
Barracuda: Project Lucifer (South America) *Barracuda: The Guillotine of the Seabed* (Greece)

Directed by: Harry Kerwin & Wayne Crawford (underwater footage) **Screenplay by:** Harry Kerwin & Wayne Crawford **Music by:** Klaus Schulze **Cast:** Wayne Crawford (Mike Canfield) Jason Evers (Dr. Elliot Snow) Roberta Leighton (Liza Williams) Cliff Emmich (Deputy Lester) William Kerwin (Sheriff Ben Williams) Bert Freed (Papa Jack)

1.85 : 1, Color, 98 Minutes

SYNOPSIS A small coastal town famous for its lobster is rocked by some mysterious ocean deaths where scuba divers are torn to shreds by barracuda. Mike Canfield, a marine biologist, comes to investigate the matter. But clearly he's poking around into something he shouldn't, for soon a wealthy town magnate, Papa Jack, has him arrested by Sheriff Williams. Mike eventually begins a romance with the sheriff's daughter, Liza, and also gets the sheriff on his side regarding his investigation. Mike's research into the killer fish soon leads into a startling conspiracy involving the town doctor...

COMMENTARY As covered in a previous chapter, *Piranha* proved to be a big hit when released in 1978. Universal tried to stop its release because they felt it was a rip-off of *Jaws* until they were persuaded otherwise. Ironically, *Piranha* then spawned rip-offs of its own. The first of these would *appear* to be *Barracuda*. However, research shows that it was actually produced before *Piranha*. Details on the film are scarce, but according to the December 19, 1977, issue of *Box Office,* the film, then titled *The Lucifer Project*, had begun shooting in November of 1977 in Fort Lauderdale, Florida. It was produced by Atlas International, based in Munich, West Germany. The budget was reported to be $1.2 million. Some portions of the film were supposedly shot in the Bahamas and production wrapped in January of 1978. *Piranha* was only beginning to shoot around this time in February of 1978, so by all accounts, *Barracuda* was shot first... it just wasn't released first.[110]

Whether the producers were aware of *Piranha* or not, it has some similarities outside of the obvious (i.e., the killer fish). Like *Piranha*, the barracuda were altered via government experimentation. *Barracuda* also would seem to tip its hat to *Jaws*, as two of its lead characters are a sheriff and a marine biologist. Actually, the marine biologist kind of looks like Steven Spielberg! This is doubly funny, as the actor playing the part also directed the film's underwater footage (which is great, by the way).

Barracuda starts off with underwater credits common to *Jaws*, its sequels, and its rip-offs. Also, *Barracuda's* score is pretty darn good when stacked against its fellow rip-offs. The first scene has two scuba divers getting eaten by the fish and doesn't leave anything to the imagination. The barracudas can be seen clearly ripping their victims to shreds and are well executed. Already

---

[110] Adding to the confusion, IMDB's trivia for *Barracuda* claims that Joe Dante was asked to direct! This seems unlikely, as Dante was not yet known for horror pictures, and before *Piranha* had directed *Hollywood Boulevard* (1976).

Barracuda is utilizing better gore than *Piranha*, with severed human limbs floating through the water looking like half-eaten drumsticks.

Unfortunately, *Barracuda's* well-done opening scene is not indicative of the overall quality of the movie. Even though the barracuda and the underwater scenes they appear in are Grade A stuff (OK, OK, more like A- or B+), the surface dwellers reek of an independent movie production. The acting isn't great, and though the leads are good enough, the film is stuffed with superfluous characters and scenes that serve no real purpose.[111] Also, early on we hear people talking about an exciting real estate development in their coastal town, which sets up false expectations. Considering this is a *Jaws* rip-off, part of the formula is that the monster has to disrupt a water-based event where lots of people can potentially get eaten. But that never happens here.

We spend about another thirty minutes before we get to the next barracuda attack, where a teenaged scuba diver is eaten. In the next scene, a girl is playing fetch with her dog on the beach, and it finds the youth's severed head in the surf. Again, *Barracuda* comes off promisingly for what we think will be an exciting slaughter later in the movie. But, in fact, by this point, its most memorable fish scenes are already behind it.

As it turns out, the hungry barracuda are just the catalyst that launches our main character's investigation. As he digs deeper and deeper into the water pollution that made the fish so aggressive, he finds that its source is the town doctor. The far-out plot has said doctor's experiments intentionally giving everyone hypoglycemia. Exciting, right? The doctor is intentionally pumping the town water supply full of chemicals that cause the condition, leading to everyone being extra hungry and angry all the time. Hence, when these chemicals are dumped into the water, the barracuda get it. The starving fish then begin to devour everything in sight.

And as to why the doctor is doing this… apparently he wants people to be angry all the time so there will be no more war protestors! That way, when the next war breaks out, the nation will get right behind the war effort. Oh, and his secret benefactors? Well, as you can imagine, they're government agents.

The ending has the marine biologist and the sheriff engage in a gunfight with the two government agents. Just when the heroes think they've had it, the State Police show up to save them. The two agents come out with their hands up. But something isn't right. They give the State Police a nod, and then the whole squad

---

[111] Oddly, there's a reporter character in the film who dresses just like Carl Kolchak from *The Night Stalker*!

turns their guns on our two heroes and blasts them to smithereens. That's right. Not only does *Barracuda* have a major downer of an ending, but the killer fish don't even play into it! In fact, the last time we got a barracuda scene was over thirty minutes ago! If you call a movie *Barracuda*, then it's supposed to be about the barracuda.

I can't find much about this movie's production history, but I can only hope it wasn't filmed as intended. I would imagine the production ran out of money and had to create a new climax. Because, again, why title your movie *Barracuda* if the killer fish aren't really the focus?

After thinking about it for a while, it's my own speculation that the barracuda became the central focus after the surprise success of *Piranha*, which beat *Barracuda* to theaters by only a few months (*Barracuda* was released in West Germany in October of 1978). Considering this film began shooting as *The Lucifer Project*, I can only guess it was hastily retitled to ride the waves created by *Jaws 2* and *Piranha*.

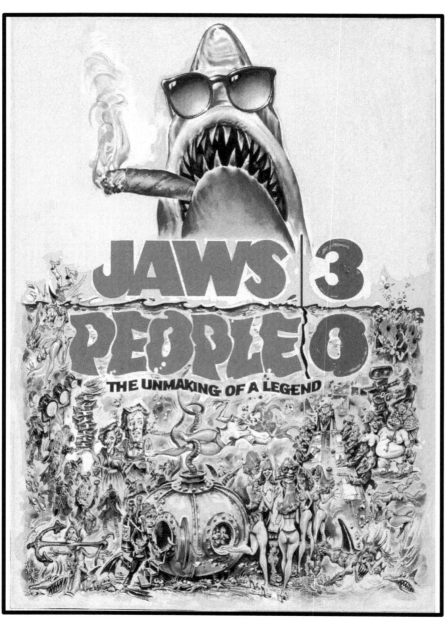

Jaws is a registered TM of Universal Pictures

National Lampoon's
JAWS 3, PEOPLE 0

Developmental Period: 1979

Treatment by: Matty Simmons **Second Draft Screenplay by:** John Hughes & Todd Carroll **Proposed Director:** Joe Dante **Proposed Cast/Characters:** Sonny [novice director] Darlene [starlet of *Jaws 3*] Mavin [evil studio executive] Marilyn [Mavin's secretary] Erma [Sonny's mother] Canterberry [executive eaten by shark] Cockatoo [French shark hunter] Butch [overweight star of *Jaws 3*] Steven [original *Jaws 3* director] **Proposed Creatures:** The Shark

SYNOPSIS A greedy studio executive, Mavin, is out to sabotage the production of *Jaws 3*. One night, the film's producer, Canterberry, is eaten by a Great White! In his will, Canterberry leaves his majority shares of the studio to his ex-girlfriend Erma, a hayseed from Idaho. Her son, Sonny, is then courted by Mavin to write and direct *Jaws 3* in the hopes that he will make the worst movie of all time. During filming, the shark attacks continue...

COMMENTARY *Jaws 3, People 0* has its roots in an unlikely—and potentially unrelated—backstory. During the lengthy shooting of *Jaws 2*, Keith Gordon, the actor who played Doug (one of the teenaged sailboaters) wrote a spoof of the *Jaws 2* script. It seemed to be based more on behind the scenes shenanigans than anything else. In *Jaws 2: The Making of a Hollywood Sequel,* he recalled that, "I don't remember many of the specifics but it was just full of all the absurd things that were going on, like the shark sinking and the wild lives that the kids were leading."[112] Gordon co-wrote it with Tom Dunlop.[113] Someone gave the five to ten-page script sample to a friend. Before the authors knew it, the script had circulated through most of the crew—even David Brown! Initially, Gordon was mortified that Brown read his spoof, but was relieved to find that Brown liked it. Just how much Brown liked it may have been underestimated at the time. It cannot be confirmed whether or not Gordon's *Jaws 2* spoof inspired *Jaws 3, People 0*, but on the *Making of Jaws 2* DVD feature, Brown and Zanuck both mention that as *Jaws 2* was winding down, they were already thinking of doing *Jaws 3* as a parody. Again, no proof that Gordon was the genesis of the idea, but if he wasn't, that's certainly quite a coincidence. Furthermore, Billy Van Zandt remembers that Brown called him about the *Jaws 3* spoof. "He asked Keith Gordon and I if we would be interested in appearing in *Jaws 3, People 0*," Van Zandt said.[114]

Whatever its true origins, the project was announced a few days after April Fool's Day in *Variety* on April 4, 1979. It was labeled as a joint production between Universal Pictures and *National Lampoon* Magazine

---

[112] Smith and Pisano, *Jaws 2: The Making of a Hollywood Sequel* (Kindle Edition)

[113] Billy Van Zandt also recalled writing a 40 page treatment with Gordon called *Murder in My Sanitarium* during filming.

[114] Phone interview with the author. Also, *House of Hammer* #21 reported on the alternate scenes in *Jaws 2* where Van Zandt's character either lived or died. The magazine joked about how Van Zandt's character lived, and so he could go on to appear in *Jaws 3*. This was just a joke on the magazine's part, which makes it ironic that Van Zandt actually was asked to play in *Jaws 3*!

(fresh off hits like *Animal House*). The germ of the idea came from the head of the magazine himself, Matty Simmons, who had hoped that three of the magazine's executive writers could flesh out the entire script.

As is usual in Hollywood, several people took the credit for the idea, including Zanuck and Brown back during shooting of *Jaws 2*. Nancy Anderson's "Hollywood Hotline" column suggested that it was Chevy Chase's idea!

> Pondering this success plus the success of "Jaws" and "Jaws II," Chevy Chase suggested that Universal make a picture with the title "Jaws Meets Animal House," or vice versa.
>
> The executive to whom he presented the notion was intrigued and said he'd discuss it with Simmons and with the Brown-Zanuck company which produced "Jaws I and II."
>
> He did, but Simmons was chilly to the idea, because he's planning a sequel to "Animal House," set six years later, and didn't want the title contaminated through a "Jaws" connection.[115]

Whether they birthed the idea or not, Zanuck and Brown were on board with the idea and would executive produce. On July 29, 1979, more details were revealed in the *Hollywood Reporter*, which stated that the screenplay was being written by John Hughes and Todd Carroll. The article also claimed that the new movie would feature members from the original film. What this actually implies is uncertain, considering I saw no mention of the original characters in the script I read (in an interview with IGN, Matty Simmons claimed that Richard Dreyfus would have appeared, though). All I saw were spoofs of Steven Spielberg and Peter Benchley. Even MCA Universal president himself Sid Sheinberg was set to cameo! Presumably, he would play one of the executives in one of the film's early scenes. The lead actor, the article claimed, would be Roger Bumpass,

---

[115] https://newspaperarchive.com/richardson-daily-news-aug-24-1979-p-2/

JAWS UNMADE

SHARK BITES: KEITH GORDON'S *JAWS 2.5*

ACCORDING TO *THE JAWS 2 LOG*, ON PAGE 112, KEITH GORDON
TITLED HIS SPOOF "JAWS 2.5: SECOND REVISED RENEWED UPDATED
SCREENPLAY." THE FAUX SCRIPT OPENS WITH TWO SCUBA DIVERS
WEARING "MINIMAL RUBBER"—IN FACT, THEY ARE NAKED.
PRODUCER DAVID BROWN THEN CUTS IN SCREAMING, "THAT'S AN
R!! THAT'S AN R!" PARODYING THE STUDIO'S FEAR OF AN 'R' RATING.
ALSO, ONE OF THE SAILBOATS WAS NAMED *THE TEGAN*, A NOD TO
THE FACT THAT THE ORIGINAL MIKE BRODY, ACTOR TEGAN WEST,
WAS WELL-LIKED AND MISSED BY THE CAST AFTER HE WAS REPLACED
BY A NEW ACTOR. IN THE SPOOF SCRIPT, *THE TEGAN* WAS PILOTED
BY, WHO ELSE, AN UNEMPLOYED ACTOR...

who had starred in the *National Lampoon's* music and comedy roadshow titled, *That's Not Funny, That's Sick* from 1977 to 1978.

Principal photography was set to begin on October 7, 1979. That same month, the project would end up being canceled. Supposedly, Steven Spielberg did not like the script as it made fun of him and his film. According to an interview with Matty Simmons and IGN, Spielberg threatened to walk off the studio lot if the film was produced. Joe Alves also remarked that he did not like the script, as it made fun of the arduous making of the first *Jaws*, which was still a sore subject for many involved. Even though two and a half million dollars' worth of pre-production had already been spent on the picture, Universal executives shut it down. Shortly after, Zanuck and Brown left Universal. Simmons pondered selling it to another studio, but as Universal owned the Jaws franchise, his chances his chances of getting it made were slim.

As usual, though, there are alternate explanations as to why the project was shut down. Joe Dante, the proposed director, said on Gilbert Gottfried's podcast that the main problem was that the Lampoon's people wanted it to be R-Rated, while Universal wanted it PG. Dante confirmed that Bo Derek was approached and agreed to star, though it's uncertain if she signed any contracts.

Yet other sources say Universal executives simply felt that a straight *Jaws 3* would perform better, and once they did a comedy version there would be no returning to a serious version.

Whatever the reason that *Jaws 3, People 0* sunk, the *Los Angeles Times* reported on the project's cancellation in their October 17th issue.

But had the film been shot, just what would we have seen? We were to open with the title, naturally. "Jaws 3" would pop up first followed by "People 0" for the full comedic effect. We are in the water, but only later do we realize we are in a swimming pool! We settle into Peter Benchley's study, where he is writing the script for—what else?—*Jaws 3*. He can only bring himself to write the title before he gives up and goes outside for a swim in his pool. As he dives in, we hear the familiar theme music, and somehow, he's eaten by Jaws![116]

In the next scene, Benchley's coffin is ceremoniously dropped into the sea—but it won't sink. The mourners are horrified as seagulls descend upon it, and so the captain of the boat turns a submachine gun on the gulls. The coffin, now peppered with bullets, sinks into the depths.

The camera pans over to reveal the filming of *Jaws 3*. There a director named Steven gets the bad news that Benchley never finished the script for *Jaws 3*, to which he reacts with great outrage. Not only that, but the star of the movie is also a washed-up overweight actor.

"I've given enough of myself to these lousy fish movies. I quit!" he yells. As he gets up, we can finally see that he is literally missing an arm and a leg!

The next scene is meant to be evocative of the first *Jaws*—same concept and ambiance—only with elderly studio executives around a bonfire with attractive young women who hang to their every word. One executive, Canterberry, stands out, as he is on the phone going on a tirade about the production of *Jaws 3*. One of the girls, Darlene, can tell he is stressed and offers to take him out for a swim.

The two run onto the beach, much like the boy and girl from the first film. However, here it is Darlene who

---

[116] Some sources erroneously describe this as Steven Spielberg getting eaten, maybe in another draft it was, but not here. Furthermore, I believe that the swimming pool gag may have stemmed from a nightmare scene in Howard Sackler's *Jaws 2* treatment.

ends up staying on the beach while the old man goes out into the water and is eaten by the shark. Nothing particularly funny happens in my opinion—the shark eats a buoy which I don't think is very clever—but had it actually been filmed and directed skillfully, perhaps it would've come off well.

The aftermath of the scene, which showcases Canterberry's remains is funny, though. His false teeth with a cigar still clenched in between them is found amongst some seaweed, along with an expensive watch.

From here we transition to Mecca Studios, "where movies are a religion." A board meeting is occurring to discuss the death of Canterberry. Though at first they intend to honor his memory, Mavin, another executive, begins to berate Canterberry and makes it clear that this is his studio now. The discussion turns to the in-development *Jaws 3*. One executive suggests shutting it down which launches Mavin into a tirade where he proclaims that *Jaws* and *Jaws 2* "made more money than the Buick-Division of General Motors, the Episcopalian Church and the March of Dimes combined."

Next, the execs are incensed to learn Canterberry left his studio shares to his ex-girlfriend Erma, the mother of Canterberry's illegitimate son, Sonny, who works in a lint factory in Idaho (don't ask). After what reads as a very unfunny scene (to me at least) we transition to Canterberry's funeral—a very funny scene. As the priest drones on about how humble Canterbury was, we would have panned over to his coffin surrounded by an "obscene assembly of flowers and banners." Amongst the mourners is an entire front row of young, attractive blondes.

None of the people there are respectful, and in the middle of the funeral, Mavin is talking to the other executives about Canterberry's will, and how Erma will now be the head of the studio. There's also a cameo written here for Robert Redford. One of the execs mentions wanting a meeting with Redford to his secretary, who we presume will call him on the phone later. Instead, she stands up in the middle of the funeral and calls to Redford in the back row!

From the funeral we cut to Sonny in a theater with his girlfriend, Wendy, watching a bad sci-fi movie. Sonny is so enraptured by the film he doesn't even notice Wendy trying to put the moves on him, and the scene mostly exists to establish that Sonny wants to be a director. Right after this, he gets the news from his mother that she's been named the new chair of Mecca Studios.

There's a scene of Sonny and his mother, Erma, being accosted in the airport by a Hare Krishna that predates similar scenes from *Airplane!* released the next year.[117] Eventually, Marilyn, Erma's new secretary, comes to greet them and in the process rescues them from the Krishna, who she beats up and stuffs into a locker.

Erma and Sunny are taken to Mavin's mansion. Naturally, he is none too happy about the situation, but like a snake, puts on a deceptively charming face. He takes Erma out to a special swing he's had constructed over an ocean cliff—for the view he says.

He pushes Erma on the swing over the ocean. That's when the Jaws theme starts up again. Erma catches on to what Mavin's trying to do and clutches at his chest as the swing comes back towards him. She grabs him by the tie, and it is he who is jettisoned into the ocean below. However, the shark doesn't attack him and strangely pushes him back to shore.

Marilyn and Sonny observed the incident, and so Marilyn suggests that they need an "expert" to handle their shark problem. Enter the character of Pierre Cockatoo, a Frenchman and the polar opposite of Quint, who lives on a luxury yacht. Marilyn gets Pierre to be a consultant of sorts on their *Jaws 3* debacle.

Meanwhile, Mavin, who always wanted *Jaws 3* to fail, asks Sonny if he would like to direct the film! Sonny's new take on *Jaws 3* harkens back to his favorite sci-fi film. He comes up with a plot where some of the Amity Islanders are aliens, prepping for the invasion of earth. One of the aliens assumes the form of a giant shark to create panic at the beach and ruin Amity's tourism. When Sonny suffers from some writer's block, he teams with the old writer of *Chihuahua's From Hell*, called the Bell Captain within the script. However, the Bell Captain changes the story to become about "A fish from outer space who decides to chuck it all and become a chiropractor in a tiny coastal village."

---

[117] *Airplane!* would itself spoof *Jaws* in its opening scene.

A horrified Marilyn looks at the script and says, "This is worse than television, no it's worse than daytime television!" However, the argument is made that it's just the sort of movie that idiots will love, and Marilyn changes her tune. "I don't know Sonny. It might just be shitty enough to work."

From here we cut to another truly good spoof scene:

A mass of screaming bathers runs at camera in an extreme version of the water evacuation scene in *Jaws*. More people, more terror, more confusion. They are carrying children, towels, ridiculous beach gear and water toys. It should have the look and feel of a true dramatic scene.

Sonny calls cut and considers the take a "keeper" until his assistant director informs him that he had the people run the wrong way—into the water instead of out of it. The AD then simply suggests they fix it by running the film backwards! It gets worse as Sonny meets "Bruce #3," which isn't even an animatronic shark, but a mere shark costume that is very fake looking. It is then inhabited by a paunchy Caucasian and a small Japanese man in scuba gear

"And the audience won't even know that it's a fake shark?" Sonny asks the effects director. He responds, "Shashufi [the Japanese man] played the original Godzilla!"

The effects director insists that the shark suit will look real in the water. Had the movie been made, they were going to insert archival shark footage here to bring Bruce #3 to life so that the effects director's statement would humorously end up being the truth.

The first shark attack scene is then filmed with the two stars, Butch and Darlene. In the first take, the shark's dorsal fin falls limp, and they lose track of Bruce #3. Announcing that the shark is broken, they break for lunch. As Darlene climbs back onto the boat, the real shark comes up behind her and bears his teeth unseen, to everyone but the audience. A little later, Bruce #3 reappears, having been mysteriously ripped in half (though the stuntmen survived). Then the crew spots a real shark fin in the water and figures out that a real shark is on the loose.

Darlene complains that she could have been killed, being in the water with a real shark. "Did you see *Jaws*?" she asks Sonny sarcastically.

He responds, "I saw *Jaws* twenty-five times and *Jaws 2* twenty-three times. It wasn't as good."

Cockatoo goes to work to try and catch the shark by diving in a bathysphere. He sprays himself in a special perfume that will attract the shark so that he can then "fill him full of a big hole." As it is, Cockatoo has a cannon mounted onto the bathysphere. However, his two assistants lower him into the water too quickly. He hits the sea bottom, which causes the cannon to fire accidentally. The cannonball strikes the boat above and it explodes.

However, this was all at the behest of Mavin, who paid the assistants to drop the bathysphere. Marilyn is then informed that Cockatoo has killed the shark, and the production may safely resume.

Around this time occurs a comical love scene between Sonny and Darlene. It is noteworthy because it precedes a similar love scene from *Naked Gun 2 ½: The Smell of Fear*. In that scene, Leslie Nielsen and Priscilla Presley's foreplay is accompanied by suggestive images, Egyptian obelisks being raised into the sky, rockets launching, etc. Here it is the same thing: 13th Century Warriors ramming a castle door with a battering ram, a woodpecker wildly pecking a tree, Babe Ruth hitting a home run, etc. It's enough to make me wonder if the producers or someone involved with the *Naked Gun* series saw the *Jaws 3* spoof script and used the idea in *Naked Gun 2 ½*.

The end set-piece of *Jaws 3, People 0* is the filming of the climactic final sequence of the faux *Jaws 3*. In the movie within a movie, Jaws is to save Darlene and following that will be a water ballet. As Sonny and Marilyn discuss the scene, the boat is rocked from underneath. They run to look over the side and see a familiar dorsal fin. To make matters worse, it is headed straight for a group of chorus girls on a platform in the water! The shark's dorsal fin slices the platform in half, causing some of the girls to tumble into the water. Marilyn then orders the cameras to start rolling as this will be the ultimate "snuff movie." Sonny is incensed by her lack of concern. Marilyn says, "We're all going to die, we might as well die with a film in the can!"

The shark continues to attack the boat, causing it to rock back and forth. In the chaos, Sonny and Erma tumble into the water. Marilyn, meanwhile, informs the secondary writer that they are in the middle of script changes (i.e., the current shark attack) and to revise the ending. This was, of course, a parody of the situation on *Jaws 2* when Carl Gottlieb was rewriting the film as it was being shot.

> MARILYNN
> Good. The shark has decided he's a monster first
> and a humanitarian second.

> BELL CAPTAIN
> Great! I used that in "Meatloaf
> from Mercury!"

The chaos continues in the water, where singers cling to the overweight Butch, who is so fat he floats and cannot possibly sink. Another man spots a porpoise and proclaims, "Look! A porpoise! They've been known to save men from shark attacks. We share common language skills! We're saved!"

The porpoise then surfaces, and in a squeaky porpoise-like voice says, "Blow it out your ass!"

Things get zanier and zanier amongst the carnage as one man fails to realize he has been attacked by the shark. He sees a familiar pair of shoes attached to some severed legs in the water. "Hey! Those are my shoes!" he yells.

In a send-up of Lassie, a man instructs his border collie to leave the ship and go get help. Below deck, the writer continues to pound out page after page, handing them to Marilyn, as the water rises within the sinking ship. A helicopter then enters the fray. Over a PA, the pilot informs the panicked swimmers that he is not licensed to help them! As an employee of the radio station KROK he says,

> While we are not required to assist you, we can inform you that the temperature is 81 degrees, winds southeasterly thirteen miles per hour, skies are

clear. Traffic is snarled on the Harbor Freeway, there is an overturned truck on the San Diego Freeway. Allow for extra travel time throughout the area.

The special effects director is taking action at least. A rickety shark cage has been assembled, and he hands the scuba diver a spear gun. "When the shark attacks, shoot this into his mouth. It's a mixture of yard mushrooms and ordinary bathroom germs." The terrified diver is then lowered into the water. From above, the effects director watches the cage jerk violently (the shark is obviously attacking it) and says, "We'll give him a minute or two to orientate himself."

Eventually they haul the cage back up, but it has been crunched down to the size of a basketball! The diver clings to it totally naked (the shark having apparently eaten his clothes but not him).

We cut back to Butch, who now has "seven men, two women, his mother and the collie clinging to him." But, the chaos has died down. The water is littered with dead bodies and body parts. The shark has disappeared, and the few survivors keep a look out for it. Suddenly it bursts from the water, flashing its mighty teeth. Sonny comes on deck with a gun, and as the tension mounts aims it at the shark and mutters, "Awright, you son-of-a-bitch!"

And then, nothing. The shark even stops swimming as if he, too, is disappointed by the sequence of events. The gun has failed to fire because it is only a prop gun. Sonny then goes on to berate the shark. Overall, it's pretty anticlimactic. Sonny yells at the shark, and it leaves. That simple. Presumably, the scene might have gotten punched up in a new draft.

We cut to the opening night of the movie. It is fairly amusing, and one of the better bits is as follows:

We see a section of seats filled, with people in formal attire, furs, jewels; beautiful show people. They are eating popcorn as regular people do, spilling some in their laps, licking buttery fingers, eating large finger-fulls, some are shaking candy into their mouths from boxes. A lovely woman reaches between her legs to the floor and brings up her Coke, which she slurps from a straw. They are behaving like regular people at a regular show. Their heads turn as the *Jaws 3* party comes in and down the aisle. They position their popcorn between their legs and brush the salt off their hands and applaud.

As we hear the movie play out, it is indeed a space invasion story set on Amity Island just as Sonny always wanted. Butch is playing a sheriff's deputy, presumably Roy Scheider's, though this is never really hinted at. It gets pretty zany, as we watch the audience but only hear lines from the film like, "Come to think of it he [the shark] could be in the hot tub, let me get my laser gun!"

Meanwhile, Mavin is out at sea on a rowboat angrily berating the shark, which seems to be bashfully swimming in circles around him. It's now apparent that Mavin hired the shark to sabotage the production. Mavin states that since he didn't kill the crew, he will. Mavin begins to row back to shore with some sticks of dynamite—our clue that he intends to blow up the theater. But, the shark seems to have had enough and begins to chase Mavin to the shore. Mavin manages to scramble onto the pier just evading the shark. "Candyass! Eat Me!" he screams. Then the shark bursts from under the pier, and it's implied that does just that. He also eats the dynamite—or so we think. We cut to the movie, where the alien shark has just exploded.

The audience applauds, they loved it. As they exit the theater, they react in shock to what they see outside. The real shark didn't die, and neither did Mavin.

The shark —Huge and very real stands upright on his tail. Next to him, hanging by a rope on a hook is a completely bound Mavin. He is also gagged and soaking wet. He is very much alive and we can see that despite the ropes and gag, he is squirming and cursing.

PULL BACK TO EXT. THEATER

Show the theatre. Pan up to marque which says: "COMING SOON: JAWS 4."
FADE OUT

THE END

As you can see, though undeniably hilarious in some ways, the script definitely had a few flat moments that could have been smoothed out in later rewrites, or possibly through on set improvisation had filming commenced. That said, Joe Dante stated in *Just When You Thought It Was Safe* that "the corporate take on the movie was pretty restrictive — I went to work and they handed me storyboards that were already drawn!"[118] Dante gave the script high marks though and saw several different drafts of it. Dante even remembered cutting and pasting the different drafts together in his office.

Perhaps the real irony of the situation is that *Jaws 3-D* turned into exactly the overblown, ludicrous sequel that the fake "Jaws 3" was in this script in some ways. While this script presents the overblown premise of an invading alien shark, audiences considered the real *Jaws 3-D*, where the big fish attacks Sea World, to be far out as well.

---

[118] Jankiewicz, *Just When You Thought It Was Safe*, pp.194.

John Sayles'

SEA DRAGON OF LOCH NESS

Script Date: March 5, 1979

First Revised Screenplay by: John Sayles **Proposed Cast/Characters:** Bill Guzak [world renowned diver], Marcella Yost [shark expert], Kit Guzak [Bill's teenage daughter], Sir Kevin Mason [retired adventurer], Campbell [evil oil company owner] **Proposed Creatures:** Nessie, sharks

SYNOPSIS Construction on an illegal, underwater pipeline accidentally awakes a giant, prehistoric monster. The creature is none other than Nessie, who uses an undersea tunnel that connects Loch Ness to the ocean to go back and forth between the two. At the same time, Sir Kevin, a wealthy English naturalist, launches an expedition to find Nessie after a recent sighting in the lake. Sir Kevin hires one of the world's greatest divers, Bill Guzak, along with Dr. Marcella Yost, who has recently developed a new shark anesthetic, to search for Nessie. The investigation, which discovers the undersea tunnel, draws the ire of the evil oil executives out to keep the pipeline a secret at any cost...

COMMENTARY Very little is known about this script from *Piranha* writer John Sayles outside of its contents. Or, I mean to say, I don't know if any major studio ever considered the scenario. Being a solid, well-written story coming off the recent successes of *Jaws 2* and *Piranha* in 1978, the main reason this movie didn't get made, I would assume, is that it would have been costly. In addition to Nessie herself, the film would have required extensive underwater shooting with expensive submarines. Location shooting at Loch Ness, along with finding an oil derrick, may have also seemed intimidating to potential investors. The screenplay was also developed at the same time that Hammer's long-gestating *Nessie* was in its death throes. In fact, in either 1977 or 1978, Twentieth Century Fox had contacted Hammer in regards to their movie having the same name as a Nessie production they had in development! So, perhaps *Sea Dragon of Loch Ness* was the film in question? Considering that Sayles revised his screenplay, this would indicate that someone was interested in it. As for one last aside, *Nessie* and *Sea Dragon* have a major similarity in that in both, the monster attacks an oil derrick.

Though it went unproduced just like Hammer's *Nessie*, many fans like myself wonder what *Sea Dragon* would have been like if it had. After reading the script, I would describe *Sea Dragon* as one of those respectable monster movies that's absolutely solid in its storytelling, and yet would probably upset monster fans because there's not enough of said monster. The script is similar to *Jaws* in that the creature doesn't get fully revealed until late. In fact, Nessie doesn't get a full-body shot until the ending action sequence. Before this, we might see a massive eye, a hump, a flipper, but never the full body.

But, the full-on entrance of the monster during the final act sounds quite spectacular on paper. Sayles writes,

> We HEAR one more CRY, then the beast swims out of the shadows. More like an island than a

creature, covered with barnacles and scars, it is immense, truly magnificent, and coming right TOWARD US shrieking with fury, its cry booming off the cavern walls.

As to Nessie's bigger than normal dinosaur size, there is a down-to earth explanation for this (or, down to earth compared to the one in Hammer's version where the beastie was enlarged by a mutagen). Sayles goes with the reasoning that reptiles never stop growing (which is true). Nessie is very old; henceforth she's very, very big.

The human characters are also solid. And, considering it is they, not the monster, who carries the script, this is fortunate. The lead is the world-renowned scuba diver Bill Guzak. Opposite him is the shark biologist Marcella. The two's relationship is predictable, but still excellent, as they do the usual routine where they hate working together initially but are an item by the story's end.

Marcella is possibly developed better than Guzak, and an actress like *Orca's* Charlotte Rampling would have suited her well. One of the better scenes has Guzak underestimating Marcella's abilities in the water. As he brags about his daughter, Kit, almost breaking a world record when it came to female divers, Marcella informs him that it was her record whom Kit failed to beat!

Speaking of Kit, the antagonistic teenaged daughter of Guzak, she just might be the script's best character. Though she may come across as annoying for some, she presents a teenaged character that was pretty well developed for a supporting role in a 1970s monster movie. Proving that odd couplings are always the best, Kit has some touching scenes with the more refined Sir Kevin. Initially, Kit belittles him, thinking he's just an armchair adventurer who's never done anything dangerous in his life. Sir Kevin chides her by saying that's not true. After all, he survived one of the most trying events of his life: "An afternoon with the world's most obnoxious teenager."

Later, after Kit has a close encounter with Nessie when she dives in the loch, Sir Kevin gifts her a gold medallion. Kit recognizes it as being from a famous shipwreck. She asks Sir Kevin how much he paid for it, thinking he bought it. To her shock, he was one of the divers that recovered it. Sayles' dialogue here is particularly good.

                    KIT
        The Santa Veronica dive was years ago.

                  SIR KEVIN
                 So was my youth.

                    KIT
                (looks at him)
        It was in the worst currents in the Caribbean.

                  SIR KEVIN
             Positive you don't want it?

                    KIT
        You risked your neck for this, can't give it away.

               SIR KEVIN (smiles)
              What are treasures for?

As for similarities to *Jaws*, I wouldn't say that there are very many. The most notable one is a *Jaws*-style POV shot from the monster's perspective as it watches Kit swim above her, but it doesn't attack. There's a great, atmospheric scene where two men are dynamite fishing on the loch on a foggy morning. After several explosions, they hear a mournful roar, not unlike a foghorn. Suddenly a towering black shape drifts towards them from within the fog and overtakes their boat before we transition to another scene. Some might argue that this descended from the fisherman scene in *Jaws*, but I don't think so myself. Aside from all that, there are two notable shark scenes in the script. We are introduced to Marcella underwater in scuba gear as she tests her underwater anesthesia on the sharks. Later, Marcella and Guzak must fend off hungry sharks in an underwater tunnel. A shark is also found bitten in half within the loch (this might have been attempting to draw attention to the fact that Nessie is a bigger beast than Jaws).

The script's oil storyline, in some ways, forms the backbone of the plot, and brings to mind Bert I.

Gordon's *Devil Fish* project, in which oil interests would also figure prominently into the plot. Considering it was developing around the same time, one has to wonder if great minds were simply thinking alike, or if there was a more direct connection.[119]

The climax of the story has some similarities to *Jaws 3-D*, which *Sea Dragon* predates. The ending sequence comprises of Guzak and Marcella coming into conflict with the hired goons of the oil company while underwater. The oil company doesn't want the duo to report on the underwater pipeline they discovered while searching for Nessie. So, from their underwater headquarters, they send a submarine out to battle the sub that Guzak and Marcella are piloting. A tussle occurs between the submarines (both have machine arms), which awakens Nessie. The beast comes in and attacks the enemy sub, which had remotely detonated an underwater mine. After she's destroyed the sub, Nessie attacks the villain's underwater observation deck, coming straight at the glass like the shark in *Jaws 3-D*. But instead of just breaking the glass,

> The beast pushes the habitat completely over -- it crashes on its side, seams cracking and gas bursting out, the last light in the cavern going out with a huge flash and roar -- we STAY in the darkness for a moment, then HEAR the CRY of the BEAST once again.

Sayles's script is good about having its cake and eating it too. It's clear that Sayles wants Nessie to be a sympathetic figure, but he also wants her to menace the heroes at the film's end. Nessie is established as being sympathetic in that she doesn't harm Kit as she watches her swim mid-way into the script. She only attacks the oil company's submarine after the explosion goes off, so she naturally views the sub as a threat. Guzak's submersible then becomes guilty by association, allowing Nessie to also chase after the heroes once she's done with the bad guys.

---

[119] Sometimes studio heads will take a liking to a certain aspect of a script, and then instruct a writer to inject it into another storyline that they consider to have a higher chance of success.

Nessie chases the heroes into the ocean and grabs the sub in her mouth. Marcella uses some helium jets to blast them free of the beast, and then discharges a dye tank to obscure them from the dinosaur's view. When that's not enough, she uses a massive dose of her shark tranquilizer to subdue the creature.

However, in the struggle, Nessie managed to damage the sub's engines, so it's not moving. Their only hope is a rescue, which Kit and Sir Kevin orchestrate over the radio. The Navy dispatches a specially trained seal (as in the actual animal) to swim down with a tow line to the sub. But Nessie is awake again, and she's watching. She doesn't harm the seal, but when she sees the sub being towed to the surface, she grips it in her jaws again. Knowing they have no other option, Guzak and Marcella swim to the surface on their own while the monster remains distracted by the sub. The duo makes it to the Navy ship above where Sir Kevin and Kit are waiting. They joyously reunite, and then Nessie breaks the surface. She roars, and then like a whale that's leapt into the air, dives back under the waves in front of her awed spectators.

Following this is one final scene, an epilogue set within a pub at Loch Ness. The pub, along with a local drunkard, Old Man McDuff, had been a reoccurring element throughout the script, with McDuff a knowing old-timer who had seen the monster several times. As everyone in the pub revels in the news that Nessie has finally been proven to exist, McDuff looks saddened and walks outside. He stands on the shores of the loch.

McDUFF

They'll be at you like pack hounds, now. Wi their ships an plane an fancy equipment. But ye'll ootwait em all, won't ye? Like all the ones before. And ye'll coom back ye will, Ye'll coom back to Loch Ness .

We PULL BACK SLOWLY, KEEP MOVING BACK till McDuff is a tiny silhouette against the moonlit, eerie Loch Ness.

No Laughing Matter
UP FROM THE DEPTHS

Release Date: June 29, 1979
Alternate Titles: *Jurassic Jaws* (Japan)

Directed by: Charles B. Griffith **Special Effects by:** Santos Hilario (as Sandy Hill) **Screenplay by:** Anne Dyer & Alfred Sweeney **Music by:** Russell O'Malley **Cast:** Sam Bottoms (Greg Oliver) Susanne Reed (Rachel McNamara) Virgil Frye (Earl Sullivan) Kedric Wolfe (Oscar Forbes) Charles Howerton (Dr. David Whiting) Denise Hayes (Iris Lee) R. Lee Ermy (Lee)

Spherical, Metrocolor, 85 Minutes

SYNOPSIS Dr. David Whiting and his assistant are studying the ocean when an undersea earthquake occurs. It awakens a prehistoric fish that eats Whiting's assistant. The fish goes on to terrorize the swimmers at a new Hawaiian resort to the horror of the manager. He offers a huge reward to anyone who can catch the fish. Dr. Whiting and a local swindler/treasure hunter, Greg Oliver, go out to capture the fish alive with Rachel

McNamara, the hotel's publicity officer. Dr. Whiting is bitten by the fish but doesn't die until he's dredged back up onto the boat. Greg stuffs his body full of explosives and tosses him back into the water. The fish eats the body, Greg flips the detonator, and the threat is over.

COMMENTARY In 1975, Roger Corman noticed that Vincent Canby, the *New York Times* film critic, had compared *Jaws* to one of his own films, only bigger. Corman had Canby's comment in mind as he watched the movie. In the documentary *Machete Maidens* Corman said, "When I saw *Jaws* I said, 'I'm in trouble, and my compatriots are in trouble.'"

Corman's first attempt at a *Jaws*-like production, *Piranha*, was a big hit with audiences. His second attempt, which Joe Dante referred to as the "Filipino rip-off version of *Jaws*," was not. However, complicated behind the scenes shenanigans and a somewhat lazy development process marred the film badly.

Corman decided to produce his next underwater horror film in the Philippines, and as such, farmed it out to his producer friend there, Cirio Santiago. Corman cobbled the story concept together out of two of his previous films: *Monster from the Ocean Floor* (1954) and *Creature from the Haunted Sea* (1961). In *Monster from the Ocean Floor,* a pretty girl comes to a Mexican village and falls in love with a local marine biologist there while a sea monster runs loose. *Creature from the Haunted Sea* was similar but added lost treasure into the mix. Corman combined all those plot points and then picked and chose select elements from *Jaws*, *Jaws 2*, and *The Deep*. According to Chuck Griffith, *Up From the Depths'* director, the trouble started when Corman dumped all these elements in the lap of his secretary Anne Dyer. As it was, Dyer was not a professional screenwriter.

"We had it written by one of the typists or secretaries in the office who didn't have any thoughts of becoming a writer," remarked Griffith.[120] A Corman veteran by then, having written movies such as *The Little Shoppe of Horrors*, perhaps it's no surprise that Griffith wisely tried to turn the film into a comedy. However, the

---

[120] Graham, "An interview with Charles B. Griffith," *Senses of Cinema* (April 15, 2005).

producer, Cirio Santiago wanted it to be a serious film and fought the comedy aspect. "It became somewhat of a dilemma because you've got two films going on simultaneously," said the star, Susan Reed, in *Machete Maidens*.

According to Griffith, another reason that the script was never truly finished by a professional was that Corman didn't want to pay anyone from the Writers Guild. Griffith commented, "...so the idea was that I would use my director's prerogative to polish up an impossible script."[121]

Griffith tweaked the story, which Corman called *Up From the Depths*, into a comedy called *Something's Fishy*. "The Filipinos were crazy about it," Griffith said. "They made a funny-looking fish for it, and we were all set to go, but they sent the script to Roger, figuring he would love it, and of course, he hit his desk and told them to fire me and everybody else."[122]

As is common in film history, the filmmakers gave different quotes in different interviews. Take this comment of Griffith's from *Little Shop of Genres*, in which he stated:

> I think Roger did it to punish me, to send me out to The Philippines where I didn't know what I was getting into. I was making an action picture, but The Philippines people were all so depressed, and they had made this goofy-looking fish with bug eyes. I told them that we'll make it a comedy, and their eyes lit up![123]

This statement would seem to imply that Griffith decided to turn it into a comedy upon seeing the monster maquette. The other story he told made it sound as though he came up with the spoof angle as he was polishing the script. Further adding to the confusion, Joe Dante claimed that Corman didn't mind the comedic tone in of itself so much as he wanted it to

---

[121] Koetting, *Mind Warp*, pp.168.
[122] Ibid.
[123] Graham, "An interview with Charles B. Griffith," *Senses of Cinema* (April 15, 2005).

match the advertising, which promised another horror thriller.

Whatever the case, filming in the Philippines was an absolute nightmare. Like the shark in *Jaws*, the creature constructed by the effects crew didn't work like it was supposed to. And that was just the full-scale model. Apparently, there was a large head prop that was meant to be operated by a diver. But it was too heavy and went unused, and only test footage of the prop exists.

The original mon-star of *Up From the Depths* in a photo taken on location by Jess Griffith. © Jess Griffith

Compounding the problem was the Filipino crew, who didn't show up for work reliably. Extras would show up dressed inappropriately for their scenes (for instance, wearing ballroom attire on the beach and vice versa). The speedboat propellers became damaged by the coral reefs and didn't work properly as well.

Under the circumstances, and despite protests from Santiago, Griffith shot the movie like it was a comedy. Griffith edited the film in Manilla, and the first cut was 106 minutes long. Griffith remembered sending the movie to Corman on a plane back to the States a day before he left. "So I sent back a comedy on one plane, and I arrived on the next one. By the time I arrived,

Roger had already cut 75 minutes out."[124] Or, what I assume Griffith meant to say was he cut the movie down to 75 minutes. This was apparently a shorter rough cut, as the final version clocks in at 85 minutes.

The monster as it appears in the final cut. © 1979 New World Pictures

The other ten minute's worth of footage was new special effects scenes with a better-looking monster—which is still bug-eyed and somewhat goofy looking. The new fish was designed by future Oscar winners Chris Walas and Robert Short, with Walas shooting new monster scenes for Corman to replace the goofy ones from the Philippines. Because the new footage was shot after principal photography had wrapped, this necessitated some choppy editing to insert the new monster into Griffith's original footage. Therefore, glimpses of the monster are all very brief, and it's only when we see it for too long that it looks a little subpar. Otherwise, the quick shots are decent.[125]

Whether Corman cut 75 minutes out as Griffith claimed, or just 31 minutes, either way, there's a lot of cut footage (and a different monster design) out there, constituting the original comedic cut of *Up From the Depths* as a lost film. Despite Corman's best efforts, many vestiges of this idea remain in the final cut. For starters, star Sam Bottoms name is flashed across the shaking butts of some native dancers (I assume that's not a coincidence). The whole credits sequence has a

---

[124] Ibid.

[125] The interpretation of the creature on the poster is certainly intimidating. I know I noticed it at Blockbuster as a kid and would have been too afraid to rent the movie even if my parents would have let me.

light, goofy air to it that suggests a comedy, which is in stark contrast to the bloody pre-credits sequence that opened the film. In it, a girl is eaten by the monster, which we don't see (we only see an eruption of blood in the water). Nothing about this particular scene suggested a comedy. After the credits, the girl's bloody remains wash into the shallows where some kids notice them. A portly man then wades through them and becomes covered in gore. His wife, unaware of the gravity of the situation, comes to clean him off and laments, "I can't leave you alone for two seconds without you getting into a mess."

Another decent scene plays soon after, where some tourists are conned into buying a fake, reproduction tiki statue (so far, the comedy aspect is working). The tourists are being conned by the male lead, Greg, basically a beach bum who runs a racket on visitors. He takes the same tourists out on a fake hunt for lost treasure, scuba diving near the site of a shipwreck where he plants trinkets for them to find. During this scene is when the monster is finally glimpsed, but wisely, only pieces of the beast are seen, which makes it more effective.

One of the comical tourists. © 1979 New World Pictures

Shooting some of the new SPFX scenes for *Up From the Depths.* © 1979 New World Pictures

The monster gets a full-on reveal at the 50-minute mark when it encounters some cliff divers jumping into the water. After that, it attacks a boat containing Greg and Rachel, the female lead. Still, all shots of the monster are very brief. The monster continues its reign of terror, eating a topless starlet in an underwater photoshoot, then storms the beaches, chasing swimmers onto the shore. This causes a massive panic on the beach, which would have been funny if this movie was an all-out spoof. After all, why run and scream on the beach if the monster can't come on land to get you? Eventually, a few of the characters even point this out as the National Lampoons-type chaos continues. Though there had been moments of satire and comedy earlier, they were somewhat subdued and were not exactly spoof-like. The beach scene is directed in the style of no holds barred comedy—a pretty significant tonal departure considering that the past ten minutes had been a non-stop gore-fest. Perhaps Roger Corman couldn't bear to cut the scene because even he knew it was a great *Jaws*-spoof? On the other hand, the retention of the scene by Corman is extremely odd since he supposedly wanted the picture played straight.

From this point forward, the film plays as more of a spoof. The hotel manager essentially gets his guests liquored up via free drinks, then announces a contest to kill the monster. And off the drunken amateur hunters go. It's really all pretty amusing (some drunks with a flamethrower blow up their boat). In fact, the movie works much better this way, and it's lamentable that the first half wasn't treated as more of a spoof to keep it tonally consistent. In the long run, Corman would have been better off just retaining the comical monster scenes. The new serious horror scenes clash badly with the better spoof scenes.

Despite its amusing comedic moments, the hunting portion of the story stops, restarts, and stalls again to a maddening extent and really doesn't have an exciting sense of momentum. It all ends in typical *Jaws* fashion with the monster getting blown up (and rather unceremoniously at that).

One of the better shots of the monster, which was only 12-feet long compared to the 25 foot shark from ***Jaws.***
© 1979 New World Pictures

Famous Monsters of Filmland painted a positive picture of the film when it first came out, reporting: "There's plenty of action in Anne Dyer's screenplay as the frenzied finned sea beast levels one character after another. But it is all done with a great sense of satiric fun which had preview audiences rolling with laughter. Director Griffith's bizarre comic sense comes shining through."[126]

Traditional film critics were not keen on the film at all. The *Los Angeles Times* wrote a scathing review stating, "The screenplay neither sustains interest nor creates

---

[126] Pound, "New World's Monsters," *Famous Monsters* #160 (1980), pp.13-14.

suspense...Director Charles B. Griffith allows the confusion to prevail." *Variety* took note of the film's "flipped-out sense of humour" and noted that the dubbing "must have been done blindfolded—preview audience came expecting one thing and stayed to laugh their heads off, which is the only response this Filipino-made programmer will ever elicit."

Filipino producer Cirio Santiago was so disappointed in the final film that he remade it in 1987 as *Demon of Paradise*. Again set in Hawaii, illegal dynamite fishing awakens a prehistoric lizard-man that goes on a killing spree. Scream Factory even released *Demon of Paradise* on a DVD double bill with *Up From the Depths*.

Speaking of DVD releases, though it's doubtful the cut footage still exists, is there a chance that the original *Up From the Depths* could receive the *Tammy and the T-Rex*[127] treatment one day and be "restored"? Probably not, but time will tell...

---

[127] *Tammy and the T-Rex* was a 1994 movie about a man resurrected as a dinosaur. Though the released version was edited down to a PG-13 romantic comedy of sorts, a great deal of gory footage was shot. In 2020, the old footage was edited back into the film and it was rereleased as "the gore cut."

THEY SEARCH FOR TREASURE.
THEY SEARCH FOR FLESH.

KILLER FISH

The adventure that drags you in,
pulls you under and tears you apart!

SIR LEW GRADE Presents A CARLO PONTI/FILMAR DO BRASIL Production

LEE MAJORS
KAREN BLACK
MARGAUX HEMINGWAY   MARISA BERENSON in
KILLER FISH

co-starring GARY COLLINS CHARLIE GUARDINO FRANK PESCE DAN PASTORINI
and JAMES FRANCISCUS as "Paul Diller"

Music by GUIDO and MAURIZIO DE ANGELIS Screenplay by MICHAEL ROGERS
Produced by ALEX PONTI Directed by ANTHONY M. DAWSON

FROM ENTERTAINMENT

KILLER FISH

Release Date: December 7, 1979
Alternate Titles: *Invasion of the Piranha* (Canada) *Hunt for Illegal Treasure* (Greece) *Devourers: Killer Piranhas* (Mexico) *Piranhas II - Revenge of the Killer Fish* (Germany)

Directed by: Antonio Margheriti (as Anthony M. Dawson) **Special Effects by:** Riccardo Pallottini, Augusto Possanza & Waldomiro Reis **Screenplay by:** Michael Rogers **Music by:** Guido & Maurizio De Angelis **Cast:** Lee Majors (Robert Lasky) Karen Black (Kate Neville) Margaux Hemingway (Gabrielle) Marisa Berenson (Ann) James Franciscus (Paul Diller) Roy Brocksmith (Ollie) Dan Pastorini (Hans)

Spherical, Color, 101 Minutes

SYNOPSIS A team of thieves has just stolen millions of dollars' worth of diamonds from a high-security facility in South America. They drop them in a lake to keep them hidden for one month before trying to smuggle them out of the country. The leader of the group, Paul Diller, plants killer piranha in the lake out of fear that his fellow thieves will try to take the gems in advance. Diller and his girlfriend eventually decide to retrieve the diamonds early themselves. They manage to do so and evade the piranha via a special repellent. They board a yacht along with one of their cohorts, Robert Lasky, who is unaware the duo retrieved the diamonds without him. A waterspout causes a dam to break, and during the storm, their yacht is also damaged. As the boat begins to sink into the piranha-infested waters, the truth about the diamonds comes out...

COMMENTARY *Killer Fish* is an odd film in that not only is it a rip-off of a rip-off, but it's also a more expensive yet less effective version of said rip-off. As we've already established, right or wrong, *Piranha* was labeled a rip-off of *Jaws*. *Killer Fish* is obviously a rip-off of *Piranha* made all the more pathetic by the fact that it had a much bigger budget but was less effective. Whereas you could tell *Piranha* was low budget, *Killer Fish* had expensive-looking miniatures, more recognizable stars, big explosions, helicopters, and other expensive equipment to add production value to it. The film was produced by Fawcett-Majors Productions from husband and wife team Lee Majors and Farrah Fawcett (only Majors stars in the film, though)—along with a few other companies.

The film gets off to a strong start with some expansive and impressive miniature work. A group of thieves, led by Majors, breaks into a high-security facility to steal some diamonds. The facility then ends up catching on fire and exploding via the miniature work. After this exciting pre-credits scene (followed by a disco-inspired theme song), the movie loses steam fast. As the characters hide out in South America, the film drags along, with the viewer wondering when the killer fish will finally show up.

When they do appear a full thirty minutes in, they don't make much of an impression in their debut scene. The sequence basically amounts to a stuntman just thrashing around in the water and pretending to get eaten before enough blood bubbles to the surface that he can disappear.

The first time we actually see the fish is in James Franciscus' fish tank, where we learn that he unleashed piranha into the water to guard the stolen diamonds. To retrieve them, he has some sort of piranha repellent on

The stars of *Killer Fish:* Karen Black, James Franciscus, Margaux Hemingway, and Lee Majors.

hand (however, he makes his girlfriend dive down to get the diamonds). When the woman goes to retrieve the diamonds, the shots of the piranha swimming right at her are well done at least.

The film doesn't really take off until the very last act, heralded by a waterspout that destroys a dam. The miniature work that Margheriti excelled at is on full display, and the effects are wonderful. The characters then become stranded in the middle of the lake with the motor to their yacht dead. Some of them try to make it across the lake on a makeshift raft but end up getting eaten.

A plane flying over the sinking ship spots them and tosses two rafts outside for them to use. One of them lands too far from the ship, meaning they'll have to swim for it, and the other doesn't inflate and sinks to the bottom of the lake. When a carbide lamp explodes on contact with the water as the ship sinks, it gives them the idea to use it against the fish. The carbide is used to scare away the piranha so that Majors has enough time to swim to the lake bottom and inflate the raft.

Later, Franciscus holds everyone at gunpoint and takes the raft. Majors doesn't care though; he jumps into the water braving the killer fish to swim after him for a showdown. Franciscus beats him away with a boat paddle relentlessly, and a torn and bleeding Majors has to swim back to the sinking boat. But the piranha begin to tear into Franciscus' raft. Using the ol' greed-does-the-villain-in ploy, Franciscus refuses to let go of his diamonds (if he did, he could swim to shore quick enough to survive) as the fish devour him. This basically serves as the climax of the film, and after he's been eaten, a rescue-chopper arrives to pick up the stranded boat passengers.

After this, the titular fish aren't even mentioned again, and the movie runs for another ten minutes to wrap up the diamond plot, which goes to show that the titular *Killer Fish* really weren't the focus of the film. (Greece titled the film as though it was about sunken treasure, which probably helped to subvert expectations.)

Though it has a lot of nice production values, this movie probably holds more appeal for miniature enthusiasts and Lee Major fans than it does aquatic horror connoisseurs.

SPECIAL SECTION

KILLER CROCODILES

It should come as no surprise that when *Jaws* inspired a new genre of killer-fish themed movies that other producers would think to take the formula and replace the fish with giant, aquatic reptiles. Toei in Japan might have been the first to tackle the *Jaws*-genre from this angle via *Legend of Dinosaurs*. But, in using said dinosaurs, they may have shot themselves in the foot as dinosaurs were still associated with the B-Movies of old. Other producers' ideas were a little more down to earth when compared to Toei's dinosaurs. They chose to focus on another type of ancient reptile, one that still survives today: the crocodile.

The first film to propagate the giant crocodile idea may have been *Crocodile Fangs* (1978). This one hailed from South Korea, and very little is known about it. However, because some of its footage was supposedly edited into the Thai produced *Crocodile*, released the very next year in 1979, it is often confused for that film. Supposedly, the plot for *Crocodile Fangs* revolved around a Korean doctor on vacation in Thailand. When his wife and daughter are eaten by a giant crocodile in the river, he vows revenge and spends the rest of the movie trying to get it. As in *Jaws*, he is aided by two other men, a scientist and a boat owner. However, this plot outline is very similar to *Crocodile*, so I'm not certain if *Crocodile* was a quasi-remake that borrowed elements from *Crocodile Fang's* plot, or if the plot I read for *Crocodile Fangs* was wrong.

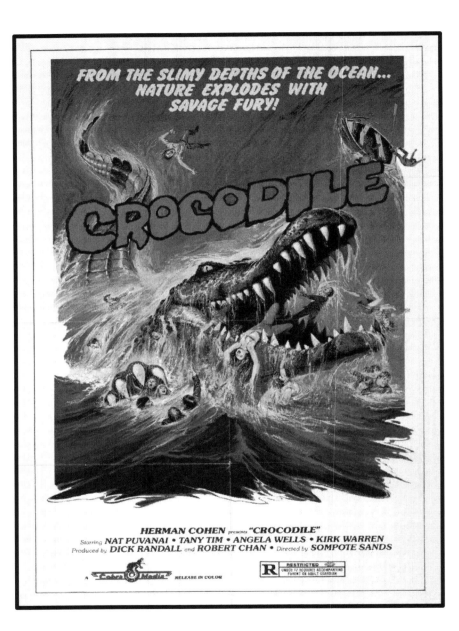

Crocodile was produced by Sompote Sands of Thailand's Chaiyo Studios. Sands was a producer of a dubious nature who claimed that he owned the rights to Japan's Ultraman, among other things. Once, he also illegally produced a movie starring Toei's Kamen Riders. It should come as no shock that in the late 1970s he too jumped on the *Jaws* bandwagon with *Crocodile*. And, whether it was a remake of *Crocodile Fangs* or not, it did allegedly use some footage from that film. It has the same core concept that I gave for *Crocodile Fangs*; only it begins with two doctors living in Thailand as opposed to visiting. In this case, both men's significant others are eaten by a giant crocodile in the ocean.

Crocodile is both parts *Jaws* and *Godzilla*. Though the story structure and style is similar to *Jaws*, the crocodile has been mutated into a giant form due to atomic testing in the ocean like *Godzilla*. And, like Godzilla, the crocodile's scale changes throughout the picture. When interacting with humans, it's close to the size of the shark in *Jaws*. However, whenever the live crocodile is set loose in a miniature village, it's closer to being King Kong or Godzilla sized!

The movie's ending is evocative of *Jaws*, as the two doctors set out on a boat with an experienced fisherman to kill the croc. To bait the beast, they use chemical compounds in some familiar looking yellow barrels. Like in *Jaws*, the monster croc eats the boat captain. Unlike in *Jaws*, absolutely everybody dies. One of the doctors straps some dynamite to himself and swims into the monster's jaws. The croc eats the man and then explodes. Unlike *Crocodile Fangs*, *Crocodile* made its way to America via Dick Randall and *Konga* producer Herman Cohen in 1981.

In 1979 also came *The Great Alligator*, starring Bond girl Barbara Bach. The Italian produced movie was more down to earth compared to its Far East brethren. It's also a lot more boring. Nor are the alligator scenes worth sitting through the whole movie for.

Outside of the focus being an aquatic menace, the film doesn't have any notable callbacks to *Jaws*. The only aspect that's similar is a scene where people become trapped on a river barge with the croc in the river, which may have been inspired by the sailboat barge in *Jaws 2*.

The king of the Crocodile movies is and always will be 1980's *Alligator* (yeah, yeah, I know, they're not the same animal exactly but c'mon...). The movie is a classic, and the only reason it's not reviewed in full is that I don't consider it a rip-off of *Jaws*. True, I'm sure the *Jaws* franchise helped get it off the ground, but it's not terribly similar to any of the Jaws films. However, it may have started out as a generic *Jaws* rip-off before John Sayles was brought on board to rewrite it.

Sayles recalled in *Starlog* #94 that he was called in to rewrite the film by director Lewis Teague. "The original script had been knocking around for quite a while," Sayles told Steve Swires, and then elaborated that the film was already pre-sold to several foreign territories.[128] In other words, the producers had to make the movie, but the script they had was apparently not very good. "We have problems with the plot, the dialogue, and the characters," producer Brandon Chase told Sayles.

"What else is left?" Sayles asked.

"Well, it's the right length," Chase replied.[129]

So, as he did on *Piranha*, Sayles kept the concept and the title and started more or less from scratch.

Since *Alligator's* success, a whole subgenre of giant killer crocodile movies was spawned, notably influencing *Killer Crocodile I* and *II* (1989 and 1990), *Alligator II: The Mutation* (1991), and *Lake Placid* (1999) to name a few. Today, much like the deluge of CGI sharks, there is a nearly innumerable amount of post-2000 CGI crocodile/alligator movies on the market.

---

[128] Swires, "John Sayles," *Starlog* #94 (May 1985), pp.44.
[129] Ibid.

King of the Rip-Offs
THE LAST SHARK

Release Date: April 2, 1981 (Italy); March 5, 1982 (U.S.) **Alternate Titles:** *Great White* (U.S.) *Shark* (U.K.) *The Last Jaws* (Denmark) *Jaws Returns* (Japan) *Jaws '81* (China) *Shark 3* (Spain) *Son of Jaws* (Turkey)

Directed by: Enzo G. Castellari **Special Effects by:** Antonio Corridori **Screenplay by:** Vincenzo Mannino, Marc Princi, Ramón Bravo (uncredited) & Ugo Tucci (story) **Music by:** Guido & Maurizio De Angelis **Cast:** James Franciscus (Peter Benton) Vic Morrow (Ron Hamer) Micaela Pignatelli (Gloria Benton) Joshua Sinclair (Governor William Wells) Giancarlo Prete (Bob Martin) Stefania Girolami Goodwin (Jenny Benton)

1.85 : 1, Eastmancolor, 88 Minutes

SYNOPSIS Port Harbor is a peaceful seaside community on the cusp of a huge regatta. However, when it becomes apparent that a Great White shark is stalking the area, gubernatorial candidate William Wells refuses to close the beaches against the advice of shark experts Peter Benton and Ron Hamer. Wells has a shark net put up, but the Great White tears through it on the day of the regatta and goes on a killing spree. Benton and Hamer take to the seas to kill the shark...

James Franciscus in *The Last Shark*. © 1982 Film Ventures

COMMENTARY Of all the Jaws rip-offs, *The Last Shark* is easily the best and the greatest of the bunch. Though its fake shark has more notoriety than the one that would later appear in *Jaws: The Revenge*, it's a commendable effort from Italian filmmaker Enzo G. Castellari, director of notable spaghetti westerns like *Keoma* (1976).

Naturally, the movie apes *Jaws* plenty, but it doesn't go so far as to copy the three male lead character structure like *Grizzly* did. In fact, there's only a Quint stand-in, Ron Hamer, as played by Vic Morrow. The performance is downright hilarious at times because of the way Morrow sporadically implements a Scottish accent for the character at random! Every time he says "great white" his Scottish accent is particularly thick, but then it disappears, and he talks with no accent at all! Though Hamer's wardrobe is usually evocative of Quint's, there are scenes where he wears outfits that Quint wouldn't be caught dead in—which is exactly what makes Hamer the perfect Euro-Quint rip-off.

James Franciscus' lead character is a horror writer and shark expert named Peter Benton, who I can only assume was a tribute to Peter Benchley (maybe the producers thought if they paid tribute to Benchley they wouldn't get sued?)! There are no equivalents of Hooper or Sheriff Brody, though gubernatorial candidate

William Wells is certainly meant to be the authority figure that ignores the shark.

As *The Last Shark* came out in 1981, it copies not only *Jaws* but also *Jaws 2*. The opening scene, where the shark stalks a man while windsurfing, is presumably a nod to the shark attacking the water skier in *Jaws 2*. In this case, the shark (unseen) sneaks up on the man and bites a chunk out of his surfboard. The man turns around to find part of his board chomped off—a nice visual, but a little silly considering this likely should have toppled the windsurfer over. The scene is no tease, though, and eventually, it gets the man (though we don't see the shark yet).

JAMES FRANCISCUS   VIC MORROW

THE LAST SHARK

A FILM BY ENZO G. CASTELLARI

Soon after this, we are introduced to Benton, typing on his typewriter while surrounded by shark jaws. His teenaged daughter comes in to inform him that one of their friends (the windsurfer) went missing. Benton and his daughter take his boat out to search for the man and come across the vessel of Hamer, who's dressed up in his best Quint attire. Benton and Hamer do happen to find a chunk of the wind board together. Hamer quips, "One thing's for sure, it wasn't a floating chainsaw [that did it]."

About this time the shark swims under the duo's two boats, knocking into them. The impact knocks Benton's daughter into the ocean. Cue the shark's POV watching her legs flutter in the water, and *The Last Shark* does its job as far as suspense goes. Just in the nick of time, Benton pulls his daughter in, not knowing the shark was just about to get her.

Our next *Jaws* imitation occurs when Benton and Hamer show the board fragments (with obvious bite marks) to Wells, who dismisses the incident stating that a boat propeller could have done it. Our heroes urge the authorities to shut down the beaches until the shark is dealt with but they refuse, stating too much money has already been spent on the regatta. The authorities don't take things seriously until an abandoned boat is towed into the harbor. Upon closer inspection, Hamer finds a severed arm inside floating in some water.

To his credit, Wells doesn't entirely stick his head in the sand where the shark is concerned. He at least pays to have shark nets cordon off the area where the regatta is to be held. Naturally, the shark tears through the net, which is lined with red buoys. One of them becomes entangled on the shark. This is obviously a nod to the yellow barrel trick from *Jaws*. However, that was an idea devised by Spielberg to signal the shark's presence so that they wouldn't have to rely on Bruce the mechanical shark (which was always broken). Here, it's just another nod to *Jaws*.

The regatta scene is well handled. Though likely inspired by the sailboat scenes in *Jaws 2*, the regatta scene in *The Last Shark* actually would have been worthy of a *Jaws* movie itself. In this case, before we see the shark fin, we see the red buoy pop out of the water and start following the windsurfers. One by one, they get knocked over as the shark plows underneath them. Oddly, it doesn't eat them, though. Instead, it singles out a man in a boat with a megaphone. It comically comes under the boat, causing it to knock the man— really a stiff dummy—high into the air in an explosion of water. As the man treads water, the huge shark head prop surfaces behind him. And, if you love semi-fake looking sharks, this one's a beauty. It's really not as bad as people riff on it for and might be better than or on par with the Bruce from *Jaws: The Revenge.*

The shark's next big scene comes when Benton and Hamer hunt it underwater in scuba gear with explosive tipped spears. The shark looks even better underwater, actually. The scene, where the shark corners the two men in an undersea cave, is fairly exciting. The duo escapes back to their boat on the surface and decides to try again later. As they depart the area, they notice Wells' boat out on the water.

Unbeknownst to Benton, it's not Wells, but Wells' son and his friends out to kill the shark. Among the friends is Benton's daughter. The teenagers lure the shark to the surface with some meat hooked to the end of a long pole. As the shark tugs on the pole, it rips loose, and the pole knocks Benton's daughter into the water. This time the girl doesn't escape unscathed, and the shark bites off her leg. The sequence may have been inspired by the Bo Derek scene in *Orca*, but truthfully the *Orca* scene is more graphic. Here, we don't see the shark bite her leg off as the editing is a little choppy. Mostly we see the shark swim away with the leg in its mouth, and then we cut to an ambulance to signal that the girl is still alive.

Feeling guilty, Wells tries the same trick as his son only in a chopper. In this case, meat is attached to a winch from the helicopter as it hovers over the water. Considering that the shark's already been established as a very heavy 35-footer, this is obviously a bad idea. It's also *The Last Shark's* attempt to top the chopper scene in *Jaws 2.* As you can imagine, the shark takes the bait and pulls the chopper towards the water. However, the winch line breaks, which saves the chopper but jostles it so hard that Wells falls into the water. The suspense mounts as the pilot gets the chopper low enough over the water that Wells can grab onto the landing gear. As Wells is being pulled out of the water, out pops the shark to bite his legs clean off! Wells loses consciousness and falls into the water. Foolishly, the pilot hovers low over the water in a vain hope that Wells will regain consciousness. Instead, the shark lunges at the chopper and drags it under—one-upping *Jaws 2* in the concept of the scene, if not its overall execution.

The end portion of the film has Hamer and Benton going out to sea with explosives to do the monster in. Through a series of unfortunate events, Hamer becomes entangled in a wire that has also become attached to the shark. Like Captain Ahab in *Moby Dick*, Hamer gets whisked away into the ocean with the shark as Benton watches in horror.

To better explain the final scenes, it should be explained that *The Last Shark* contained a notable subplot throughout concerning a TV news reporter. The reporter gleefully films the carnage at the regatta and becomes determined to capture more shark footage. So, by the picture's end, he's rigged a huge rack of ribs underneath a rickety old pier on the docks. He's invited a professional shark hunter to come slay the shark once it grabs the ribs. A group of onlookers has gathered for the occasion—on the pier. The huge shark comes along to munch on the ribs and ends up detaching the pier from the dock.

Still from the climax of *The Last Shark.* © 1982 Film Ventures International

Therefore, a hapless group of people (and the worthless shark hunter) are dragged into the water. As this happens, the reporter doesn't even call for help and enjoys the footage he's getting of the panicked people trying to evade the shark, which periodically pops up to chomp the pier. Eventually, the shark breaks away enough of the structure that some of the people fall into the water. One man swims frantically back to the remaining wood planks. His cohorts pull him up only to discover his bottom half is completely missing!

Benton comes along in Hamer's boat and pulls up alongside the ruined pier, rescuing the survivors. At one point, Benton steps onto the pier to help someone on his boat, and the shark ends up pulling the pier away, causing Benton to become stranded on it next. Suddenly, Hamer's dead body, strapped with explosives, surfaces (remember, he was attached to the shark's body). The shark surfaces too, and Benton grabs the remote detonator from Hamer's dead body. As much as he hates it, he allows the shark to take his dead friend's body. At the right moment, Benton hits the ignition switch, and the shark is blown in half underwater.

The movie's last scenes have Benton on the docks with his wife. Benton is hounded by the reporter who caused all the trouble for a comment on the day's events. Benton punches him in the face. He and his wife get into their car and drive away as the credits roll.

Audiences were warm to *The Last Shark* not only in Europe but in America as well (as *Great White*), where it grossed $18 million in one month of release. And one month of release was all it got in the States. Though *Jaws* gets ripped off left and right today in too many CGI shark movies to count, back in 1982 mimicking *Jaws* was still a punishable offense in Universal's eyes. Universal had tried to block the film's American premiere, but Universal's attempt was denied by the U.S. District Court. Later, Federal Judge David V. Kenyon did agree that the film was too similar to *Jaws* and had it pulled from theaters on Universal's behalf.

In all the oceans of the world
nothing is more feared than...

GREAT WHITE
THE TERROR BEGINS MARCH 5TH

"GREAT WHITE" TEASER 1-SHEET "A-1"

© 1982 Film Ventures International

Critics weren't kind to the film in the U.S., either, as the *Boston Globe* compared the shark to a Macy's Thanksgiving Day parade balloon and the *Monthly Film Bulletin* pointed out its inferiority to *Jaws*.

Sadder still for *Last Shark* fans, had the mechanical shark used during filming not been damaged, Castellari planned to produce *The Last Shark 2*.

A Tale of Two Directors
PIRANHA II: THE SPAWNING

Release Date: November 5, 1982
Alternate Titles: *Piranha II: Flying Killers* (alternate title)
Piranha II - The Vampire Fish (Portugal)

Directed by: James Cameron & Ovidio G. Assonitis
(uncredited) **Special Effects by:** James Cameron
Screenplay by: James Cameron, Charles H. Eglee &
Ovidio G. Assonitis **Music by:** Stelvio Cipriani **Cast:**
Tricia O'Neil (Anne Kimbrough) Lance Henriksen (Steve
Kimbrough) Steve Marachuk (Tyler Sherman) Ted
Richert (Raoul) Ricky G. Paull (Chris Kimbrough) Leslie
Graves (Allison Dumont) Albert Sanders (Leo Bell) Ancil
Gloudon (Gabby) Tracy Berg (Beverly) Phil Colby (Ralph
Benotti) Hildy Maganasun (Myrna Benotti) Carole Davis
(Jai) Connie Lynn Hadden (Loretta)

Spherical, Technicolor,
94 Minutes (Theatrical Cut)/84 Minutes (Director's
Cut)

SYNOPSIS Chris Kimbrough is a relatively normal American teenager except that he lives on a Caribbean island with his divorced parents. His mother, Anne, is a scuba diving instructor while his father, Steve, is a sheriff. When one of Anne's students dies mysteriously, Anne and Steve argue about what caused the incident and how to handle it. Eventually, the duo learns that a new super species of flying piranha is to blame. And the creatures' emergence couldn't come at a worse time. Chris is out at sea, serving as the cabin boy for a rich boat owner and his teenage daughter. Meanwhile, a beachfront hotel is having a special event where the guests will all descend on the beach at midnight to witness the spawning of a rare breed of fish. However, the piranha have already devoured all the rare specimens, and they will be the fish meeting the hotel goers on the beach...

COMMENTARY The smash success of *Piranha* in 1978 guaranteed a sequel, no surprise there. What is surprising is how long it took to get off the ground. After all, wasn't Roger Corman known for getting movies off the ground fast? Well, for starters, Corman only had a one-picture deal for *Piranha*, so he wasn't guaranteed a sequel option (Jeff Schechtman and Chako Van Leeuwen still had franchise rights). Instead, the sequel was optioned by Warner Bros and Italian producer Ovidio G. Assonitis (*Tentacles*). Reportedly, it was Warner Bros who wanted the fish to fly. Assonitis wasn't wild about the idea but went with it.

Like *Jaws 2*, *Piranha II* went through several directors, and that included after the movie began shooting. During pre-production, the chosen director was Miller Drake. Like Joe Dante, Drake had been a trailer director/editor in the New World trailer department. Drake developed a story with Charles H. Eglee wherein a character from the first film returned. Specifically, a dead character. Drake had the crazy idea that the mad scientist played by Kevin McCarthy would come back. Though mutilated badly, the character had survived somehow. "I pitched this idea of bringing Kevin McCarthy back, all chewed up and mutilated from the previous movie," Drake told EW.[130] "He was on an abandoned oil rig and he was developing these flying piranhas out there to get revenge, or whatever. I think we were going to bring Barbara Steele back and have him kill her by smashing her head through a fish tank."[131]

However, Drake was Schechtman and Leeuwen's choice, not Assonitis. Once he could, Assonitis got rid of Drake. As something of a control freak, Assonitis looked for inexperienced directors that he could control through intimidation. Apparently, he didn't feel confident he could do that with Drake... and so he hired James Cameron. Yes, that James Cameron. The future director of some of the biggest blockbusters of all time made his debut on *Piranha II*. Initially, he was only to direct the special effects scenes, but that all changed once Drake was fired, and Assonitis witnessed Cameron shooting in person.

According to Cameron in *Crab Monsters, Teenage Cavemen, and Cady Stripers*, he got hired while he was working on *Galaxy of Terror* for Roger Corman. Assonitis just happened to be on set when Cameron was filming a special effects scene involving worms crawling across a severed arm. Supposedly Assonitis said to another producer friend, "If he's that good with worms, I wonder what he can do with actors?"[132]

Cameron accepted the job, but had only three weeks to prep for the shoot, nor was he told that most of the crew was Italian—and only spoke Italian. Cameron worked relentlessly to not only revise the script but create the piranhas (which he hand-painted himself). Usually, a picture will have a director and a special effects director, but poor Cameron was pulling double duty.

As to how Cameron changed the script, some have theorized he probably gave Tracy O'Niel's character more to do. She was a much more proactive heroine when compared to similar characters from the time

[130] Collis, "Fishy Business," Entertainment Weekly (August 18, 2010) https://ew.com/article/2010/08/18/cameron-piranha-3d-dante/
[131] Ibid.
[132] Nashawaty, *Crab Monsters, Teenage Cavemen, and Candy Stripe Nurses*, pp.181.

period. This was indicative of future Cameron creations like *Terminator's* Sara Connor. (Speaking of *Terminator*, during a fever-induced nightmare during the shooting of *Piranha II*, Cameron dreamt of killer robots...)

Early on, it was clear to Cameron that this was not really his picture. Assonitis would change major stretches of dialogue at will. The next step in his taking over the production was his announcement to Cameron that he was appointing himself the second unit director. Assonitis said it was to help speed up production, but what he ended up filming was topless scenes of women that were nowhere in the script (notably, a few topless scenes do not appear in Cameron's cut of the movie).

Cameron shot for a little over two weeks before Assonitis decided he wasn't right for the job (Assonitis told him his footage was incoherent, which was an outright lie). Assonitis then began directing the picture himself! Later, upon returning to the U.S., Cameron learned that his hiring was a ruse from the get-go. Warner Bros distribution deal with Assonitis needed an American director at the helm (if audiences saw it was a directed by an Italian they might dismiss it as low budget trash right off the bat). So, Cameron was hired to shoot just enough footage to warrant keeping his name on the film, and when he had shot enough, Assonitis took over.

Cameron might have let the whole thing slide until he realized that his name was going to be plastered across Assonitis's potential abomination of a film. Cameron traveled back to Rome to confront Assonitis. Oddly enough, Assonitis began to play ball with Cameron, allowing him to see some of the footage. It would even seem that Cameron might be able to finish the movie, or if nothing else, edit it. Eventually, Cameron learned that Assonitis was already editing the movie.

Like the hero in one of his future films, Cameron took matters into his own hands and broke into the editorial department one night! Cameron didn't know which reels were which because they were all in Italian. Eventually, he found the reel marked "Fin" and decided to edit the movie backwards, starting with the ending. Eventually, Assonitis and his goons discovered what was happening and put a stop to Cameron's recut. However, many of

Cameron's editorial changes made their way into the final cut.

Piranha II was released to little success in theaters. Audiences perhaps couldn't get behind the idea of flying piranha, and the *Jaws 2* wave had subsided. The movie was a critical and commercial bomb and only turned a profit later via VHS releases and cable broadcasts. Speaking of VHS, when Cameron told Warner Bros how he had been booted out of his own film, they allowed Cameron to edit his version in a direct-to-video director's cut.[133]

Overall, *Piranha II* is a bigger movie than its predecessor. The locations are more exotic (it was filmed in Jamaica as opposed to Texas), and there is a great deal more underwater footage. The effects are also better (as they should be), and one can tell this sequel had a higher budget (but only slightly). Though too far-out for some, the piranha attacks in this film are more entertaining—in my opinion, at least.

The idea for the ending is inspired. The main event is the surf-side spawning of a rare breed of fish that beaches themselves on land during the spawning process. A hotel owner has organized a contest among the hotel guests to see who can catch the most fish. This naturally coincides with the flying piranha bursting out of the tide just as the contest begins, with flying piranha launching themselves at the guests. Some of the panicked guests jump into the swimming pool as they run towards the hotel. This, of course, just gives the fish an even greater advantage.

The climax gives the leads parallel missions, and Anne actually has the more daring of the two. While Anne is risking her life to plant explosives within the sunken ship that the piranha call home, Steve is looking for Chris by helicopter. He finds his son, and in one the most face-palming moments of cinema, he jumps out of his chopper, letting it crash into the ocean and explode! He does this so that he can swim over to a yacht, commandeer it, and rescue Chris and his girlfriend. (Why not write Steve in a co-pilot or something so Steve

---

[133] For a more scholarly comparison than what I offer in this book as to the differences between the two versions, see this article from movie-censorship.com at: https://www.movie-censorship.com/report.php?ID=501743

could dive into the water without destroying a perfectly good chopper?) Steve has to rescue the teens because they are currently floating right above the shipwreck that's set to explode. Steve gets them onto the yacht while Anne barely escapes from the piranha after plating the bombs.

While the helicopter scene might be dumb as rocks, Anne's escape from the wreck is great. It's similar to the first film's ending but done better. Here, Anne sees the yacht's anchor getting pulled away and grabs onto it, and it whisks her away from the explosion in the nick of time. James Bond couldn't have done it any better.

Now that I've established what was good about the sequel—or at least what I thought was good—we will now discuss the differences between the two cuts. The Cameron cut begins with the credits right away, whereas the theatrical version has a pre-title scene, some of which was cut from Cameron's version. The theatrical cut opens on a raft next to a buoy at sea. It is night on the ocean, and two lovers are having some... difficulties. They decide to take a dive down to a sunken ship beneath them.

The two begin to do below the water what they couldn't do above it, and then the piranha swarm interrupts their tryst. In Cameron's cut, after the credits end, we are introduced to the divers already under the water. Their surface scenes have all been removed (therefore, we're unaware of their previous issues). Furthermore, the piranhas' POV shots as they approach the couple are tinted red in Cameron's version (for that matter, all Piranha POV shots in his cut are red-tinted). When the couple is eaten, we cut to a shot of their raft above the water, which was actually the first shot of the theatrical cut. Watching them side by side, I have to say I prefer the theatrical cut's opening, with the credits displayed after the killing.

The next scene that Cameron removed from the theatrical cut was a scene of two topless women (Jai and Loretta) on a yacht. Other than showing off their breasts, it reveals that they've run away from home. Presumably, Cameron didn't include this scene because it was one of the scenes that Assonitis directed. Next, a scene between Steve and Anne talking at the docs is rearranged. In the theatrical cut, the scene precedes a sequence of one of the yacht girls (now clothed and on land) stealing some food. In Cameron's cut, the dock conversation comes after this scene.

The next significant alteration is the big reveal that the piranha can fly. As a nurse is inspecting the dead body of a piranha victim, a piranha pops out of his stomach in a nod to the *Alien* films. It then leaps out of the body and bites the poor nurse on the neck, killing her in a memorable scene.

After establishing that the fish can fly, the next scene to feature them occurs that same night. Jai and Loretta (now established as unlikable characters) are out on their yacht late at night. Suddenly the piranha begin leaping out of the water and attacking them.

Cameron chooses to reveal the fish in a different order. In his version, the attack on Jai and Loretta comes before the autopsy attack. It's also got at least one additional shot that I noticed. In the theatrical cut, a fish suddenly bites Loretta's neck from the side. Cameron's version has a shot of the fish flying directly at the camera before it gets her neck. When Loretta falls into the water, there's a few additional shots of the piranha swimming under the water to attack her in Cameron's cut. Also, Cameron's version of the scene is unscored, whereas the theatrical cut plays the piranha's theme. The theme doesn't come in until we transition to an underwater POV shot present in both versions (but Cameron's is tinted red).

The next piranha kill, where the fish kill the son of Gabby, a fisherman character, is also altered. In one of the shots of piranha flying in the air towards the camera, the sound effects are different between the two versions. When the flying fish attack Gabby's son, the scene is unscored in the theatrical cut but has music in Cameron's version that sounds a little similar to the famous score from *Psycho*. This is followed by a scene of Chris's parents worrying about him, and then Steve takes the helicopter out to the yacht. Hovering over the boat, Steve learns that his son has snuck off the ship with the rich owner's daughter. However, this scene happened earlier in the theatrical cut.

The theatrical cut goes from the young fisherman's death to Chris and the rich guy's daughter on an island, then to Gabby finding his dead son, then to Anne and

Steve's talk by the chopper. Essentially, Cameron combines the two chopper scenes and eliminates the daytime scenes of the teenagers on the island (there is a scene where Chris and his new girlfriend frolic around an island during the day). In Cameron's version, we have the two leads say goodbye at the launch pad, and then the scene of Gabby finding his dead son. Then we get the yacht scene that appeared earlier in the theatrical cut (so, again, originally it was a separate helicopter trip on a different night). From here, we cut to the teenagers on the island at night. Remarkably, either Cameron has tinted the daytime footage to night, or he must have shot a version of the scene set at night. Other than the night and day differences, the scenes are identical.

The flying piranha in action. Piranha II © 1982 Warner Bros

As to the ending where the fish have a feeding frenzy on the hotel guests, there's a particularly gruesome scene that's been left out of Cameron's cut. In it, a deputy, half eaten by the fish (and looking like a zombie) stumbles out of the water alive. The scene where Gabby fends off the fish is also scored differently between the two versions. And, finally, Cameron chooses to end his version of the scene with a shot of all the dead bodies on the beach, which was used earlier in the theatrical cut. Overall, Cameron's decision to end on that shot was the right one.

This is the last of the truly significant differences, and ultimately both versions have their merits but are similar enough to the point that if you've seen one, you've seen them both.

SHARK BITES: PIRANHA 3

DESPITE THE FACT THAT IT WAS A FAILURE, THERE WAS STILL TALK OF A *PIRANHA 3*. JOE DANTE RECALLED THAT CHAKO VAN LEEUWEN WOULD CHECK IN WITH HIM EVERY COUPLE YEARS FOLLOWING *PIRANHA II* TO SEE IF HE WOULD BE INTERESTED IN RETURNING TO THE FRANCHISE (BUT DANTE DECLINED). *PIRANHA II* PRODUCER OVIDIO G. ASSONITIS WAS ALSO GOING TO DO *PIRANHA 3* IN THE EARLY 1990S. A POSTER FOR THE PROSPECTIVE FILM WAS ADVERTISED IN *VARIETY*, LISTING OLIVER HELLMAN AS DIRECTOR (HELLMAN WAS ASSONITIS BY THE WAY...). IN 1995, *PIRANHA* WAS REMADE AS A TV MOVIE, BUT IT RE-USED ALL THE SPFX SCENES FROM THE ORIGINAL! IN 2010 THE FRANCHISE RECEIVED A PROPER REBOOT IN THE FORM OF *PIRANHA 3D*.

Poster for Assonitis's *Piranha 3*.

Developing
JAWS 3-D

Script Date: August 10, 1982 (first draft)
Release Date: July 22, 1983

Directed by: Joe Alves **Screenplay by:** Carl Gottlieb, Richard Matheson, Michael Kane & Guerdon Trueblood (story) **Music by:** Alan Parker **Cast:** Mike Brody (Dennis Quade) Kathryn Morgan (Bess Armstrong) Phillip FitzRoyce (Simon MacCorkindale) Calvin Bouchard (Louis Gossett Jr.) Sean Brody (John Putch) Kelly Ann Bukowski (Lea Thompson)

2.39 : 1, Color, 99 Minutes

SYNOPSIS A string of mysterious deaths haunts the opening of a new exhibit at Sea World called the Undersea Kingdom. Park engineer Mike Brody and his girlfriend Kathryn, a dolphin trainer, investigate and find that a baby Great White shark is responsible. The baby shark is captured by Kathryn and an underwater cameraman, Philip. The shark is put on display in the park, but it dies in captivity. As it turns out, the 35-foot mother shark birthed the infant in the park's lagoon and has been loose in the park all along...

The shark in *Jaws 3-D* was Megalodon-sized at 35 feet!
© 1983 Universal Pictures

COMMENTARY A year after the *Jaws 3, People 0* debacle was settled, the October 29, 1980 edition of the *LA Times* announced that Alan Landsburg Productions was going to produce a third Jaws film. Universal was involved too, of course (they had to approve the project), but to a slightly lesser extent than they had been on the last two movies. The *Times* reported that the script was by one Guerdon Trueblood, but there is evidence to the contrary.[134]

In actuality, one of the most respected names in science fiction had come up with the initial story outline for *Jaws 3*. That man was *I Am Legend* writer Richard Matheson (who had also written Steven Spielberg's *Duel* movie, elements of which popped up in *Jaws*). Of the mix-up, Matheson told Tom Weaver:

---

[134] Trivia on IMDB states that Guerdon Trueblood's concept was not initially a *Jaws* movie, and was apparently just another shark movie until the studio tied it into the *Jaws* franchise.

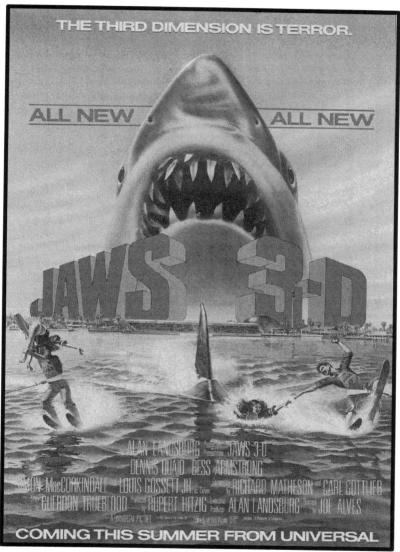

© 1983 Universal Pictures

© 1983 Universal Pictures

I wrote an outline which was really very interesting —and I found out later, when the picture was done and I saw the credits, that they gave the credit for the story to some other writer! And I had never read anything by him![135]

Matheson's treatment is not set in a waterpark, but an inland lake. The story was birthed by the same real-life New Jersey shark attack that inspired Peter Benchley's *Jaws* novel. Matheson's twist on it was that a great white swims up a saltwater river until it becomes trapped in a lake. There it terrorizes an unsuspecting fishing community. A novel concept overall, even if it wasn't as fun as a shark loose in Sea World.

But then studio meddling reared its ugly head. Executives wanted characters from the first two films brought in to lend continuity.[136] One of my own qualms with *Jaws 3-D* was that it brought back the Brody boys. It seemed too implausible to have them encounter yet another giant shark all the way down in Florida. More than that, it was unnecessary, as the character's lineage adds nothing to the story aside from Sean's fear of the water.

Matheson hated this as well, and makes sure to point out in interviews that including the brothers was forced upon him. Worse still, apparently a few executives even wanted it to be the same shark from *Jaws 2*! In other words, the burned up shark had survived being electrocuted. I'm guessing one of the executives thought that would explain why the shark was all the way down in Florida: it was there to get revenge on the Brody boys. Or, maybe the executive was a fan of horror movies like *Friday the 13th*? Because, no matter how many times Jason or Michael "died," they always came back. Maybe that was the idea?

Thankfully cooler heads prevailed, and the shark was allowed to be a new animal, albeit ten feet longer than the previous big shark. Matheson wrote a first draft along with another writer identified as Michael Kane in

---

[135] Weaver, *Science Fiction Stars and Horror Heroes*, pp.318.
[136] They probably wanted Roy Scheider back, and the actor was so worried that they would ask him that he signed on to do *Blue Thunder* (1983) just so that he would be unavailable!

SHARK BITES: MICKEY ROONEY IN *JAWS 3*?

ONE OF THE PRODUCER'S BIGGEST DEMANDS WAS THAT THEY
WANTED A SPECIAL ROLE WRITTEN JUST FOR MICKEY ROONEY!
MATHESON WROTE A SPECIAL ROLE FOR HIM AS A CLOWN THAT
WAS SO TAILORED TO ROONEY, THAT WHEN HE DROPPED OUT, THE
PART WAS USELESS AND HAD TO BE REMOVED. NOTABLY, THERE IS
NO CLOWN CHARACTER IN THE FIRST DRAFT SCRIPT, THOUGH.
PERHAPS IT WAS IN AN INITIAL TREATMENT?

August of 1982. Soon after, Matheson had enough and quit, so writer Carl Gottlieb was brought in to finish the story.

News outlets continued to report on the film with various titles. The August 28, 1981 edition of the *L.A. Times* called it *Jaws 1982*. This was a nod to the *Airport* movies that denoted the sequels not by their number, but by the year they were released. The article also stated that the film was to be directed by Mel Stuart. Whether this was misinformation or not, the production designer on the first two Jaws films, Joe Alves, was hired to direct. Further confusing the matter, in an interview with the *Albuquerque Journal* on July 17, 1983, Alves implied that *Jaws 3* began as a modest TV movie. Alves then claimed that he convinced Sid Sheinberg and MCA chairman Lew Wasserman to make it a feature film in 3-D. There are other conflicting versions of how the 3-D decision came about. For instance, supposedly *Jaws 3-D* canceled a 3-D remake of *Creature from the Black Lagoon*. John Landis, a producer on the remake, claimed that when MCA head Sid Sheinberg saw his *Creature* test footage, he exclaimed, "What a great idea! But why do the Creature? Let's do *Jaws 3-D!*" Ironically enough, *Jaws 3-D* borrowed quite a few ideas and gimmicks from *Revenge of the Creature* (1955), also released in 3-D. However, the writers have claimed in interviews that this was purely coincidental. On *Animal Icons: Jaws*, it is implied that while Alves was location scouting at Sea World he came up with the 3-D idea. He said as he was walking through an underwater shark tunnel looking at the real sharks that the 3-D idea hit him.

Matheson's first draft is structurally similar to the finished film with the same characters and the same setting.[137] Matheson and Kane's script begins exactly the same way as the finished film, 3-D fish head gimmick and all, so it's safe to say the 3-D aspect was already decided upon when they wrote it. The only notable difference in the beginning is that, after watching the ski team practice, we go straight to Calvin Bouchard addressing the press and giving exposition on just what the Undersea Kingdom is supposed to be, including a special section just for sharks.

When a reporter asks what kind of sharks, this serves as our introduction to the Kathryn Morgan character, who explains all the different types of sharks on display (notably, they don't have a Great White). In the film, we are introduced to Kathryn via Mike, who goes to visit her. Here, we are introduced to Mike via Kathryn. As in the film, Mike comes to see her as she's working with her dolphins. The cameraman character, Philip, barges in on their conversation on a crane, wanting to get footage of the dolphins! This scene also makes it very clear that there is a rivalry between Mike and Philip, and that Philip wants Kathryn. In the film, Philip's attraction to Katheryn is downplayed, and he is introduced with some fanfare as a celebrity.

The early differences continue to be minor and relatively uninteresting: Mike meets Sean at the airport instead of at Sea World, etc. And yet, that said, the airport scene warrants a little discussion. Sean's apprehension towards the water and sharks is established when Mike makes a joke that he'll get him a job at Sea World "shoveling shark shit."[138] When Sean gives him a look Mike explains that he's joking, and the only place he'll see sharks is from within the underwater restaurant in the lagoon. "I'll eat at McDonalds," Sean quips. As the conversation continues, talk turns to their father. Sean was to show Mike a recent Polaroid of Sheriff Brody scowling (presumably they were just going to use a pre-existing photo of Roy Scheider).

---

[137] To play it safe, the theme park wasn't called Sea World and was alternately Marine World and Underwater World.

[138] I should mention this script has a subplot about Sean and Mike wanting to work together that was dropped by the time filming started.

SHARK BITES: STEVEN SPIELBERG ON *JAWS 3*

IN JUNE OF 2011 SPIELBERG WAS INTERVIEWED BY BRIAN VESPE OF *AIN'T IT COOL NEWS*. SPIELBERG REVEALED THAT NOT ONLY WAS HE OFFERED *JAWS 2*, BUT *JAWS 3* AS WELL. SPIELBERG ALSO SAID THAT ALTHOUGH HE COULDN'T COME UP WITH A STORYLINE TO HIS LIKING FOR ANY SEQUELS, HE DID COME UP WITH "A VERY, VERY GOOD SCENE WHICH I THOUGHT WOULD HAVE BEEN GOOD FOR A SEQUEL SOMEDAY." KEEPING HIS CARDS CLOSE TO THE VEST (AND PERHAPS THINKING IT COULD STILL BE USED ONE DAY), HE DIDN'T REVEAL WHAT THIS SCENE WAS.

> MIKE
> How is he? Still fighting crime?
>
> SEAN
> Last week he broke up a major counterfeiting ring. Gang of kids were using slugs in the Pac-Man games.
>
> MIKE
> (laughing)
> Big bust! He confiscate their water pistols?
>
> SEAN
> Booked them all at Baskin-Robbins.
>
> MIKE
> (appreciating)
> That's Dad...

Though a nice little scene, I can only assume its purpose was to remind audiences that these are the Brody children. Anyhow, back to the airport scene, this is also where Sean meets Kelly (the water skier), unlike the film where they meet in a bar.

In one of the following scenes, Mike and Kathryn go diving to inspect the broken gate at the entrance to the lagoon. In this iteration, Mike is much less comfortable in the water and at one point the dolphins scare him with a surprise entrance. The sub they are piloting has an electrical malfunction, requiring them to swim back to the surface. Naturally, this is where the baby Great White makes its entrance. When Mike sees it, a flashback to his traumatic scene from *Jaws* was to play for an instant.

As in the film, the dolphins provide the lovers with a quick rescue. Upon reaching safety, Mike comments on the blackness of the shark's eyes. "Don't think about it. It's over," says Kathryn. "It's never over...Here comes another six years of bad dreams," Mike quips. During the capture of the Great White, Mike was to have another flashback to *Jaws*, this time the scene in the lagoon where he saw a man get attacked by the shark. (There were plenty of good flashbacks to choose from *Jaws 2*, but curiously none were alluded to in the script).

After the shark's capture, they take note of how young it is right away (but make sure to mention it's big for its age). This somewhat undercuts the reveal of the mother later, so the revised version in the film is better (in the film they don't learn it's a baby until after it's dead). And, remember the scene of Mike interrupting a tryst between Sean and Kelly with a bullhorn? Here this scene happens right after the capture of the shark (in the film it takes place well before it), and Mike uses the P.A. system instead.

Notably, the scene where Mike walks the baby shark with Kathryn in the pool in the movie is different in the script. Here it is Philip who does so rather than Mike. Philip uses this as an opportunity to flirt with Kathryn. The two would seem to share a moment when the shark awakens, and he helps to get her out of the water, but, by the next scene, she's back in bed with Mike. As we cut away from this romantic interlude, the mother shark is revealed in the lagoon. Again, the film chooses to let us think that the baby shark is *the* shark before the reveal of the mother on the Undersea Kingdom's opening day.

Speaking of opening day, this script has yet another scene of Mike stating his distaste for sharks when he refuses to walk through the shark tunnel in the Undersea Kingdom. Kathryn makes him, but eventually Mike can't take it and collapses against the wall stating,

"It's back." At first I thought the script was going all *Jaws: The Revenge* on us, and he was psychically sensing the giant shark, but no, he's talking about his hydrophobia. "My dad had it, and I don't know if you can inherit it or what, but I got it, and I hate it. I can't stand it!" he says before dashing out of the tunnel. As he does, the giant mother shark watches.

Things progress similarly to the finished film with the baby shark dying while on exhibit, though Kathryn gets there once it's already dead rather than witnessing it happen. In the meantime, Mike and Sean have a conversation about working together. Sean then asks Mike if there are any plans to get married in Amity, which gives the script another chance to remind us these are the boys from the first two movies all grown up. Sheriff Brody is mentioned again as well. This is probably a good spot to mention that the subplot from the film about Mike getting transferred to Venezuela isn't in this draft, and instead, the romantic subplot/conflict is about him and Kathryn's wedding date. Shortly after this, a dead Sea World worker is discovered floating in the water.

However, there is no scene of Mike and Kathryn inspecting the body as in the film. In the movie, Kathryn determines that a huge shark killed him due to the bite radius. In this script, we don't see her examine the body. Instead, Mike is having a drink at the bar in the Undersea Kingdom when Kathryn comes in to show him a gigantic tooth she found in the man's body.

The shark's true reveal is a doozy and comes moments later. It's similar to the reveal in the film also set in a bar, only without Calvin there. As Mike stares into his glass, he mutters some R-rated profanity, "Oh, no... not again. A thirty-five-foot f---in' shark...what's wrong with my family? First my father... now me..."

Let's go to the script for the full effect:

> MIKE sees something REFLECTED in his glass. He leans forward, curiously, watching whatever it is growing larger and larger.

                    MIKE
              What the hell...

He turns and SEES

190 JAWS!

In all it's full, awesome, HORRIFYING form. Mouth open, it tries to eat the viewing glass, then turns. Its body thunders against the window, shaking it as people SCREAM and panic for the door.

And now we come upon the portion of the script that you really want to know about: Jaws loose in Sea World. The same tropes are mostly all there, plus some that didn't make the final cut. Remember that time that the Fonz' jumped the shark on *Happy Days*? Well, it happens here too. In this case, a water-skier does a jump off the ramp and looks below him as he flies over a giant shark and utters holy you-know-what.

Oft times, these screenplays envisioned a sequence that the effects team couldn't pull off or that the budget wouldn't allow for. In the film, we see Sean and Kelly get attacked while riding bumper cars (or rafts, really) in the water. The script's version is much cooler. In this version, Sean and Kelly are on an underwater gondola ride. The gondolas cycle through the water, going deep into the lagoon underwater and then are pulled up out of the water on cables.

Naturally, the shark comes upon Sean and Kelly while they are under the water. Sean spots the fin of the monster first, then makes out the full form as it swims towards them. Naturally, they are being pulled up out of the water as it rapidly approaches. The tension mounts as they hope they will be pulled out before the shark can reach them... they break the surface, and the shark seems to dive out of sight. But Sean keeps his eyes glued to the glass bottom. The shark then lunges from out of the water and bites the bottom of the gondola, dragging it back into the water as it breaks open! A terrifying scene, to say the least.

One of the more famous visuals from *Jaws 3-D.*
© 1983 Universal Pictures

We would then jump-cut to an ambulance racing through the streets, and then to Mike pacing the halls of a hospital. Sean has survived (and has even retained all of his limbs), but Kelly is dead. In the film, the two lovebirds make it out unscathed (Kelly gets a bad cut on her leg from one of the shark's teeth, and that's it).

The plan to deal with the shark is quite different in this draft too, as Mike suggests catching it in a huge net. Philip, who keeps an underwater grenade on his person, suggests blowing it up, but Mike explains that would ruin the filtration system. As this is a "construction job," this gives Mike (an engineer, remember) a role to play in the climax. In the film, this is accomplished by having the shark damage one of the underwater tunnels; hence Mike needs to scuba dive to repair it and keep the people inside from drowning. This excellent scene hadn't been thought up yet.

The plan with the net turns into a disaster. Though the shark is caught, it eats Philip in the process, and the beast's immense weight allows it to break free. In doing so, it topples Mike's crane into the water. Mike crashes into the lagoon and gets his foot caught in part of the discarded net's webbing. However, as a safety precaution, Mike was wearing a wet suit complete with a tank and respirator. He puts in the ventilator and escapes the netting just as the shark lunges at him. He loses a flipper in the process, and when it floats to the surface, Kathryn momentarily thinks he has been killed. Not wanting to give up hope, she boards the mini-sub from earlier and takes to the lagoon. Meanwhile, an underwater chase occurs between Mike and the shark. Mike takes refuge in a cave, which the massive shark bumps into, causing a cave-in. Kathryn tries to dislodge some of the debris with her sub while her dolphins run interference on the shark.

Mike is freed and clambers into the craft. But it's not a happy ending yet, the shark attacks the sub, taking it into its jaws and shaking it. But, the shark grabbed the rear end of the vehicle. Kathryn turns on the propellers in the back and cuts the beast's mouth badly. The shark lets them go, but now the propellers are jammed up. They evacuate the sub and swim for the artificial sunken galleon (with a little help from the dolphins, who give them a lift there). Once the duo is inside, the shark butts its head into an opening, but its torso gets stuck, and it can go no further. The shark backs up and rams it again, but still can't fit inside. As it does so, the dolphins attack and butt its sides.

Mike and Kathryn swim out of the galleon via a different opening they've spied. They make a mad dash for the surface, but the shark is already on their tail. The dolphins come to their rescue again, and a high-speed chase occurs between the shark and her prey.

412 THE CHASE

> Shots alternating between Mike and Kathryn being pulled along by the dolphins and the giant shark pursuing them, getting closer and closer. When it becomes apparent that the shark is going to overtake them, the dolphins make a sharp turn and elude its heavier, straight-forward impetus.

The dolphins get the duo to the exterior of the Undersea Kingdom control room (which features a special chamber for scuba divers to enter into from outside). Mike and Kathryn are able to enter just as the shark reaches them. Once the water is drained from the room, the two enter into the main control room with the rest of the staff. But they haven't a moment to spare. As

SHARK BITES: *JAWS 3-D* VS. *JAWS III*

A FEW SEQUENCES WERE ACTUALLY ALTERED FOR THE TV AND HOME VIDEO MARKET. NOTABLY, THE TITLES ARE REDONE AND THE MOVIE IS NOW JUST "JAWS III". A SHOT FROM THE ENDING, WHERE THE SHARK'S JAWS SHOOT OUT TOWARDS THE AUDIENCE WHEN IT EXPLODES, IS REMOVED.

in the film, the shark rams through the glass, flooding the room (notably, Calvin is not in this iteration of the scene). In the film, only one technician dies in the chaos, but in this version, multiple people do. One gets slammed into the wall from the water pressure, another is eaten by the shark, and another is crushed under a piece of equipment.

For added suspense, Mike's air tank begins to run out, so Kathryn must share her oxygen with him. In another deviation, the shark is itself injured as it has a huge glass shard poking into its side. Just as the shark has the lovers cornered, Philip's dead body emerges from the shark's mouth, still clutching his grenade. In the film, Mike merely takes the pin out with a hook so it can detonate. Here, it is a bit more suspenseful. The hook only dislodges the grenade from the dead man's hand and rolls between the shark's teeth. In between the snapping of the monster's maw, Mike swiftly grabs the grenade! While Kathryn distracts the shark, Mike pulls the pin and then shoves the grenade into its mouth.

And from here on out, events play out as in the film—with the shark getting blown ass-backward out of the control room.

It's tough to say which draft of the script is superior, but the biggest loss, in my opinion, is the underwater gondola attack. Furthermore, a few of the unused concepts from this script would make their way into *Jaws: The Revenge*, namely the flashbacks to the first film and Mike's scene in the sunken ship.

The film was a huge success upon release despite being critically panned. Nearly everyone who worked on the film doesn't have anything good to say about it. When asked about it years later, Dennis Quade reportedly said, "I was in Jaws what?" When asked by

Tom Weaver what he thought about the finished film, Richard Matheson answered:

> I'm a good storyteller and wrote a good outline and a good script. And if they had done it right and if it had been directed by somebody who knew how to direct, I think it would have been an excellent movie. *Jaws 3-D* was the only thing Joe Alves ever directed; the man is a very skilled production designer, but as a director, no.[139]

In recent years, the film has been reevaluated as one of the first movies in the "amusement park gone wrong" genre popularized by *Jurassic Park*. For some fans, it is even the favorite among the *Jaws* sequels—myself unabashedly among said *Jaws 3-D* fans.

Some *Jaws 3-D* tie-in merchandising.

---

[139] Weaver, *Science Fiction Stars and Horror Heroes*, pp.318.

Cliff Twemlow

THE PIKE

A cold relentless killer
from the murky depths

Fake Fish
THE PIKE

Developmental Period: 1982

Screenplay by: Cliff Twemlow **Proposed Cast/Characters:** Mike Watson [tabloid journalist] (Jack Hedley) Unnamed Female Lead (Joan Collins) Ulysses Grant [Scottish longbow expert] Supporting Role (Linda Lou Allen) **Proposed Creatures:** The Pike

SYNOPSIS Mysterious deaths plague Lake Windermere, the largest natural lake in England. Mike Watson, a tabloid journalist recovering from a failed marriage, is at the lake when an angler is attacked by a 12-foot pike! Watson begins an investigation into the monstrous fish and discovers that not all is as it seems...

COMMENTARY Having seen giant killer sharks, octopi, orcas, and swarms of piranha, in 1982, someone finally concocted a giant pike fish. That someone was actor/screenwriter/film library composer (not to mention former nightclub bouncer) Cliff Twemlow, who wrote *The Pike*. Twemlow didn't start the story out as a script either. Playing it smart, he wrote it as a novel that could later be adapted into a screenplay. Even the book's page count is close to a script's length at 160 pages, further evidencing that Twemlow was writing a movie in the form of a novel.

The story was unabashedly inspired by *Jaws*. Once again, a tourist destination is the feeding grounds for an aquatic killer. The big event, rather than the 4th of July, is a beauty pageant called Miss Lakeland (this also would've given the movie an excuse to showcase plenty of bikini-clad girls). And though the main character is a reporter rather than a sheriff, there are stand-ins for Hooper and Quint in the form of a marine biologist and Ulysses Grant, a Scottish longbow expert. Coincidentally, as Twemlow considered this the "freshwater equivalent of Jaws," it also mirrored Richard Matheson's unmade *Jaws 3*, set in an inland lake. Though its doubtful Twemlow knew of Matheson's abandoned idea, *The Pike* was written around the same time that *Jaws 3* was being developed.

Despite all the similarities to *Jaws*, *The Pike* has a very different ending sure to disappoint most monster fans. If you were one of those kids—like me—who always hated it at the end of the *Scooby-Doo* episodes to find that the monster was a fake, then you'll also hate this ending. As it turns out, the monstrous pike was really a manmade submersible disguised as a monster pike the whole time!

Twemlow managed to assemble a small cast for the film and even had a scale Pike built by Ulvertech Engineering. Among the cast were Joan Collins, TV hostess Linda Lou Allen, and Jack Hedley. Twemlow and the cast made several appearances on British TV shows to try and drum up interest in the film.

The death of the film came during what was supposed to be something of a final production launch at Low Wood Centre. There Joan Collins and the cast gathered to pose with the 12-foot robotic Pike for journalists and photographers. The mechanical Pike was placed in the water and failed to perform, just like Bruce in *Jaws*. *The Pike* movie was dead from then on, though the resulting article wouldn't give you that impression. It read:

The Super Pike Meets Superstar

The 12 foot mechanical pike—star of the film with the same name, was launched on Lake Windermere for tests yesterday.

It was supposed to jump out of the water and roll its eyes for the benefit of cameramen, but it refused to budge. So divers coaxed it through the water.

But Joan Collins saved the day when she announced she was interested in a part in the film.

The glamorous star posed with the pike on the water's edge. Jack Hedley of Colditz fame was also present at the launch and may also star in the film.

The film is due to be shot entirely in Windermere later this summer. Producers reckon it will take eight weeks to complete the filming.

The Pike

The pike was manufactured by Ulvertech at a cost of a quarter of a million dollars. It took seven months from the drawing board to its first tests on Windermere.

The film is based on a book written by Cliff Twemlow who will also take part in the film. It is being produced by City Major Ltd.

Though the production was canceled, the mechanical fish was retooled by the Ulvertech engineers until they got it working. The fish then performed for two years at a Japanese robotics exhibition! There visitors could operate the monster's jaws via joystick. Likewise, a "dummy" fiberglass version of the beast was later loaned to the Low Wood Water Sports Centre. Supposedly you can still see it there to this day.

Behind the scenes still of the mechanical fish.

GRIZZLY II:
The Predator

Originally Shot: 1983
Proposed Release Date: 2020
Alternate Titles: *Grizzly II: The Concert* (alternate title)
Grizzly II: Revenge (release title)

Directed by: André Szöts **Special Effects by:** Nick Maley
Screenplay by: Ross Massbaum, David Sheldon, Joan
McCall & Géza Jánossy (rewrites/uncredited) **Music by:**
Bernard Herrmann (stock music) & Robert O. Ragland
Cast: Louise Fletcher (Eileene Draygon) Steve Inwood
(Nick Hollister) John Rhys-Davies (Bouchard) Deborah
Raffin (Samantha Owens) Deborah Foreman (Chrissy
Hollister)

Color, 97 Minutes

SYNOPSIS When the unusually large mother of a pair of
grizzly cubs finds her young murdered, the twenty-foot
tall bear goes on a murderous rampage. The killings
couldn't come at a worse time, as Yellowstone National
Park is on the verge of holding a huge summer rock
concert. Despite being pressured to close, the park

superintendent refuses to do so. A French hunter, Bouchard, is called in to exterminate the bear, which has killed three teens, a park ranger, and some poachers so far. The concert goes forth as planned, but it's interrupted by the giant bear, which goes on a rampage. The creature is eventually killed via electrocution on stage.

COMMENTARY Being the hit that it was, *Grizzly* should have secured a sequel long before it eventually did, but *Grizzly II* didn't begin shooting until 1983. And, it wasn't actually finished until the year 2020. Thus begins the long and storied history of one of the greatest success stories in the realm of lost films...

The story was written by original *Grizzly* writer David Sheldon and his actress wife, Joan McCall. Though it is known that Sheldon was approached about writing a sequel by producer Ed Montoro, it is not known exactly when this occurred (but presumably it was right after the picture started making money). Oddly, Montoro had trouble securing funds for the sequel and eventually gave up. Then, producer Joseph Proctor approached Sheldon about his script, and Sheldon agreed to give it to him on the condition that he got to direct. That didn't happen.

Sheldon got swindled out of the director's chair due to difficulties securing a suitable filming location in the U.S. The problem was that the centerpiece of the movie was a rock concert held in the middle of Yellowstone National Forest. Proctor, knowing that filming a rock concert would be near impossible due to shooting restrictions in the U.S., decided he would fare better by shooting the entire picture overseas. Suzanne C. Nagy, a Hungarian economist, was brought on as a producer on the tentatively titled *Grizzly II: The Concert*. "This movie would never be able to get a permit in the United States," Nagy remembered to *The New York Post* in 2014. "To make a huge concert on film in a rural area, it was almost impossible. Getting all the environmental permits, etc."[140]

---

[140] Tucker, "Clooney and a killer bear," *New York Post* (June 29, 2014) https://nypost.com/2014/06/29/the-star-studded-film-youll-probably-never-see/

© GBGB International

Proctor settled on shooting in Hungary and secured a director in the form of André Szöts, who had never shot a major film before in his life. The cast and crew were then flown off to Hungary. David Sheldon didn't find out about it until they were long gone.

To film the all-important concert scene a Russian military base was secured as the venue. Instead of simply recreating a rock concert like a normal film would do, the producers staged a real rock concert, even charging the "extras" $15 per ticket to attend! The concert was marketed as a three-day event, and 50,000 people ended up attending.[141]

---

[141] One has to wonder, who profited off of the ticket sales? Did it go into the budget, or Proctor's pocket?

SHARK BITES: *GRIZZLY II's* SUPERSTARS

ONE OF THE REASONS *GRIZZLY II* IS STILL REMEMBERED IS DUE TO THE FACT THAT IT OFFERED EARLY ROLES TO FUTURE MEGASTARS: GEORGE CLOONEY, LAURA DERN, AND CHARLIE SHEEN. THOUGH THEIR NAMES SHINE BRIGHT ON THE POSTER FOR THE COMPLETED FILM, THEY WERE REALLY JUST THE SACRIFICIAL TEENAGERS TO BE EATEN BY THE BEAR (REPORTEDLY, THEIR SCREEN TIME AMOUNTS TO FIVE MINUTES). BY THE EARLY 1980S, THE *FRIDAY THE 13TH* FRANCHISE WAS IN VOGUE, SO NATURALLY *GRIZZLY II* WOULD HAVE SCENES OF TEENAGERS TRYSTING IN THE WOODS AND GETTING EATEN BY THE BEAR. CLOONEY AND DERN WERE THE MAIN COUPLE, AND BRUCE DERN WAS REPORTEDLY VERY ANGRY WHEN HE FOUND OUT THAT THEY TRIED TO CONVINCE HIS SIXTEEN—YEAR-OLD DAUGHTER TO DO A NUDE SCENE. A BODY DOUBLE WAS USED INSTEAD, BUT DERN SR. WAS ANGRY NONETHELESS. LAURA DERN REMEMBERED THE SHOOT IN BUDAPEST POSITIVELY WHEN ASKED ABOUT IT BY THE AV CLUB IN 2011. AS FOR CHARLIE SHEEN, REPORTEDLY HE TURNED DOWN THE LEAD IN *THE KARATE KID* TO DO THIS FILM INSTEAD! IT'S A CHOICE HE REGRETS TO THIS DAY. IMAGES © GBGB INTERNATIONAL

John Rhys Davies as Bouchard. © GBGB International

The bands present were mostly from Hungary (keep in mind, the movie was still set in America) but a few also came from England and America.[142] According to trivia on IMDB, which can sometimes be of dubious veracity, the concert scenes were filmed without the participants' knowledge after a performance by Nazareth. Supposedly, the concert-goers were not told that the band used for filming was not actually a real band![143] Adding to the troubles, the second-unit director reportedly had a "nervous breakdown" before the scenes were filmed.

Original *Grizzly* co-writer Harvey Flaxman, not involved in *Grizzly II*, humorously commented on the set-up, likening the "American rock group" played by Europeans to the "wild and crazy guys" from *Saturday Night Live* played by Steve Martin and Dan Akroyd. "That was a movie that should have not been made where it was made," Flaxman succinctly summed it up in a *Grizzly* documentary.

But the misplaced rock concert might have been the least of the film's problems. This time, there was no

---

[142] These included Toto Coelo, the New Wave group that sang "I Eat Cannibals Part 1." According to the *Grizzly II* website, also present were The Predator, Set the Tone, The Dayz, and KFT.

[143] If IMDB is to be believed, this also made for the largest gathering in Hungary since the Hungarian Revolution of 1956!

Teddy, or real bears of any kind on the production supposedly. Instead, all the main bear scenes would be accomplished via animatronics and "a guy in a bear suit." Reportedly, the animatronic rarely worked, and the bear suit looked terrible. This, and other problems, necessitated some rewrites. And who did they get to rewrite the script? Well, they couldn't get Sheldon as Proctor had already screwed him out of the director's chair, and so the on-set caterer was hired to do the rewrites. Why? Well, that we don't know, but presumably there was some reason behind it.

And, even before the mishaps with the mechanical bear, Proctor disappeared from the production along with most of the film's money. In a 2014 interview, Proctor denied that he took the funds. Proctor told the interviewer this from his jail cell at the Los Angeles Federal Prison, where he was carrying out a five-year sentence for tax evasion.

I had always assumed Proctor's departure came about midway through the shoot, but according to Nagy on the official *Grizzly II* website it happened after the concert was shot! According to Nagy, "The first day of shooting was the most important event—a Woodstock-style concert where a gigantic grizzly bear attacks people. It was a fantastic and mesmerizing day. Everything worked out– the weather, the rock bands, the 40,000 audience."[144]

Nagy continued to explain how shocked she was when Proctor left with the funds, and how she then had to refinance the movie and finish the 45 day shoot herself. Quite a feat for the producer! Nagy managed to finish most of the principal photography, but as stated earlier, the effects footage with the bear was apparently deemed unusable in the end. Sadly, there was no money left to finish the special effects scenes by this time. Adding to the troubles was the fact that Proctor wouldn't relinquish his rights on the film until four years later. Free of Proctor, Nagy made a deal with Cannon Films in 1987 to finish the movie. It was more bad luck for Nagy, as Cannon found themselves in financial troubles and would fold a few years later.

---

[144] https://www.grizzly2revenge.com/about

The *Grizzly II: Revenge* release poster. © GBGB International

And, for twenty plus years, the *Grizzly II* footage sat in a Paris film lab, while the soundtrack was located in a vault in New York. A workprint of the film was screened in 2007. The bear itself only appeared during the end concert scenes, and preceding this, scenes featuring the bear consisted of a blank screen.

Still from the climax, featuring the animatronic grizzly.
© GBGB International

Initially, Nagy had no interest in completing the film, but stated she would sell the rights to anyone who wanted to complete it. An anniversary piece on the unfinished film in 2012 by the *New York Post* may have helped to change her mind. A few years later, she began to actively pursue finishing the film along with producer/screenwriter Ross Massbaum.

"In 2018, the time was right to rethink the Grizzly movie and create a challenging new narrative with a new message which could fill the missing part in the movie," Nagy wrote on the website. "Restoring the old footage was a great challenge. But in the summer of 2019, we got a clean, super crispy digital transfer from London. During the waiting period, we worked on the new script and re-erected the film from its dormant stage."[145]

As of right now, the most exciting developments on *Grizzly II: Revenge* (the final title) are yet to come. If all goes to plan, by 2020, the film will be released onto home video, along with a making of documentary and an elaborate behind the scenes book entitled: *Swimming Among Sharks: The Story Behind the Making of Grizzly II: Revenge.*

---

[145] Ibid.

MONSTER SHARK

Release Date: September 7, 1984 (Italy)
Alternate Titles: *Devilfish* (U.S.) *Revelation in the Red Ocean* (France) *Shark: Red in the Ocean* (Italy) *Devouring Waves* (Australia) *Jaws Attack 2* (Japan)

Directed by: Lamberto Bava **Special Effects by:** Germano Natali & Ovidio Taito **Screenplay by:** Gianfranco Clerici, Dardano Sacchetti, Hervé Piccini, Vincenzo Mannino, Luigi Cozzi & Sergio Martino (story) **Music by:** Fabio Frizi **Cast:** Michael Sopkiw (Peter) Valentine Monnier (Dr. Stella Dickens) Gianni Garko (Sheriff Gordon) William Berger (Professor Donald West) Iris Peynado (Sandra Hayes) Lawrence Morgant (Dr. Bob Hogan) Cinzia de Ponti (Florinda) Paul Branco (Dr. Davis Barker) Dagmar Lassander (Sonja West)

Spherical, Eastmancolor, 90 Minutes

SYNOPSIS Along the Florida coast, a secret military experiment has combined the DNA of an octopus, a dolphin (for intelligence), and the prehistoric Dunkleosteus. The sea beast goes on a killing spree that attracts the attention of researchers Peter and Stella. Their investigation, in turn, attracts the attention of the military, which wishes to cover up the monster's existence...

COMMENTARY It's both surprising and a little disappointing that it took this long for one of the Bavas to do a movie in the *Jaws* genre. Mario Bava and his son Lamberto Bava were two of Italy's most accomplished and respected horror directors. Nor were they averse to jumping on the bandwagon as it were. (For instance, in 1976, they almost produced their own take on *King Kong* called *Baby Kong*.) As it is, their take on *Jaws* is too little too late.

In watching *Monster Shark,* I wasn't sure if I was seeing a bad cut of a mediocre monster movie, or just a plain bad monster movie. The editing leaves a lot to be desired. For instance, when a man who's lost his legs[146] to the monster is dredged out of the water, the whole sequence is curiously interrupted by shots of the female lead training her dolphins! However, this choppy feel isn't because the original editor was inept; it's because what most of us see is a TV cut of the movie. Naturally, it was edited down for blood and violence, and it wasn't done skillfully either. This is sadly the version that's made its way onto most streaming sites. Even aside from the bad editing, there are still some real groaners in *Monster Shark*, chief among them a badly acted death scene for the villain, Dr. Davis.

The monster rears its ugly head in *Monster Shark*.

---

[146] Real amputees played the victims.

And yet, all that said, *Monster Shark* is still the last of the great *Jaws* rip-offs, in my opinion. True, more rip-offs like *Deep Blood* and *Cruel Jaws* would follow, but those films used stock shots of real sharks rather than new footage of mechanical ones (*Cruel Jaws* used footage from *The Last Shark*, though). *Monster Shark* at least featured a bonafide, well-designed animatronic monster to terrorize its cast with.

In many ways, I feel like this movie is what people wanted *Tentacles* to be, as there are plenty of shots featuring the monster's appendages plucking people off their boats. In fact, the monster is revealed in the very first scene terrorizing a couple on a yacht with its tentacles.

As a shark-octopus hybrid, the monster predates *Sharktopus* from 2010 and is a fine creation in my book. The creature gets plenty of screen time and isn't the least bit camera shy. And, because the monster's cells can regenerate when severed from the main body, the heroes really have to rack their brains as to how to kill it. They end up luring it into the Everglades and setting it on fire. Surprisingly enough, the ending doesn't use the regeneration ploy as sequel fodder, and the two leads can apparently live happily ever after.

Shot in Florida with a very limited budget, several of the movie's stars defended the film, stating that Bava was a great director and that the budget was simply too low for the type of movie they wanted to make.

Monster Shark was a little too late to the party whereas the Jaws franchise was concerned. While *Jaws 3-D* was still a financial hit, it was poorly received critically, and many found the concept of a giant shark at Sea World a little too far out. Elsewhere, *Piranha II: The Spawning* was neither a critical or commercial success. Therefore, there was little interest in *Monster Shark* upon its release in Italy on September 7, 1984. The film didn't see a theatrical release in the U.S. until November 14, 1986. It was distributed through Cinema Shares International, which had notably released *Godzilla vs. Megalon* and other Godzilla sequels to the U.S. in the late 1970s.

Developing
JAWS: THE REVENGE

Release Date: July 17, 1987
Alternate Titles: *Jaws 4* (multiple countries) *Jaws 87* (Japan) *Jaws: The Return* (working title)

Directed by: Joseph Sargent **Special Effects by:** Ira Henry Millar **Screenplay by:** Michael de Guzman **Music by:** Michael Small **Cast:** Ellen Brody (Lorraine Gary) Mike Brody (Lance Guest) Jake (Mario Van Peebles) Carla Brody (Karen Young) Thea Brody (Judith Barsi) Hoagie Newcombe (Michael Caine)

2.39 : 1, Color, 90 Minutes

SYNOPSIS When Sean Brody is killed in the waters of Amity Island, Ellen Brody becomes convinced that a Great White shark is targeting her family due to events of the past. She travels to the Bahamas to be with her son Michael, who works there as a marine biologist, with his wife, Carla; daughter, Thea; and friend, Jake.

Soon Michael and Jake come across a huge Great White shark and try to track it. Meanwhile, Ellen is distracted in a budding romance with an island pilot, Hoagie. One day at the beaches, Thea is targeted by a Great White shark but escapes. An enraged Ellen takes a boat out to sea to settle the score once and for all...

COMMENTARY There's a rule about sequels. No matter how poorly the previous film was critically received, if it made plenty of money, there will be another sequel. *Jaws 3-D* was panned by critics but had the second-biggest opening weekend of 1983, right behind *Return of the Jedi*. Coincidentally, that summer also saw the release of *Superman III*, which, likewise, was also a money maker but a critical dud. In a further coincidence, 1987 saw both the fourth Superman movie and the fourth Jaws arrive in theaters. Both were critically panned certified box office bombs this time around.

It's unknown what exactly got the ball rolling on *Jaws 4* (probably an executive with dollar signs in his eyes).[147] Supposedly, the first two movies had recently attained extremely high ratings on TV, something that Sid Sheinberg took note of. According to Sheinberg's wife, Lorraine Gary, Sheinberg came home one day and said to her, "We've got to have a hit movie this summer and I think we can do another *Jaws*."[148] A shocked Gary thought that he was teasing, but he wasn't.

Sheinberg wasn't the only one thinking of *Jaws* sequels. So was Universal Studios head, Frank Price. In an interview in *Just When You Thought It Was Safe,* screenwriter Steve DeJarnatt (*Miracle Mile*) said that he wrote a *Jaws 4* for Price but that Sheinberg "threw it out and came up with something his wife could do."[149]

DeJarnatt's script, like the original *Jaws 3*, was satirical, but not an all-out spoof. The tone would've

---

[147] Nothing wrong with that, by the way, so long as the sequel is good.

[148] Gary as quoted in *Newsweek*. Retrieved from: www.denofgeek.com/uk/movies/jaws-the-revenge/42396/jaws-the-revenge-how-the-sequel-went-so-horribly-wrong?fbclid=IwAR0h5TlhfEJVVqMQZXwHmyCrdxg1TSlbFCISNGRDRlOqCpUnNpFKuJ-EnQ8

[149] Jankiewicz, *Just When You Thought It Was Safe*, pp.185.

been established in the very first scene, wherein we are duped into thinking the opening is set during medieval times. A princess who looks like she's from the Middle Ages walks along the beach. Eventually, we learn this isn't actually set in the past—she has a Walkman—she's just working at a renaissance fair. She goes out to take a swim, much like the girl in the first *Jaws*. Eventually, a shark begins to stalk her in the waters. Just when we think she's a goner, a shark "ten times bigger" than the other one bites it in half, inadvertently saving the girl. Actually, if DeJarnatt was serious about the size, I have to wonder if he was going the Megalodon route?

The story was to be set in Malibu, California, with a cast of "surf punks." The lead character was an Australian surfer. The film's end would have had the man's girlfriend swallowed whole (and alive) by the mega-shark. He kills it somehow, surfs it onto the shore, and then would have cut his girlfriend out of its stomach![150]

Apparently, this got the ball rolling on *Jaws 4*—or, *Jaws 87* as it was initially called (the producers were so embarrassed by *Jaws 3-D* that they didn't want the new film to be titled "Jaws 4" by association). I don't know what the next sequence of events was, but in late September of 1986, director Joseph Sargent got a call from Sheinberg to make a fourth Jaws movie. According to him, there was no script (apparently because Sheinberg threw it out). Sheinberg more or less told Sargent he wanted a story that was similar to the first film, where the drama was driven just as much by the human characters as it was the shark. In other words, Sheinberg wanted Sargent to make it personal. And make it personal he did...

In an interview 20 years later, Sargent admitted that the concept was born out of desperation. "We thought that maybe if we take a mystical point of view, and go for a little bit of ... magic, we might be able to find something interesting enough to sit through."[151]

[150] Ibid.

[151] Rutkowski, "Joseph Sargent Interview," *Archive of American Television* (March 9, 2006).

SHARK BITES: THE SAGA OF VENGEANCE

IF YOU'LL REMEMBER THE *JAWS 2* NOVEL REVEALED THAT BRUCETTE
GAVE BIRTH TO SOME LITTLE SHARKS BEFORE SHE DIED. WELL, GUESS
WHO THE SHARK IN *JAWS: THE REVENGE* IS SUPPOSED TO BE IN THE
MOVIE'S NOVELIZATION? YOU GUESSED IT, THE *JAWS: THE REVENGE*
SHARK, NICKNAMED "VENGEANCE" BY FANS, IS THE SON OF BRUCE
AND BRUCETTE. NOT ONLY THAT, HE IS THE FATHER OF BRUCETTA,
THE SHARK FROM *JAWS 3-D*! NO, I AM NOT MAKING THIS UP. THIS IS
INDEED VENGEANCE'S BACK STORY. NO WONDER HE WANTED
REVENGE ON THE BRODYS!

On the note of "a mystical point of view," *Jaws: The Revenge* seems like it's missing a subplot, and there's evidence that this is indeed the case. The novelization, said to be based upon the original script, would seem to answer that nagging question: how does the shark find the Brody's, and why does it want to kill them? According to the novel, the shark is the tool of a voodoo witch doctor who has a grudge against Michael! While as bizarre as anything else, it does at least offer an explanation.

The novel has a few other deleted scenes that may have been in the script at one time or another. The first one has Amity PD discovering Sean Brody's body. It also has a bit more for the shark to do, such as killing a windsurfer and also an island gangster who befriended Ellen. One of the more significant subplots explained that Hoagie had been smuggling drugs onto the island. Scenes revealing this were shot and then deleted during post-production (because producers felt that it took away from the main premise).

One of the scarier scenes had the voodoo witch doctor, Papa Jacques, stealing Thea's sand pale. He bewitches it, which somehow hypnotizes Thea and causes her to walk outside during the middle of the night. In the nearby waters (the house is on the beach, remember) the shark waits. Just when she is about to wade into the water, she is stopped. The cause of the bad blood between Mike and Papa Jacques is a little mundane. Mike feels that he is exploiting the islanders, the two have an altercation, and from then on Papa Jacques uses voodoo to control the shark!

Jaws: The Revenge © 1987 Universal Pictures

SHARK BITES: JAWS 3-D PART II?

REPORTEDLY JOSEPH SARGENT BRIEFLY CONSIDERED SHOOTING *JAWS: THE REVENGE* IN 3-D. HE CONTACTED THE COMPANY THAT HAD SUPPLIED THE CAMERAS FOR *JAWS 3-D* BUT SARGENT WAS ADVISED BY THE COMPANY THAT THE CAMERAS MAY NOT WORK CORRECTLY IN THE BAHAMAS DUE TO THE CLIMATE, SO THE IDEA WAS DROPPED.

Voodoo aside, a lot of people also wonder just whose idea it was to center a whole film around Ellen Brody? Though one would think that this movie probably started off in hopes of Roy Scheider returning in the lead, apparently the plan was always to focus on Ellen. That said, Scheider made the comment that, "The only way I would reprise my role is if I were to be killed off at the beginning of the movie." The producers took this to heart, and the original idea was for Martin to get eaten rather than Sean! When Scheider asked for $1 million to film the scene, the script was tweaked to have Martin already dead (Ellen claimed that fear of the shark returning one day killed him), and Sean would be the shark's victim.[152] As to why Ellen was chosen over Martin, there were several reasons. One, everybody knew by that point that Scheider would not anchor another Jaws film. Two, Gary was Sheinberg's wife. And three, Joseph Sargent already had a working relationship with Gary and wanted to work with her again.[153]

Even without Scheider, *Jaws: The Revenge* is something of a reunion. Notably, Mrs. Taft returns, as does the secretary from the police station. Even Mrs. Kintner is in the living room for Sean's wake![154] Other cameos were planned for Hooper and the mayor. Murray

---

[152] Actually, Sean's death is our first clue that this movie is retconning *Jaws 3-D* out of existence, as the Sean in that film hated the water and had moved far inland to get away from it.

[153] Sargent had worked with her on 1973's *The Marcus-Nelson Murders* and he had won a Directors Guild of America Award.

[154] If you'll remember, she's the woman whose son was eaten by the shark in *Jaws* and she absolutely hated Martin. She seems quite happy in the wake scene for *Jaws: The Revenge*. Maybe she's giddy that Ellen can now share in the pain of losing a son to a shark?

Hamilton was meant to have a short part in the beginning Amity scenes, but he passed away before filming began.

Hooper's cameo was going to be via a phone call to the Brodys to offer his condolences for Sean's death. Young Thea would answer and identify him as "Uncle Matt." Carla was going to refer to Hooper as her "second favorite marine biologist" to show how close they all were. The scene lasts long enough that Michael and Hooper are able to reminisce about Martin dressing up as Santa at a Christmas gathering where Hooper was present. The scene was to end with Michael calling for his mother to come talk to Hooper.[155]

There are two different versions of *Jaws: The Revenge*, the U.S. theatrical version, and the overseas theatrical version/U.S. home video version. In the original theatrical cut, the shark doesn't explode. Ellen rams the boat into the shark, and it hemorrhages blood from its mouth. It then falls limp into the water, bleeding all the way down. Jake does not miraculously resurface alive either. We fade out on the characters at sea and then fade into Ellen hopping into Hoagie's plane. Before she leaves, she asks Michael if he's sure he's OK (referring to Jake's death).

When this ending proved unpopular, it was reshot. The new ending had the shark explode upon impact! Stock footage from the original *Jaws* was also used to show the headless corpse sinking to the bottom of the ocean. The characters then regroup in the water and shockingly find Jake to be awake, alive, and bleeding badly from the shark bites. Despite all the blood, Jake seems to be in good spirits—giving the scene an unintentionally campy feel. The epilogue on the plane is the same, only Ellen says to take care of Jake (since he's now alive).

This new ending was decided upon the day after the film opened in U.S. theaters to a chilly reception. The new ending still wasn't able to help the film, which flopped in all markets. Nor was the revised ending the only alternate cut. Now cognizant of just how ludicrous

---

[155] The *Jaws: The Revenge* novel makes a mention that the two once had an affair—something that happened in the Peter Benchley book, not the movie!

Man's Greatest Fear Has Risen Again.

LORRAINE GARY LANCE GUEST MARIO VAN PEEBLES KAREN YOUNG and MICHAEL CAINE
A JOSEPH SARGENT Film "JAWS THE REVENGE" Music MICHAEL de GUZMAN Music MICHAEL SMALL

Still from the ending, which was famously reshot.
Jaws: The Revenge © 1987 Universal Pictures

the plot really was, the TV version began with narration stating, "Since time immemorial events have taken place with no evident reason for their happening. Such phenomena has been man's dilemma and the subject of constant philosophical discussion. When there is no factor motivating an event, no case of cause creating effect, what triggered the action? Fate or circumstance? What you are about to see concerns such an event. Maybe you can determine whether we are dealing here with circumstances or fate." The TV version also included a bevy of deleted scenes to further pad out the run time.[156] Curiously, it ends the same way as the theatrical cut, though.

---

[156] The extra scenes in the TV version included an extended taxi ride where Michael points out Neptune's Folly to Ellen; Michael and Jake singing on Michael's front porch (placed early in the movie, in fact the wrong spot, as it was meant to take place right before the duo go out to search for Ellen); a scene where Hoagie is regaling Ellen with a story about bananas when suddenly the shark emerges to eat part of the barge; a shot of the shark diving from the surface when Jake is down on the seabed, and another shot of the shark diving after eating part of the barge; Hoagie gambling at the casino; and finally Ellen telling Michael a bad joke about an Egyptian pharaoh (also in the wrong spot).

Since its release, *Jaws: The Revenge* has gone on to become the butt of an innumerable amount of Hollywood jokes. It also killed the franchise, which has yet to resurface to this day. That said, every once in a while comes reports of another big fish named "Jaws" lurking in the waters of Development Hell...

DEEP BLOOD

Release Date: 1989
Alternate Titles: *Wakan* (working title) *Sharks: The Challenge* (working title) *Blood in the Abyss* (Italy) *Shakka - Beast of the Depths* (Germany)

Directed by: Raffaele Donato (as Raf Donato), Joe D'Amato (uncredited) **Special Effects by:** Brian Wood **Screenplay by:** George Nelson Ott **Music by:** Carlo Maria Cordio **Cast:** Miki (Frank Baroni) Allan (Allen Court) Ben (Keith Kelsch) Ben's father (Charlie Brill) John (John K. Brune) Elizabeth (Margareth Hanks) Sheriff Cody (Tody Bernard) Native American man (Van Jensens)

Academy Ratio, Color, 90 Minutes

SYNOPSIS One day at the beach, four boys—John, Miki, Ben, and Allen—are told of a dire prophecy by an old Native American man that the gods will send a shark monster to terrorize the sea. Years later, on a summer break from college, John is killed by a large shark. And he's not the only one. Soon the boys deduct that the prophecy is coming true, and it's up to them to defeat the shark...

COMMENTARY One wouldn't think that a movie as despised as *Jaws: The Revenge* would have been subject to its very own Italian rip-off, but it was. *Deep Blood* came out only two years after *Revenge* and had a quasi-similar story in the form of another shark who makes it personal. In this case, the shark attacks four childhood friends because it is the physical incarnation of some sort of mythical monster sent by the gods!

Considering that most of the movie focuses on a group of childhood friends destined to fight an evil force, I have to wonder if this story was also inspired by Steven King's *It*. However, *It* wasn't made into a TV mini-series until after this film wrapped production, so perhaps it was a coincidence.

Though an Italian combination of *Jaws: The Revenge* and *It* might sound interesting, *Deep Blood* is not what I would call a thrilling story. In fact, you can tell that it's *probably* going to be a bad movie right away. The opening shots have the boys roasting burnt hotdogs on the beach to some generic piano music that sounds like it was composed by Maurice Jarre on Xanax. But, you *know* it's a bad movie when the first spoken dialogue is a heavy exposition dump about how the boys are the reincarnations of ancient Native American warriors destined to fight an evil shark monster one day.

And as to why this shark monster is the incarnation of an ancient curse... well, that's explained about as well as why the shark is after the Brodys in *Jaws: The Revenge*. As the story progresses, the idea isn't greatly elaborated upon outside of the opening remarks.[157] The boys more or less remember the story told to them by the old man at the beginning of the movie and take recent events to mean the prophecy is being fulfilled (recent events being a shark killing folks).

The first shark attack is a sort of inverse to the Kintner boy scene in *Jaws*. In this case, rather than a mother watching her son get eaten, the son watches his mother get attacked on a raft. This is accomplished via shark POV shots and quick cuts of blood in the water

---

[157] One character makes mention of a Native American legend that the monster ate a whole village! Presumably, he meant a whole village's worth of people, not that it somehow came on land and did it.

and the woman thrashing about. The child actor looks amused by it all rather than terrified, though.

The second shark attack scene isn't much better than the first. And by that I mean the adult actor watching his friend getting eaten isn't any more convincing than the child actor from earlier. Nor do we see much of the shark outside of the dorsal fin.

And, if you're into the whole fake-looking giant shark thing, this movie might disappoint you because it uses real, archival shark footage.[158] In fact, it appears to me that that's all this movie used, despite claims that a giant shark head was constructed for certain scenes.[159] In an interview in *Spaghetti Nightmares* on page 79, D'Amato claimed that they made a mechanical shark's head. Either the shark head looked so real that I confused it for the stock shots, or the version I saw edited it out because I saw nothing to me that looked like a fake shark head. So, in that sense, this movie stands out from other *Jaws* rip-offs like *The Last Shark*. And though it may be more realistic, it's also a lot less fun.

Real sharks aside, the movie has a low budget feel overall (due to the performances more than anything else). However, there was apparently enough money available for the producers to splurge on extras and a small helicopter. For instance, there's a large scale search mounted for the shark that involves multiple boats and the chopper. During the hunt, a shark is shot from a helicopter and killed.

As this happens midway through the movie, we know this can't be the right shark. Of course, this same plot point occurs in *Jaws* when a shark is caught, but its bite radius doesn't match the bodies of the victims. In *Deep Blood*, as Ben watches the dead shark hauled up onto the dock, the old Native American man from earlier randomly pops up behind his shoulder and says, "Don't believe everything you see." The man soon vanishes without a trace and doesn't appear again for the rest of the film.

---

[158] *Deep Blood* and *Last Shark* use the same archival footage of real sharks. I don't know if *Deep Blood* stole it or bought it.
[159] IMDB features a still from *The Last Shark* among the images credited to *Deep Blood*. This scene from *Last Shark* does not appear in *Deep Blood*.

Not long after this scene, there's what appears to be an homage to the opening of *Jaws* to confirm that the shark is still on the loose. In this case, a trampy blonde having an affair with a guy in a van runs out into the ocean for a moonlight swim. The real shark footage here is used to good effect, and this time we see some excellent stock shots of a shark's mouth opening up to devour its prey.

Perhaps even more so than *Jaws: The Revenge*, I suppose this film is really out to mimic *Jaws*. Though the main characters are the three surviving boys, there's also a prominent mayor character. There's even a sheriff character named Sheriff Cody (rhymes with Brody)! At the end of the second act, the young men board a boat with Ben's father, a fisherman, to kill the shark. Naturally, this is meant to be evocative of Brody and Hooper going out with Quint on the *Orca*. Notably, one of the boys remarks on how much he hates slinging the chum into the ocean, just like Brody did in *Jaws*.

The movie gains some good momentum as they head out to sea...and then loses it for an interminably long stretch (or, about 20 minutes). The boat gets called back into the harbor by the police via helicopter. Back on land, the story drags to a halt, and it seems as if the film is just trying to find things for the characters to do before we get close enough to the end to kill the shark (gotta hit that 90-minute mark to make it feature length!).

Then, when they finally do get back out to sea, there's a lot of padding shots of the characters scuba diving to the sunken ship. "What's the deal with the sunken ship?" you ask. Well, I couldn't tell you, but their mission is to blow it up. The best that I can figure is that they think it's the shark's lair (it isn't). And it's not just me; other reviewers also puzzled over the sunken ship subplot (maybe it was another way to ape *Jaws: The Revenge* which had a prominent set-piece revolving around a sunken ship). Anyhow, the boys set up explosives to kill the shark, the shark shows up, and ship and shark go boom (via stock footage from *The Last Shark*). End of story.

Deep Blood was produced by schlock European horror producer Filmirage headed by Joe D'Amato. It was D'Amato's desire to shoot the film in America and in English. Wanting someone with a good command of the language, he hired his English dialogue coach from *Red Coats* (1975), Raffaele Donato, to direct. Donato had expressed interest in directing in the past, and so D'Amto gave him the shark picture. As it turned out, Donata only directed the opening scene set on the beach. That was all it took for him to decide he didn't like directing and quit. D'Amato directed the rest of the film after that, but still gave Donata the primary director's credit.[160]

D'Amato filmed the picture predominantly in Florida, though he also shot a few scenes in a New Orleans aquarium and along the Mississippi River. The underwater footage was shot back in Europe, in Ventotene, and also a Roman swimming pool.

Surprisingly, the film was actually financially successful, even in Japan![161]

---

[160] He did this because he had already directed quite a few films recently, and didn't want people to think his production company was a one man show.
[161] This, according to the book *Spaghetti Nightmares*.

SPECIAL SECTION

Jaws is a Registered TM of Universal Pictures

JAWS: THE RIDE

The Jaws ride at Universal Theme park in Orlando was a beloved attraction from 1993 to 2012. However, it was preceded by a lesser-known Jaws ride in 1990. Like the films, it too went through an interesting developmental process.

The origins of the ride go back to 1976 when the Universal backlot ride showed a *Jaws* themed scene. In that case, the shark pulls a fisherman under the water and blood bubbles to the surface.

Planning for the full ride began in the late 1980s (perhaps in anticipation of the release of *Jaws: The Revenge*). The storyline of the ride was that you were part of a group touring Amity Island when the shark attacks your boat. As was the case during shooting of the movies, the shark rarely worked. What it was supposed to do was to grab the boat and drag it across the lagoon. At the end, the skipper would shoot the shark with a grenade launcher!

To go into further detail, the ride would begin with Amity having just recovered from a "shark problem." A dead prop shark is hung in the town square (which visitors could snap photos in front of, naturally), and Mayor Vaughn believes, therefore, that said shark problem is now over. You would then board the boat *Tours One* with Skipper Herb to go out to Lighthouse Cove. The skipper would explain to you that he's been given a grenade launcher to ward off any potential shark attacks!

The boat would pass by Quint's shack, and you would then overhear a rather loud argument between Chief Brody and Quint. Obviously, this wasn't meant to be any kind of sequel to *Jaws*, but a sort of retelling of *Jaws* that you got to be a part of. In Quint's opinion, the shark hanging in the town square is the wrong shark. Your skipper would then tell you not to worry about it because Quint is just drunk today and doesn't know what he's talking about.

The boat would make its way to Lighthouse Cove, and when rounding a corner, another boat, *Tours Three*, is found sinking into the depths. Bloody clothes were to be spotted in the water, but this was removed from the tour once it actually got going (perhaps to tone it down). A good scare is one thing, but blood would have made the ride less appealing to families. The shark would then make its presence known, and the skipper would fire two grenades at it which miss. Chief Brody would then radio your boat and advise the skipper to unload the passengers at the boathouse. You would then make your way to Jay's Boat House (a nod to Universal Studios Florida President Jay Stein).

The scene set within the darkened boathouse would change and evolve over time. The first idea was the "less is more" approach by only hinting at the shark's presence in the dark. But it was suggested the shark should show itself by lunging at the boat. There was also to be some gore in another iteration of the scene that dated back to 1987. In this case it was to be a Coast Guard boathouse. Inside you would have seen the wreckage of another boat. The shark would then bump into it, causing it to turn over and reveal a dead sailor. As the ambitious sequence continued, the wrecked boat's motor would catch fire, and the shark would begin tearing the boathouse apart as you narrowly escape.

The shark would follow you outside and sink its teeth into one of the pontoons. Your skipper would then use their bang stick to force the shark's jaws off the boat, but this idea was discarded while the ride was being constructed. Instead, the shark would simply let go of the boat on its own. Then your skipper would fire a grenade into the shark's mouth, it would submerge, and then you would witness an underwater explosion representing the end of the shark.

The ride opened in 1990 but lasted only three months before Universal gave up on it. The shark often malfunctioned, and the scene where it bit the pontoon and pulled the boat rarely worked. Eventually, Universal decided to start again but make the ride less complex. For instance, instead of blowing up at the end, the shark would bite an electrical cable recreating the ending from *Jaws 2*. From there, the other differences were fairly minor, renaming the tour boats *Amity Six* and *Amity Three*, Skipper Herb became Skipper Gordon, and so on.

So, as you can see, not only did the Jaws movies go through a myriad of ideas, so did the ride!

Sources:

McNeil, Dustin & J. Michael Roddy. *Adventures in Amity: Tales From The Jaws Ride.* (2018, By the Authors).

Defunctland. "The History of Jaws: The Ride." YouTube Video, 2017. www.youtube.com/watch?v=qO7dslkMbF0&t=311s

Yesterworld Entertainment. "The Jaws Ride You Never Got To Experience." YouTube Video, 2017. www.youtube.com/watch?v=yBsYVDlYkhs

Origins of the
BEAST

Script Date: 1992

Proposed Director: John Carpenter **Treatment by:** Peter Benchley **Screenplay by:** John Carpenter **Proposed Cast/Characters:** Whip Darling [fisherman] Talley [marine biologist] Marcus Sharpe [Navy pilot] Manning [millionaire] **Proposed Creatures:** Giant Squid, baby giant squids, sperm whales

SYNOPSIS When a Bermuda fishing village is puzzled by mysterious disappearances at sea, only veteran fisherman Whip Darling suspects the truth: that an Architeuthis dux, or giant squid, is to blame. As evidence, Darling has found two claws from the massive beast's tentacles at one of the accident scenes. Backing up Darling's theory is Talley, a marine biologist. It is Talley who entices a man named Manning, the millionaire father of one of the squid's victims, to fund a hunt for the monster. The mayor beats the team to the punch, searching for the squid in a mini-sub which the sea monster destroys. Darling becomes depressed, as one of his crewmates perished on the sub with the mayor, and decides to withdraw from the hunt. However, the bereaved father of the victims takes ownership of Darling's mortgage and forces him to help him and Talley hunt down the squid. Darling reluctantly agrees and enlists the help of his friend Marcus Sharpe, a local Navy pilot. The four men go out on a boat and are able to lure the squid to them with hormones that Talley harvested from a deceased giant squid he'd found in the past. Manning is killed in an accident, and as the squid tries to sink the boat, Darling manages to wound the creature severely. The blood in the water attracts the squid's natural enemy, the sperm whale, which finishes off the beast. Darling, Sharpe, and Talley return to land, unaware that the squid's spawn lurks in the deep...

COMMENTARY Similar to the turn of events wherein *Jaws 3, People 0* developed into the straightforward *Jaws 3-D*, Peter Benchley's original version of *Beast* was a comedy. Benchley apparently had the idea of an aquatic monster spoof germinating for quite some time. When his editor, Tom Congdon, disliked Benchley's first run of chapters on *Jaws*, Benchley tried to tweak *Jaws* into a comedy as well until it transitioned back to a straight thriller. The initial draft of the novel that eventually became *Beast* ran 200 pages and was entitled *The Last Monster*. It is dated August of 1990.

When *The Beast* TV mini-series was coming out in 1996, Benchley offered a few comments on the development. "I began this book as a comedy. I wrote 200 pages of what I thought was a fall-down hilarious comedy and I consulted with my editor at Random House," Benchley told *The Buffalo News*.[162] "I said I have this great idea for this comic thriller. She said her initial reaction is you can't do it because a comic thriller is almost an oxymoron. They don't work generally."[163]

Instead, his editor convinced him to do the story straight, though Benchley had reservations about repeating *Jaws*. To acknowledge this fact to his readers,

---

[162] Pergament, "Attack of the Giant Squid," *The Buffalo News* (April 25, 1996). https://buffalonews.com/1996/04/26/attack-of-the-giant-squid/
[163] Ibid.

he included an in-joke reference to *Jaws*. "I couldn't do the book without making a self-referential statement. That really risks people thinking this person has gone out of his mind if he thinks this is a new subject."[164]

Just as his Bermuda diving trip back in the early 1970s had inspired *The Deep*, it also helped to birth *Beast*. In an interview with *The LA Times,* Benchley mentioned a return trip to Bermuda in 1979 with a "fisherman pal" who served as the inspiration for the lead character in *The Beast*. Presumably, this "pal" was the same man who inspired Robert Shaw's character in *The Deep*—that being real-life diving legend Teddy Tucker. Again, I don't know this for a fact, but as Tucker was a friend of Benchley's based out of Bermuda, he's the most likely candidate. During the 1979 trip, Benchley and his friend decided to try and entice a giant squid to the surface. "The first time we went out we took cables--48 woven strands of stainless steel--down to 3,000 feet with hooks and lights and baits," Benchley told *The LA Times.*[165]

Benchley didn't catch a monster, but he did see evidence of one. "When we brought the cables up the next day, we discovered they had been bitten off at 2,000 feet!" Benchley said, and then added, "I don't know what the first impulse was to turn it into a book, but it was based on, like, 12 or 15 years of looking for him."[166]

By 1991 *Beast* was published and was another bestseller for Benchley. Naturally, movie studios noticed. "*Beast* was sold to Universal as a feature, but, after receiving scripts from both me and John Carpenter, the studio deemed it too expensive – around $30 million," Benchley said in an interview.[167]

The Boston University archives provides dates for Benchley's first few cracks at the script. The first treatment was done on June 10, 1991, and a second treatment followed a week later. The full script, written

[164] Ibid.

[165] King, "That's One Mean Mollusk," *LA Times* (April 28, 1996) https://www.latimes.com/archives/la-xpm-1996-04-28-tv-63810-story.html

[166] Ibid.

[167] http://www.peterbenchley.com/articles/peter-benchley-the-father-jaws-and-other-tales-the-deep

by John Carpenter, is dated September 4, 1991, and is listed as being 119 pages. As archives typically don't allow photocopying of screenplays, the only way to know what the Carpenter script looks like is to book an appointment with the university.

"Jaws 5"
CRUEL JAWS

Release Date: September 26, 1995 (Italy)
Alternate Titles: *Jaws 5: Cruel Jaws* (U.S. Home Video)
Jaws '96 (Japan) *The Beast* (working title)

Directed by: Bruno Mattei (as William Snyder) **Special Effects by:** Larry Mannini, John Meads & Ernest Stark **Screenplay by:** Robert Feen, Bruno Mattei & Linda Morrison **Music by:** Michael Morahan **Cast:** Scott Silveria (Billy Snerensen) Richard Dew (Dag Snerensen) David Luther (Francis Berger) George Barnes, Jr. (Samuel Lewis) Carter Collins (Ronnie Lewis) Natasha Etzer (Gloria Lewis) Jay Colligan (Tommy Snerensen) Kirsten Urso (Susy Snerensen)

Spherical, Eastmancolor-Kodak, 96 Minutes (Japan)
93 Minutes (U.S.)

SYNOPSIS Dag Snerensen is a widower with three children: marine biologist Billy, teenager Tommy, and Susy, confined to a wheelchair due to a horrible accident. Dag owns a beachfront aquarium desired by evil hotel magnate Samuel Lewis, in cahoots with the mob. Lewis has given Dag 30 days to pay off his aquarium, or else he builds a new hotel there. Amidst the family drama, a huge Tiger Shark begins killing swimmers in the area, including Lewis's son, Ronnie. Dag and his two sons hit the high seas to kill the shark in hopes of securing a reward that will pay off their aquarium.

COMMENTARY *Cruel Jaws* is quite possibly the most notorious *Jaws* rip-off there is. Notice I didn't say best known—or best—that distinction shall always belong to *The Last Shark*. No, *Cruel Jaws* is labeled as notorious for having the audacity to advertise itself as "Jaws 5" and also the fact that it illegally "borrowed" footage from *The Last Shark* and *Deep Blood*. The hybrid film, which used the previous two films' shark footage in a new storyline, was also ballsy enough to rip a few quick shots from *Jaws* and *Jaws 2*. The shots are so brief that perhaps the producer, Bruno Mattei, hoped no one would notice (or at least not Universal's lawyers). But, they did, and *Cruel Jaws* is no longer eligible for home video release on DVD in the U.S.[168] Back in the days of VHS, it was given the title of *Jaws 5: Cruel Jaws* in America and *Jaws '96* in Japan. In 2015, Scream Factory planned to give it its first-ever Blu-ray release (paired with *Exterminators of the Year 3000*), but the illegal usage of pirated footage and music[169] canceled those plans.

Have no fear, though. You're not missing much, and if you think you are, you can easily find this movie online for your viewing pleasure.

You can tell from the first lines of dialogue—awkwardly delivered and chock full of exposition—what kind of a movie you're in for, and it's not good. As it was, the actors were all first time performers—or relatively first time performers—and one was even a professional Hulk Hogan impersonator! That's not to say they're not likable, just that the actors are inexperienced. For a *Jaws* rip-off, there's actually not too many character stand-ins. The sheriff is a minor character and in no

[168] It is available in Europe.
[169] It even uses a few cues from John William's famous *Star Wars* opening title crawl!

way the lead, while the real-estate mogul is downright wicked compared to the mayor in *Jaws*. Billy is a Hooper stand-in, though, and is about to go on a six-month voyage on a research vessel. He even has some of Hooper's lines, explaining that sharks do three things: eat, swim, and make baby sharks.

The shark appears within the movie's first two minutes to chomp on some scuba divers and then sink a boat (via some of the worse miniature shots from *The Last Shark*). However, it's not as exciting as it sounds due to choppy editing—and the editing has to be choppy to mix the footage of several different movies into one.

Overall, this film has the most shameless *Jaws* callbacks of any the rip-offs to come before it. The first is the discovery of a dead body on the beach. Billy is brought in by the sheriff to examine the body and deducts that it was a gigantic Tiger Shark, but the authorities refuse to believe the news. Not only do they refuse to cancel an upcoming regatta, they also try to claim the man died in a boating accident! In many ways, the exchange between Lewis and the Sheriff is a line for line remake of the same scene in *Jaws*! Our next *Jaws* callback has a blonde go for a moonlit swim where she gets eaten by the shark while her boyfriend watches from the beach.[170]

Even *Jaws 3-D* gets ripped off. For starters, there's a significant pair of dolphins in the film, watched over by Susy. And, remember that scene where Sean Brody makes out with Kelly in the lagoon, and Mike sneaks up on them with a bullhorn? Well, even that scene gets recreated with the character of Ronnie!

It's almost pointless to talk about this movie's best shark scenes because they are all lifted lock-stock and barrel from *Deep Blood* and *The Last Shark*. With the footage also comes plot points from the two films. *Deep Blood's* shark hunt, where a shark is shot from a helicopter, is reprised here. And the regatta is written into this film solely to make use of footage from *The Last Shark*. Following the regatta attack—which you might consider to be a great scene if you didn't know it was stolen from a better movie—there's another line for line

---

[170] Actually he does venture into the water before she gets eaten, but he survives the scene.

redo of a scene from *Jaws*. In this case, Billy and the sheriff accost Lewis at the hospital and inform him that he's going to post a $100,000 reward to kill the shark. This doesn't entirely make sense, because Billy plans to kill the shark with or without the money, so it would seem they just wrote the scene in to copy *Jaws*. Oh, and Billy calls Lewis a "fat f----"—can you imagine Roy Scheider saying that to Murray Hamilton?

It's at this point that *Cruel Jaws* is besieged by the pacing issues that plagued *Deep Blood* in its final act, probably because *Cruel Jaws* is copying *Deep Blood* for its own ending. As in *Deep Blood*, some good momentum is established as the heroes take to the sea to kill the shark... and then they come back because of various plot threads. Some of these plot threads are thrown in at the last second, such as the mafia being Lewis's secret backers. I'm pretty sure they were written in just so that more footage from *The Last Shark* could be utilized. In this case, one of the mafia stooges dons some scuba gear and takes it upon himself to kill the shark. Cue the scene from *The Last Shark,* where the shark chomps Vic Morrow's character in half.

Another major plot point is the shark's secret origin. While out on the high seas, Billy and Dag's boat has engine trouble. The other brother, Tommy, dives under the boat to see what the problem is and spies a shipwreck beneath them. Again, this whole scene was written to reuse footage from *Deep Blood*. Unlike that movie, where the shipwreck isn't explained very well, here, Billy claims that the wreck belonged to the U.S. Navy. Billy claims the Navy had raised a shark in captivity and trained it to be a weapon. So, this shark isn't eating because it's hungry, it's just killing because it's a secret weapon! However, this new information in no way makes the ending more exciting. Again, it just sets up the fact that the shark is territorial to the wreck. Hence that's the spot where they will kill it via the *Deep Blood* footage.

Before this happens, there are a few hilariously inept scenes. First up, Ronnie and his friends are all killed while hunting the shark. Ronnie is knocked in the water accidentally via footage from *The Last Shark*. The shark gets him, and as his friends panic, the shark rears its head out of the water. Ronnie's girlfriend, from the best

that I can tell, is either trying to douse the shark in gasoline or wants to throw the gas can in the shark's mouth (maybe she's seen *Jaws 2*?). As she does this, another friend is preparing to shoot the shark with a flare gun. Instead, the girlfriend spills gas on herself and the boat, and the flare ignites the gas and blows up the entire boat rather quickly. It shouldn't be, but in this movie, the scene is an absolute hoot.

Our next big guffaw comes when the sheriff gets it via more footage from *The Last Shark*. The famous scene with the helicopter is used to lesser effect. What makes it even more pathetic is that the chopper pilot says, "We're gonna need a bigger helicopter."

There's really not much to say about the ending if you've seen *Deep Blood* or read the chapter on it in this book. The characters are simply edited into that footage and plant a bomb in the wreckage. The shark apparently eats the bomb—again, the editing is so choppy and terrible, it was all a bit confusing. Whether he ate the explosives or not, the shark does go kaboom as usual. In another nod to *Jaws 3-D*, we end the movie on happy shots of the dolphins doing flips back at the aquarium.

Cruel Jaws was shot in Florida at a location known as Theater of the Sea. Supposedly the budget for the new footage was $300,000 though some of that may have gone towards buying some underwater footage, according to actor Jay Colligan.[171]

Ultimately, the film did dupe some viewers into thinking it was the fifth Jaws movie and is still easy to find on DVD in Europe.

---

[171] Jackson, "An interview with Jay Colligan," Mondo Exploito. http://mondoexploito.com/?p=10922

Bollywood's Lost JAWS Rip-Off
AATANK

Originally Shot: 1980s
Release Date: 1996

Directed by: Prem Lalwani & Desh Mukherjee **Special Effects by:** Sanjay Naik **Screenplay by:** Sachin Bhowmick **Music by:** Laxmikant Shantaram Kudalkar (as Laxmikant), Rameshwer Pyarelal, Ramprasad Sharma (as Pyarelal) & Kamal Singh **Cast:** Jesu (Dharmendra) Peter (Vinod Mehra) Jesu's girlfriend (Hema Malini) Inspector Khan (Girish Karnad)

1.85:1, Color, 113 Minutes

SYNOPSIS Jesu, an orphan, is best friends with a boy named Peter. When Jesu saves Peter's life one day, Peter's mother adopts the boy. In adulthood, the two adopted brothers live in the same fishing village, which lives in fear of an evil mob boss who controls the shores. At the same time, a gigantic shark appears and kills Peter right in front of Jesu. The embittered Jesu makes it his mission to do away with both the shark and the mob boss...

COMMENTARY Ever wonder what *Jaws* would look like made by Japanese special effects technicians in the early 1970s? Well, look no further than *Aatank*, made by Bollywood effects technicians in the early 1980s. *Aatank*, which translates as *Terror* in Hindi, is a movie than can be endured by only the strongest of bad movie fans. Because, in addition to having poor effects—which I thoroughly enjoyed myself, by the way—it's a Bollywood movie. And if you've endured the Bollywood version of *King Kong* (see *Kong Unmade* for that one) then you might have some trepidation over a Bollywood *Jaws*. I know I did.

Lost Film: AATANK

But, for a Bollywood monster movie, you're getting off pretty easy as there's only four or five musical scenes, and it clocks in at under two hours long (the movie in total, not the dance scene). By comparison, this movie is lightyears better than the 2 ½ hour Banglar *King Kong*. You do still get plenty of Indian melodrama though. Within the first ten minutes Jesu is whipped by a priest, Peter falls into a well, Jesu gets adopted by Peter's mother, and in the next scene, the woman is on her death bed! The sequence then concludes with the boys being separated, and we then jump into the future where both are now adults.

As the adult Jesu is Indian superstar Dharmendra, who started out as the lead man in romantic dramas in the 1960s until he switched gears to a big action star in the 1970s. And, speaking of the 1970s, despite the fact that the movie looks like that's when it was filmed, every source that I could find claimed the movie was released in 1996. Furthermore, the 1970s would be exactly the right time to rip off *Jaws*. Finally, I learned that Indian movie producers the Mukherjees started production in either the late 1970s after the success of *Jaws* or some time in the early 1980s—there are conflicting sources. For reasons that I can't uncover, the film was shut down towards the end of production. As it was, most of the film was in the can already aside from a few scenes, (and I know those effects sequences had to come from the 70s or the 80s!).

The giant shark bears down on one of its victims.

Original star Dharmendra saw to it that *Aatank* was finished.

In 1990, the lost film's existing footage came up for auction and was purchased by Bemisaal Productions. At the same time, Dharmendra saw a rough cut of the existing footage at a screening and decided to help finish the film. And literally, there are one or two new scenes of Dharmendra playing the same character even though he is noticeably older! This was done to fill in some gaps within the story, but I think a few bits of narration could have done the trick. That would have been less jarring overall. The other missing scenes were trickier, as the actors who had played those parts had passed on. Therefore body doubles were used to complete certain scenes, while in other cases, new characters altogether were created to fill in the blanks.

When finally released in 1996, it only grossed ₹6,900,000 on a ₹15,000,000 budget. This isn't necessarily surprising considering the quality of the shark effects, either.

As it is, the shark doesn't appear in the context of the story until close to an hour in (but it is glimpsed right away in a freeze-frame for the movie's opening title shot). For the sake of argument, let's say you missed the opening credits with the shark, and you've been watching the movie on TV unaware of the true premise.

You might think that it was a soap opera and nothing more.

For context, you've just watched about 50 minutes of this thing, which appears to be about the relationship between two brothers. We've just completed a very happy, upbeat wedding scene where Peter has gotten married. The newlywed bride and groom run out onto the beach in the midst of a very peppy Bollywood musical number. The wife runs out into the ocean for a swim and the singing continues. But then, the music turns ominous. We cut to a very fake looking seafloor, where what could pass for a shark toy in a bathtub is resting on the ocean bottom. The shark stirs up the mud on the seafloor as it swims towards the girl. Just when you think she's going to get it, we switch back to the happy musical number! Similar to the opening of *Jaws*, the drunken Peter stays on the beach as the beautiful girl swims. Though we saw the shark a few minutes ago—yes, there is several minutes more of singing!—it pops up unexpectedly in the middle of the song to swallow the woman whole! And what a big shark it is and is easily bigger than the one in *Jaws*.

Though scary in spite of the bad effects, I would have to compare these scenes to the killings in *Legend of Dinosaurs*. Overall, there's an odd juxtaposition between the fake-looking monster prop and the exploitive amount of gore from the attacks. Furthermore, every time we see the shark approaching, we hear a tiger's roar!

We get another shark attack scene only five minutes later. This time, Peter and Jesu are out on a small sailing craft (presumably looking for Peter's dead wife) when the shark attacks them. The effects jump back and forth between good and bad here. The scale shark fin and mouth look pretty good, but the full shark body looks like a bathtub toy. This prop jumps out of the water near the boat, causing Peter to fall into the ocean and suffer the same fate as his late wife. It is here, at the hour mark, that the film's central conflict is finally established: Jesu is going to kill the shark that ate Peter.

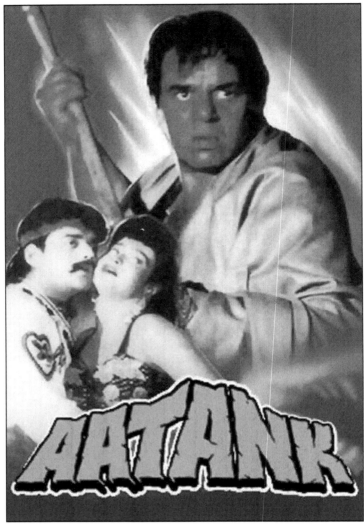

And kill the shark he eventually does. The story's climax consists of Jesu and the Chief of Police going out on a small boat to kill the shark (sound familiar?). At one point, the shark gets the boat's anchor caught in its jaws and pulls the small vessel through the water. This scene also establishes an error in the shark's scale. Whereas earlier it had the dimensions of a Carcharodon Megalodon, in this scene it is the same size as a regular Carcharodon Carcarius.

Aatank's version of the scene from Jaws 2.

The film's ending takes no prisoners. As the soap opera drama continues, Jesu's adopted son and a friend take to the waters on a sailboat at the same time that Jesu is hunting the shark. Naturally, the monster shark (Megalodon sized again) comes along and eats the friend in what is probably the movie's best remembered scene. Jesu's son manages to survive, though (the film's not that cruel).

I should also mention that the film has a badly disconnected subplot about an evil tycoon/mob-man whose been wronging the villagers for the past two hours. At the same time that the shark hunt is going on, he escapes into the waters. Jesu, taking a break from the shark hunt, chases him down. A helicopter comes to the villain's rescue. But then, in an effort to top the scene from *Jaws 2*, the shark lunges out of the water and hits the chopper, which crashes into the bad guy's boat! And it gets even better. The explosion catapults the villain into the air, and with precision aim, Jesu throws a harpoon through him!

Remember the ending of *Free Willy*? Where the Killer Whale leaps over the boy, and he touches the animal's belly as it sails over him? Well, the ending of this movie is like that. The shark jumps over the boat for some reason, and when he does, Jesu digs a harpoon into his stomach. It gets stuck, and so Jesu gets dragged into the water with the massive shark.

The dead shark, a life-size prop, washes up on the beach (Jesu survives, by the way). Once again, the scale is wrong, and it's smaller now than it was before. As the excited villagers rush to the shark, the movie ends.

So, I'll say it again, if you're a *Jaws* completist and/or a fan of 1970s era Japanese special effects, *Aatank* might be enjoyable for you. Otherwise, stay out of the water with this one.

Unleashing
THE BEAST

Broadcast Date: April 28-29, 1996
Alternate Titles: *Peter Benchley's The Beast* (U.S.)

Directed by: Jeff Bleckner **Special Effects by:** Bart Mixon, Tad Prode & Michael Walters (creature molds) **Teleplay by:** J.B. White & Peter Benchley (novel) **Music by:** Don Davis **Cast:** William Petersen (Whip Dalton) Karen Sillas (Lt. Kathryn Marcus) Ronald Guttman (Dr. Herbert Talley) Charles Martin Smith (Schuyler Graves) Missy Crider (Dana Dalton) Sterling Macer Jr. (Mike Newcombe) Murray Bartlett (Christopher Lane) Denis Arndt (Osborne Manning)

1.33 : 1, Color, 176 Minutes / 115 Minutes (edited version)

SYNOPSIS Strange deaths and mysterious incidents plague the fishing community of Graves Point in the Pacific Northwest. A helicopter unit from the Coast Guard, led by Lt. Kathryn Marcus, investigates a distress call from a pleasure craft where the occupants have vanished without a trace. Aiding in the investigation is a fisherman, Whip Dalton, who finds a strange claw embedded in a life raft. Dalton gives the claw to a zoologist, and it finds its way into the hands of Dr. Herbert Talley, an expert on giant squids. Talley and his assistant, Christopher, come to investigate, and eventually, the giant squid shows itself. The harbormaster, Lucas Graves, hires another fisherman to kill the creature, only unbeknownst to everyone he has only killed the giant squid's offspring. The mother reveals itself when it attacks an exploratory sub containing Christopher. To kill the squid once and for all Dalton sets out on his boat with Graves, Kathryn, Dr. Talley, and rich amusement park owner, Osborne Manning, whose intentions are not all that they seem...

COMMENTARY After a big-screen version of *Beast* was ruled to be too costly by Universal, the company had it adapted into a stellar TV movie/mini-series on NBC (a subsidiary of Universal) in 1996. "They hired J.B. White to turn it from a two-hour movie to a four-hour miniseries," Peter Benchley said of the project.[172]

As a TV miniseries, it was positively stellar—in my opinion, at least. In fact, it was so polished I would imagine it was an expensive production as well (which begs the question: why not just make it a theatrical release?). As far as Peter Benchley novel adaptations go, I would place this one between the best (*Jaws* and *The Deep*) and the worst (*Creature* and *The Island*). That said, more tweaks were applied to *The Beast's* adaptation when compared to *Jaws* and *The Deep*, but nor was it as bad as the alterations applied to *Creature* two years later.

For starters, the setting was moved from Bermuda to the Pacific Northwest. I would assume this was done to make the story more relatable to American viewers (and maybe even to draw comparisons to *Jaws,* which was set "close to home" so to speak when compared to faraway Bermuda). This also probably helped to cut down on production costs.

---

[172] King, "That's One Mean Mollusk," *LA Times* (April 28, 1996) https://www.latimes.com/archives/la-xpm-1996-04-28-tv-63810-story.html

From the Bestselling Author of JAWS

PETER BENCHLEY'S
THE BEAST

They said it was safe
to go back in the water.

They were wrong.

🎬 8PM KXAS-TV 5
AN NBC WORLD PREMIERE EVENT!

This version embellishes a bit on an element from the novel that didn't come into play until the novel's ending—that being the beast's offspring. In the mini-series, the baby squid serves as a red herring for the mother. In the book, the giant squid's young weren't revealed until the very end of the story as a surprise twist. The downer of an ending implied the baby squids would grow to adulthood unchallenged due to the lack of competing predators in the area. As for more minor changes, Whip Darling's name has changed to Whip Dalton in the mini-series.

In the mini-series, the titular beast is revealed accordingly, first as an unseen menace stalking a married couple in a raft after their boat sinks. Nothing of the creature is glimpsed in the scene at all. It makes its presence known when, suddenly, the wife is plucked from the raft when the husband has his back turned. Considering that the scene takes place at night it's quite frightening. Unlike a shark, which can only grab you with its mouth while you're in the water, the giant squid can use one of its lengthy tentacles to pluck you from the safety of a boat. This is a rather intriguing difference when compared to *Jaws* that *The Beast* exploits right away.

The first minor reveal of the squid occurs in broad daylight as it swims under a fishing trawler (the fleeting use of CGI is basically well handled here too). The next time we see the squid is via practical effects (thankfully, this is the case throughout most of the series). In the scene, one of the squid's tentacles wraps around an anchor and is very realistic looking. Next, the squid kills two divers, and we see it squeeze one of them to death bloodily.

We don't see the squid's full body until the very end of part one. In the episode's final moments, a fisherman kills what he thinks to be the fully grown squid. This is, of course, confusing for viewers who are wondering why the squid is dead in Part I when Part II is set to air the next night. The mother squid then shows up in all its glory, looking quite good, and teasing what's to come in Part II.

Overall, Part I is essentially an effective teaser to set up the characters and garner sympathy for them. This way, when they are either killed or mauled by the monster in Part II, the deaths will hit home. For instance, Dalton's daughter Dana began a romance with a likable character named Christopher in Part I. In Part II, the submersible containing Christopher and two other men is destroyed by the beast. In the scene, the squid wraps itself around the submersible and crushes it allowing water to flood the vessel and drown the men inside.

Next, the squid wraps its tentacles around a whole fishing trawler on a stormy night and pulls it under. Onboard is Dalton's partner, who has a pregnant wife at home. He survives the encounter with the squid, but it is implied that he will be paralyzed for life. One of Dana's friends is attacked when she goes to see the dead baby squid on display. The adult is lurking nearby and slips a tentacle through an opening into the pool to grab her baby. The tentacle then knocks the girl into the water, though she is not killed. The mama squid then drags her dead young back into the ocean. In this instance CGI is used, and it has to be said it is quite good for a TV movie circa 1996. In fact, it's still as good as or better than more recent efforts from Asylum.

Though certainly not better than *Jaws*, the ending of *The Beast* might just be more epic. The plan set forth by amusement park owner Osborne Manning, so far as everyone knows, is that he will shoot the squid with cyanide injecting spear tips. The dead body will then be towed to shore, and he will take the beast to his amusement park in Texas for display. The plan goes off without a hitch. The squid takes their bait, and Manning shoots it with two spears. However, when towing the creature back to shore, the engine gives out late at night, leaving the crew stranded. Manning then fesses up that he really shot the quid with tranquilizers so that he could take it alive, which naturally enrages Dalton and everyone else. They call the Coast Guard to come rescue them, but that isn't quick enough for the cowardly harbor master, Lucas Graves, who steals the life raft and heads home without everyone else. Dalton goes to cut the tow lines loose, but the squid wakes up. Rather than attacking the boat, once it gets loose, it makes a beeline for the unlikable Graves and kills him first. Then it returns to snatch Manning from off the side of the ship. Like the shark in *Jaws*, the beast launches itself onto the boat and begins grabbing at anyone it can. Dr. Talley is among those ensnared in its tentacles and drawn towards its snapping beak, though we don't see him get eaten.

A coast guard chopper shows up in the nick of time. To kill the squid, Dalton purposely spills several spare gallons of fuel he brought along, letting the gas run down towards the squid. Before he can light it, the squid catches his leg. Kathryn, climbing up the chopper's rescue ladder, begins to descend back down to help Dalton, but he yells at her to fire off her flare gun at the deck. She does, and the ensuing fire causes the squid to let go of Dalton, who climbs onto the ladder. As the chopper flies off, the boat explodes, killing the squid.

Overall, this is a more exciting ending than the one in the book, where a sperm whale attacks the wounded squid. Had this ending been used, this would have made the film comparable to *Tentacles*, which wouldn't be a good thing considering that film's reputation. Speaking of that film, *The Beast* blows it out of the water, though I suppose that should go without saying.

However, not many people compare *The Beast* to *Tentacles*. Most people, naturally, still compare it to *Jaws* since it came from the same author. And there are plenty of callbacks to *Jaws*—even though I would not go so far as to say this is simply *Jaws* with a squid. There's a town hall meeting scene, shots of beautiful girls seen swimming through the ocean from the

SHARK BITES: *THE BEAST* ON VHS

AFTER *THE BEAST'S* SUCCESSFUL BROADCAST IT WAS RELEASED TO VHS. BUT, RATHER THAN RELEASE IT ON TWO TAPES UNCUT, IT WAS SHORTENED DOWN TO 115 MINUTES, EFFECTIVELY REMOVING OVER AN HOUR'S WORTH OF MATERIAL. THE FIRST SCENES TO BE CUT WERE RELATIVELY INCONSEQUENTIAL, BUT A LARGE CHUNK IS EXCISED FROM THE MOVIE REGARDING THE TWO RICH MEN WHO GO SCUBA DIVING AND ARE KILLED BY THE BEAST. A SCENE OF DALTON, KATHRYN, DANA, AND HER FRIEND SWIMMING IN THE OCEAN WHILE THE SQUID LURKS NEARBY IS ALSO REMOVED ALMOST ENTIRELY. THE FOUNDER'S DAY SEQUENCE IS REMOVED, WHICH WAS IMPORTANT TO THE ROMANTIC RELATIONSHIPS BETWEEN DALTON AND KATHRYN AND DANA AND CHRISTOPHER. THE REVEAL OF THE MOTHER SQUID AFTER THE DEATH OF THE BABY IS REMOVED, IN EFFECT MAKING ITS APPEARANCE LATER MORE OF A SURPRISE (WELL, NOT REALLY CONSIDERING THIS ALL HAPPENS MIDWAY INTO THE MOVIE). THE NEXT BIG CUT AMOUNTS TO NINE MINUTES WORTH OF FOOTAGE OF MANNING TRYING TO CONVINCE DR. TALLEY TO LET HIM PARTICIPATE ON HIS NEXT MISSION, DALTON GETTING DRUNK IN A BAR, AND TWO MINOR CHARACTERS GETTING TERRORIZED BY THE MOTHER SQUID, WHO HAS ARRIVED TO RETRIEVE HER BABY'S DEAD BODY. FROM THIS POINT FORWARD, NOTHING OF SIGNIFICANCE WAS CUT.

monster's POV, and scenes of the beach being closed down. One could almost argue that the town's refusal to cancel "Founders Day" is similar to *Jaws*' 4th of July celebration, but really it's not as no festivities take place in the water, and the squid causes no real harm. There's even a callback to *Jaws 2*, which Benchley didn't write, where a mauled whale carcass washes up on the beach.

Upon release, some critics weren't kind to the film. Steve Johnson of *The Chicago Tribune* remarked, "The parallels between the two Benchley books are sufficiently evident to fuel a college course about the ethics of self-plagiarism."[173] While that might be true from a certain perspective, *The Beast* didn't deserve that harsh a criticism. Furthermore, it is still light years better than most theatrical *Jaws* imitators.

---

[173] Johnson, "Benchley's Beast," *Chicago Tribune* (April 26, 1996).

Creating the
CREATURE

Broadcast Date: May 17-18, 1998
Alternate Titles: *Peter Benchley's Creature*

Directed by: Stuart Gillard **Special Effects by:** Stan Winston **Teleplay by:** Rockne S. O'Bannon (based on the novel by Peter Benchley) **Music by:** John Van Tongeren **Cast:** Craig T. Nelson (Dr. Simon Chase) Kim Cattrall (Dr. Amanda Macy) Colm Feore (Adm. Tony Richland) Cress Williams (Tall Man) Matthew Carey (Max Chase) Giancarlo Esposito (Lt. Thomas Peniston) Michael Michele (Tauna) Megalyn Echikunwoke (Elizabeth Gibson)

1.33 : 1, Color, 166 Minutes

SYNOPSIS In the 1970s, government experiments create a shark-human hybrid which escapes from the lab, based on an island in the Caribbean. More than 20 years later, the Creature makes itself known to shark biologist Dr. Simon Chase. The creature runs afoul of the island, terrorizing not only Chase, but also his ex-wife, Dr. Amanda Macy, and their son, Max. Eventually,

Dr. Chase meets Thomas Peniston, the very scientist who created the shark with his own genes. With the help of Peniston, Chase and his family trap the mutant man shark on the island where it was created. Peniston lures the creature into a decompression chamber where he and the creature both perish.

COMMENTARY Presumably, the TV mini-series adaptation of Benchley's 1994 novel *White Shark*, renamed *Creature*, was due to the good ratings received by *The Beast*. Following the same sequence of events as *Beast* production-wise, *White Shark* was first optioned for a theatrical feature, which was then downscaled into a TV mini-series. "*White Shark* was optioned for a feature in 1994, but, again, various studios thought it would be too expensive. So it languished for a while and was finally made into a miniseries for ABC," Benchley recalled.[174] The Benchley Collection at Boston University lists one draft for *White Shark* running 118 pages dated March 25, 1994.

The storyline of the novel was quite different from the mini-series adaptation. In the book, the humanoid shark is the product of Nazi experimentation at the close of WWII. Ernst Kruger, a mad Nazi scientist, has taken an ex-Olympic triathlete turned psychotic SS officer and implanted steel talons and teeth into his body. He alters the man through surgery, giving him gills that enable him to breathe underwater. However, there's a flaw in his design. Once the man-shark resurfaces and goes back on land, he will never be able to return to the water. But it's too late for Kruger's experiment to turn the tide of the war as its coming to a close. As Germany is captured, Kruger puts the creature into a state of hibernation, places him in a sealed casket, and then he and the casket board a Nazi submarine. Said submarine is sunk not long after in the Atlantic.

Years later, divers find the wreckage and open the mysterious casket, releasing the man-beast, which kills them. A string of mysterious killings follows off the coast of Long Island, and Dr. Simon Chase determines that

[174] http://www.peterbenchley.com/articles/peter-benchley-the-father-jaws-and-other-tales-the-deep

whatever the culprit is, it has manmade metallic teeth and claws. Chase isn't able to solve the mystery until he's approached by Holocaust survivor Jacob Franks, who was forced to aid in Kruger's experiments. The man-monster comes on land and continues its killing spree until Chase and Franks trap it within a decompression chamber where they kill it.

In a twist of irony, while *The Beast* was relocated from Bermuda to the U.S. to make it more relatable for U.S. viewers, the opposite happened with *Creature*. As we just discussed, the book was set on Long Island, but the mini-series moved the setting to the Caribbean, where it was filmed on location on St. Lucia (but studio interior sequences were shot in Vancouver). Furthermore, the Nazi experiment during WWII becomes a U.S. military experiment during Vietnam with shades of *Jurassic Park* style bio-engineering that seemed just a little too ahead of its time for the early 1970s.

The character of Dr. Chase at least carries over into the film, but one of the U.S. Army scientists from Vietnam replaces the holocaust survivor.

Though it may have come from the mind of Peter Benchley, *Creature* is pretty far removed from *Jaws*. It's also quite different from *The Beast*. While *The Beast* had a certain cinematic flare that suited the 1990s, *Creature* seems more like a 1950s B-movie right off the bat. This is probably thanks to being set at a typical secret lab common to b-movies coupled with the stilted dialogue for one of the military characters. Other than that, the scenes in the lab are well-done and do a good job of teasing the mysterious creature.

Rather than a shark hunter, we focus on a shark biologist/preservationist. In his first scene, he rescues a pregnant Great White caught on a fisherman's lure. After this, the man shark terrorizes the fishermen. The scene is well played and begins when a boy tossing chum into the ocean drops his headphones. The boat pilot dips his hand deep into the water to get them out, and the shark grabs him and pulls him under. There's even a quick tease of the creature's face in the scene.

Next up, the monster kills a teen that went cliff diving. This further enrages the islanders, who think that Nelson's Great White is to blame. Nelson goes out to investigate, and the Creature tries to climb onto his boat in a very *Creature from the Black Lagoon*-type scene. It ends with Nelson chopping off one of its fingers, and it drops back into the sea.

A famous plot point from *Jaws* is repeated when a shark is killed, and everyone is convinced that the trouble is behind them, though Chase knows better. Part I ends with Chase and his ex-wife coming face to face with the monster in the lab from the episode's beginning. It offers an excellent, unrestrained look at the creature, and overall it works. A scene where it pursues them through darkened corridors is well handled and suspenseful as well. And, considering this shark can open doors when they try to shut it out, it's an interesting twist. The bipedal shark eventually collapses, and they assume it has died from being out of the water for too long. Really, it's just transforming into its next phase and sprouts more capable hands and feet.

Stan Winston's wonderfully realized Creature.

The second installment of the series is a bit more fun and basically has the man-shark on the loose for most of the story. A particularly good scene has Chase's son and the island chief's daughter looking for the beast. He feels something drip down on him from underneath a tree. He looks up into the branches, and the Creature is above him salivating! The two run away to take refuge in a house. It follows them there and bursts up from the floorboards. Scenes of soldiers hunting the monster and getting pulled into the tall reeds would seem to have been inspired by the raptor scene from *The Lost World: Jurassic Park* (1997).

Overall *Creature* was ill-suited for a TV miniseries for two reasons. First, it's not compelling enough for a two-night event, and the two episodes are padded out with needless filler. Second, horror fans might have appreciated the vicious shark monster in an R-rated gore flick unrestrained by TV standards. So, essentially, *Creature* would have likely fared much better as a two-hour theatrical release allowing for more horror and less filler.

SPECIAL SECTION
Ctrl + Alten + Del:
How a Fight with a Critic Turned One Novel into Three by Justin Mullis

Prior to its life as a string of unmade movies and then finally a big budget summer blockbuster starring Jason Statham, *Meg* was a book by author Steve Alten (b. 1959). What some readers may not know though is that there isn't just one version of Alten's *Meg* but rather three. Like George Lucas with the original Star Wars trilogy, Alten has repeatedly made alterations to his novel over the years. However, the reason for these changes may surprise you and it all starts with a bad review…

Alten's debut novel originally hit American shelves as a hardback in July of 1997 under the title *Meg: A Novel of Deep Terror* published by Doubleday (the same publisher who first released Peter Benchley's novel *Jaws* in 1974).[175] The publisher paid the 37-year-old Alten – a Philadelphia native with a wife and three kids working as a general manager at a wholesale meat plant – $2.1 million as part of a two-book deal. This was after his agent Ken Atchity had managed to convince Walt Disney Pictures to sign a $1.5-million-dollar deal for the as-yet unpublished book's film rights on the off chance that they were looking at what could turn out to be the next *Jurassic Park*.[176]

Meg is a sci-fi horror novel about the discovery of a living *Carcharocles megalodon*: a 60-foot-long extinct species of shark that swam the world's oceans roughly 2.6 million-years-ago in shallow tropical seas. The prehistoric shark is discovered in a lost world of warm water at the bottom of the real-life Mariana Trench; the deepest abyss known to man. The hero of the story is

---

[175] *Meg* actually first appeared in German and then Italian several months before its U.S. release, and appeared in the U.K. a few months after.

[176] All biographical information on Alten and the development of *Meg* courtesy of Tim Collies, "A Shark Named Meg," *Sun Sentinel*, June 23, 1997: https://tinyurl.com/ybzoe6pu & Josh Getlin, "They're All Hoping the Public Will Bite," *Los Angeles Times*, July 8, 1997: https://tinyurl.com/yboab8p7

the maverick Jonas Taylor; a super scientist cut from the same cloth as classic pulp heroes such as Doc Savage. Brawn and brains, Taylor is Dr. Benton Quest and Race Bannon rolled into one idealized Alpha Male. A former navy submersible pilot, Taylor's military career came to a tragic end when a sub he was piloting in the Trench was attacked by a megalodon resulting in the death of his crew. Because no one would believe him about the attack, Taylor is blamed for his men's deaths and has, in turn, spent the rest of his life accumulating PhDs in an attempt to show the world that these sharks still exist. When a Japanese expedition to study earthquakes in the Trench accidentally frees one of the sharks from its underwater prison, Taylor finally gets the proof he needs; but not before the meg racks up a considerable body-count.

Alten has said that the idea for *Meg* came to him in 1995 while reading an article in *Time* magazine about deep-sea exploration. He had also read Benchley's *Jaws* as a teenager which is where he first learned about the megalodon.[177] Little known fact, the shark in Benchley's book is explicitly identified as a surviving megalodon by marine-biologist Matt Hooper; a facet of the story largely forgotten due to the 1975 film adaptation in which the creature is merely an extant Great White.[178]

With *Meg* finally published and the prospect of a film on the horizon, everything seemed to be going great for Alten. Then the reviews started coming in.

One of the first reviews, published on July 20, 1997, was from the *Los Angeles Times*. Titled "Jurassic Con," the review savagely attacked *Meg* on multiple fronts ranging from allegations of multiple typos and narrative *non sequiturs* to the opinion that as a horror novel *Meg* failed spectacularly since it was "not the slightest bit terrifying." However the bulk of this bad review focused on the novel's many scientific errors, including Alten's claim that the bottom of the Mariana Trench contains

---

[177] Alten discusses the influence of Peter Benchley's *Jaws* in an interview with Sean McClannahan, "'The Meg' Author Steve Alten On the Long Road to Getting His Monster On the Big Screen," *Bloody Disgusting*, Aug. 10, 2018: https://tinyurl.com/ya8lln76

[178] Peter Benchley, *Jaws* (Ballantine Books Trade Paperback edition, 2013): 257-59.

hydrothermal vents; a plot device used to explain how a warm water lost world could exist below an ocean of cold water – something which is scientifically impossible. Likewise Alten's descriptions of the megalodon and other marine life came under fire as well with the critic claiming that they sounded less like real animals and more like imaginary aliens from another planet.[179]

Who was this critic? None other than Richard Ellis (b. 1938): an acclaimed painter of marine wild life and author of more than 23 books and 100 articles on the subjects of marine biology, paleontology, and mythology. Like Alten, Ellis had spent time in Philadelphia having graduated from the University of Pennsylvania in 1959 and worked for the Philadelphia Zoo as well as the city's Academy of Natural Sciences. Like Alten his big break came in his 30s when he landed a job at the American Museum of Natural History in New York working to fabricate a life-size blue whale model for the museum's up-coming 100th-Anniversary. After that job was completed Ellis stayed with the museum as a researcher in both the marine biology and paleontology departments. He would end up serving as a scientific consultant on Benchley's *Jaws* though he grew to regret the way the book tarnished the reputation of sharks.[180] In 1982 Ellis also joined the now-defunct International Society of Cryptozoology dedicated to proving the existence of monsters like Bigfoot, Nessie, and sea serpents.[181]

No doubt Ellis's negative review of *Meg* struck a nerve for Alten, not least because while carrying out research for his novel Alten had read Ellis's non-fiction book *Great White Shark* (Stanford University Press, 1991) co-authored with John McCosker: Chair of the Department of Aquatic Biology at the California Academy of Science and a key member of the 1975 hunt for the coelacanth

---

[179] Richard Ellis, "Jurassic Con," *Los Angeles Times*, July 20, 1997: https://tinyurl.com/y8nlrbdp

[180] All biographic information about Richard Ellis courtesy of William J. Broad, "Guard of Sea Life, Armed With Pen and Brush," *The New York Times*, Aug. 20, 2012: https://tinyurl.com/yctx5lq3

[181] Richard Ellis' involvement with the International Society of Cryptozoology is discussed in Loren Coleman & Jerome Clark's *Cryptozoology A to Z* (Simon & Schuster, 1999): 82-3.

(a species of fish that until 1938 was believed to have died out alongside the dinosaurs).[182]

Ellis, in fact, made note of his apparent influence on Alten in his review, writing: "And the most embarrassing thing about all of this is that [Doubleday] -- and the author -- are proud of what they have done... For publishing this rubbish, [they] ought to be ashamed... I am more than a little embarrassed to see that in his author's note, Alten acknowledges me and John McCosker for our book 'Great White Shark' as 'an excellent source of information on both Megalodons and great whites.' If 'Meg' is what we spawned, then we ought to be ashamed of ourselves too."[183]

If Ellis's hostility towards Alten's novel seems overblown it is worth pointing out that in his 1994 book *Monsters of the Sea* – amusingly also published by Doubleday – Ellis repeatedly attacks works of both science-fiction and horror which he feels misrepresent marine-life. These ranged from Italian B-movies like *Tentacles* (1977) to Disney's *Pinocchio* (1940); the latter for its depiction of Monstro the whale. In hindsight, Ellis may not have been the best person to ask to review a knowingly pulpy sci-fi novel about a prehistoric shark.

Despite Ellis's contempt for *Meg*, the book became a bestseller. This fact did little to placate Alten, however, who felt the need to defend himself. On August 3, the *Los Angeles Times* ran a rebuttal of Ellis's review penned by Alten, as well as a further response by Ellis. Titled "'Meg' Author Bites Back: Steve Alten vs. Richard Ellis," the rebuttal opens with Alten excusing any typos and errata which Ellis may have encountered in the novel by pointing out that he had been given an "advance reading copy... issued a full eight months prior to the release of the hardback" which hadn't gone through the final stages of editing yet.

However, like Ellis, Alten spills most of his ink on the book's science, in this case defending the claims that megalodons may not have died out before the last Ice Age and that a warm water oasis could possibly exist at

---

[182] All biographic information about John McCosker courtesy of the California Academy of Science: https://tinyurl.com/yd2k42l2

[183] Richard Ellis, "Jurassic Con," *Los Angeles Times*, July 20, 1997: https://tinyurl.com/y8nlrbdp

the bottom of the sea due to the presence of hydrothermal vents. As for any errors having to do with sharks – be they extant or extinct – Alten foists that responsibly off on Ellis since it was his book which he consulted.

Ellis, in his reply, refused to recant, commenting that Alten's excuse that Ellis had "[read] the wrong version of his book seems like a poor defense" of not only bad writing but also the propagation of scientific misinformation. Ellis belabors this latter point by explaining that while hydrothermal vents are known to exist at the bottom of the Atlantic there was (at that time) no evidence of similar vents in the Mariana Trench which is located in the Pacific. Furthermore, Ellis writes that even if such vents were to be found in the Trench they would not result in the creation of a warm water environment since warm water dissipates when pumped out into colder water. Ellis also refuses to accept responsibility for Alten's pseudoscience simply because it was his book which the author consulted, concluding that Alten must "[read] as poorly as he writes" to have come up with such a gross misunderstanding of shark biology.[184]

Formally this concluded Alten and Ellis's public debate, but Alten still wasn't satisfied. In July of 1999 Alten released his sequel to *Meg*, titled *The Trench*, published in hardback by Kensington Books.[185] In the opening chapter, "Deep Pressures," readers are introduced to a character named "Ellis Richards" described as "an obstinate man who preferred the use of bully tactics rather than concede he might be wrong."[186] Obviously it doesn't take a detective to realize who "Ellis Richards" is supposed to be. For the duration of the opening chapter Alten continues to describe his thinly-veiled caricature of Ellis in decidedly unflattering terms before having him unceremoniously killed off by

---

[184] Steve Alten & Richard Ellis, "'Meg' Author Bites Back: Steve Alten vs. Richard Ellis," *Los Angeles Times*, Aug. 3, 1997: https://tinyurl.com/yb6k3pwv

[185] In 2013 Gere Donovan Press released an eBook version of *The Trench* titled *Meg 2: The Trench* and in the UK this book is (amusingly) known as *Meg² : The Trench*.

[186] Steve Alten, *The Trench* (Kensington Books paperback edition, 1999): 11.

a red-eyed kronosaurus; an extinct marine reptile from the time of the dinosaurs which, in another bit of pseudoscience, Alten has equipped with gills like a fish.

Otherwise, *The Trench* is largely a rinse-and-repeat affair. One notable plot development however is the revelation that Taylor's original expedition into the Mariana Trench was part of a covert operation to look for a new renewable energy source which could end the United States' dependency on Middle Eastern oil.[187]

The fact that Alten decided to kill off Richard Ellis in his *Meg* sequel should not come as a total surprise. In a June 1997 interview with the *Sun Sentinel*, Alten was already joking about "taking an author's revenge on his critics" by making them "character[s] in the next book and kill[ing them] off."[188] This was before Ellis had even penned his review of *Meg*. What is surprising however is that Alten felt it necessary to attack Ellis in his fiction again; this time retroactively.

In April of 2008 Apelles Publishing issued a pocket-sized paperback version of *Meg*. This became one of the book's most popular editions featuring a cover of the megalodon killing a T. rex in reference to a scene which actually opens the novel. It was also the first edition of the book to carry the "Soon To Be A Major Motion Picture" tag even though Disney had purchased the rights to the film back in 1996.

While largely identical to the previous editions of *Meg*, the Apelles version contains one notable difference. In the book's second chapter, "The Professor," Alten inserted a scene in which a radio talk show host called "the Turk" challenges Jonas Taylor regarding his claim of hydrothermal vents in the Mariana Trench. Upon hearing the challenge Taylor reflects that: "He had heard excerpts of the Turk's recent interview with Richard Ellis, a painter and self-proclaimed expert on all things nautical who had lambasted Taylor's

---

[187] Also interesting is the decidedly minor plot point that the villain of the novel is being funded by former real-life terrorist Osama bin Laden, this being two years before the 9/11 Terrorist Attacks would make bin Laden an international figure. Steve Alten, *The Trench* (Kensington Books paperback edition, 1999): 376.

[188] Tim Collies, "A Shark Named Meg," *Sun Sentinel*, June 23, 1997: https://tinyurl.com/ybzoe6pu

research." Naturally Alten's protagonist mounts a robust one-sided defense ending with the admonishment that Ellis needs to "do some fact checking...!"[189] This time Alten didn't even bother to hide his attack on Ellis behind an uninventive pseudonym.

While Ellis does not appear to have responded to either of Alten's literary provocations, other critics in the science community did. Paleontological journalist and author Riley Black, in a September 2008 post for the website *ScienceBlogs* asked "Since when is Alten an expert?" Responding primarily to Alten's then-recent appearance on the short-lived History Channel TV series *Jurassic Fight Club* (2008) as an authority on megalodons, Black chides that "pulp fiction authors" do not count as scientific experts let alone ones with "the bad taste to have one of his scientific critics devoured in effigy" referring to the aforementioned scene in *The Trench*. Finally, for good measure, Black also points out another scientific fact which Alten got wrong: megalodon and T. rex did not co-exist.[190]

The Apelles version of *Meg* remained on shelves until December of 2015 when Viper Press put out a "Revised and Expanded Edition" of *Meg* in paperback. This version still contained Alten's jab at Ellis but, in a surprising move, fixed much of the science which Ellis had originally criticized. It even re-worked the opening scene of the megalodon killing a T. rex so that this moment now only existed as a computer simulation developed by Taylor, who makes sure to explain that the two predators never encountered one another. In addition to these scientific corrections, this new version of *Meg* also added new graphics at the beginning and end of each chapter, an additional prologue, and changed several plot points which results in spoiling the aforementioned twist introduced in *The Trench*.[191] One

---

[189] Steve Alten, *Meg : A Novel of Deep Terror* (Apelles Publishing, 2008): 14-15.

[190] Riley Black (formerly Brian Switek and here under the pen name Laelaps), "Since when is Alten an expert?," *ScienceBlogs*, Sept. 3, 2008: https://tinyurl.com/ydacsmrg

[191] To my knowledge there is no "Revised and Expanded Edition" of *The Trench* meaning that the character's surprise regarding the true nature of

thing which did not change was the "Soon To Be A Major Motion Picture" tag as this had still not come to pass. This "Revised and Expanded Edition" of *Meg* has become the default version of the novel, including being the version put out by publisher Head of Zeus to tie-in with the 2018 movie.

Despite going to lengths to correct much of the science in *Meg*, Steve Alten evidently still holds a grudge against Richard Ellis. In a June 2016 newsletter to fans, Alten brought attention to a then-recent CNN report on a new expedition into the Mariana Trench which succeeded in uncovering the presence of hydrothermal vents there. Alten expressed his excitement over this discovery by writing "Hey, Richard Ellis - you just got served!" before proceeding to expound the odd conspiracy theory that the *Los Angeles Times* had deliberately hired Ellis "to do a hatchet job on MEG because the Times reviewer was upset Bantam/Doubleday used the LA Times reviewer's quote on the book."[192] Why the *Los Angeles Times* would be upset that a quote from one of their own critics had appeared on the book's dust jacket and thus decide to hire a well-known and highly regarded naturalist to pen a bad review of said book is anyone's guess, but it sounds about as plausible as a giant extinct shark living in a superheated bubble at the bottom of the sea.

Taylor's mission from the first book now makes little sense. Similar to how the Star Wars prequels ruin the twist that Darth Vader is Luke's father.
[192] Steve Alten, "June 2016 Newsletter," June 2016: https://tinyurl.com/yam2oka8

Justin Mullis is a PhD Candidate in the American Cultural Studies program at Bowling Green State University in Ohio. He also holds a Master's Degree in Religious Studies from the University of North Carolina in Charlotte where he taught classes on the intersection of religion and science-fiction literature and film. His published work includes "Notes from the Land of Light" (*Kaiju and Pop-Culture*, McFarland Press, 2017), "Star Wars: Ritual, Repetition, and the Responsibility of Relaying the Myth" (*The Myth (Re-)Awakens*, Wipf and Stock, 2018), "Cryptid-Fiction! Science-Fiction and the Rise of Cryptozoology" (*Paranormal and Popular-Culture*, Routledge, 2019) and "King Kong: The Delos W. Lovelace Novelization" (*Kong Unmade*, Bicep Books, 2019). Justin has also written for *Adventures in Poor Taste!, G-Fan, Maser Patrol, LovecrafteZine, Henshin Justice Unlimited* and has recorded podcasts for The Film Find.

THE MEG's
Long Journey to the Big Screen

Developed: 1996-2018

COMMENTARY Before Steve Alten even finished his now classic novel *Meg*, Disney acquired movie rights to the project in 1996. Specifically, the book was acquired by Hollywood Pictures, a branch of Disney at the time. After the book was released, it became a big hit. So why wouldn't Hollywood Pictures produce a film while the book was a hot commodity? Unfortunately, it all came down to studio politics. After having drafted what Alten called "two subpar scripts"[193] (reportedly one of them gave the Meg wings!), the head of Hollywood Pictures, Michael Lynton, was fired in 1997.[194] Though Lynton's leaving had nothing to do with *The Meg*, the project was dropped. Ironically, the film wasn't dropped because the new executives thought it would flop. Just the opposite,

[193] McClannahan, "[Interview] 'The Meg' Author Steve Alten," Bloody-Disgusting.com (August 10, 2018)
https://bloody-disgusting.com/interviews/3512319/terror-deep-steve-altens-journey-getting-meg-big-screen-future-monsters

[194] According to the article on Bloody Disgusting he was fired, but more diplomatic sources claim he simply left to pursue a new position at Penguin Publishers.

SHARK BITES: JAWS: THE ORIGINAL MEG?

IN 1997, STEVE ALTEN'S *MEG: A NOVEL OF DEEP TERROR* MADE WAVES AS ONE OF THE FIRST ACTION STORIES TO HIGHLIGHT THE GIANT PREHISTORIC SHARK, THE MEGALODON. PEOPLE OFTEN FORGET THAT HOOPER EXPLAINED THAT THE GIANT SHARK THEY ARE CHASING IN THE *JAWS* NOVEL IS A REMNANT MEGALODON, EVEN IF IT'S NOT AS LARGE THE 60 FOOT PREHISTORIC VARIETY. THIS DETAIL FAILED TO MAKE IT INTO THE FILM VERSION...

they were afraid it had potential, which would mean that Lynton's project would end up being a hit. "It's all about ego," Alten lamented to Bloody Disgusting. "Can you imagine a sports franchise firing its GM and then the new GM coming in and trading all the team's best players just because he didn't draft them?"[195]

As always with the case of Hollywood, there are alternating stories as to why *The Meg* was dropped. Another goes that the film was still in development at Hollywood Pictures even after Lynton left. According to this story, the less than hoped for grosses of *Deep Blue Sea* at the box-office in 1999 sunk *The Meg* at Hollywood Pictures.

Whatever the reasons for cancellation, nothing happened with *The Meg* adaptation again until 2004, when a friend of Alten's learned that he had the screen rights to the book again. The friend, Nick Nunziata, knew Guillermo Del Toro and Lloyd Levin, who worked with Del Toro on *Hellboy*. Del Toro was interested and got the ball rolling by having Alten write a screenplay. *Twister* director Jan De Bont was also called in to help Alten with the script.[196] The project was then taken to New Line, where a frustrating amount of palavering took place between the prospective producers. One of the lesser involved ones was wanting more money, and the deal barely got signed.

Alten's hard work on the script, not to mention his novel, was thrown out the window when New Line had the script rewritten by Shane Salerno (1998's

---

[195] https://bloody-disgusting.com/interviews/3512319/terror-deep-steve-altens-journey-getting-meg-big-screen-future-monsters

[196] De Bont also worked on the original Tri-Star version of *Godzilla* before Dean Devlin and Roland Emmerich. De Bont's version of *Godzilla* was much better, needless to say.

SHARK BITES: *EXTINCT:* THE MINI-SERIES

THE SAME YEAR THAT STEVE ALTEN'S *MEG: A NOVEL OF DEEP TERROR* WAS PUBLISHED, A SIMILAR BOOK, *EXTINCT* BY CHARLES WILSON, WAS RELEASED. IT TOO FOCUSED ON A PREHISTORIC MEGALODON SURFACING IN MODERN TIMES. THE STORY KICKED OFF WITH A SIX YEAR OLD BOY WITNESSING TWO OF HIS FRIENDS GETTING EATEN BY A MONSTER SHARK IN A COASTAL RIVER. HIS MOTHER, CAROLYN HAINES, JUST HAPPENS TO BE A CHARTER BOAT CAPTAIN ON THE MISSISSIPPI GULF COAST. HAINES TAKES UP AN INVESTIGATION INTO THE MATTER AND TEAMS WITH MARINE BIOLOGIST ALAN FREEMAN TO HUNT THE MYSTERIOUS CREATURE ON A KILLING SPREE ALONG THE GULF COAST. LIKE ALTEN'S *MEG*, THIS BOOK'S MEGALODON ARISES FROM THE MARIANAS TRENCH. UNLIKE ALTEN'S BOOK, THERE ARE SEVERAL IN THIS ONE, NOT JUST ONE. BUT IN A RATHER SILLY TURN, THE SHARKS SEEK REVENGE ON HUMANITY WHEN ONE OF THEIR NUMBER IS KILLED, WHICH IS MORE AKIN TO THE SILLY JAWS SEQUELS THAN IT IS REAL LIFE. NOTABLY, THE BOOK WAS OPTIONED BY NBC TO BE A MINI-SERIES. AT THIS TIME, NBC WAS FINDING SUCCESS WITH TV MOVIES AND MINI-SERIES LIKE *THE BEAST*, WHICH WAS PROBABLY ANOTHER FACTOR IN THEIR ACQUIRING *EXTINCT*. ANOTHER REASON NBC DID SO WAS PROBABLY BECAUSE THEY KNEW *MEG* WAS IN DEVELOPMENT AT HOLLYWOOD PICTURES AT THE TIME. IT WOULD MAKE SENSE FOR NBC TO RELEASE A TV MOVIE ON THE SAME SUBJECT DURING THE HYPE FOR THE *MEG* MOVIE WHICH NEVER CAME. IN FACT, THAT COULD BE THE REASON NBC NEVER PRODUCED *EXTINCT*.

Armageddon). Furthermore, new producers were brought onto the project, and Guillermo Del Toro could sense the winds of change and left the prospective movie. And change the project New World did. The new script bore little relation to Alten's novel. This iteration of *The Meg* was inspired by *Moby Dick*, and had the crew of a Japanese whaling ship chasing down the shark. "When I read the first draft, I felt ill because I knew this was a franchise-killer," Alten told Bloody Disgusting.[197] Alten wrote six pages worth of notes, many of them pointing out scientific flaws, and gave them to Shane, who paid them no mind. According to Alten, Shane's next rewrite was even worse and more ambitious, which

---

[197] https://bloody-disgusting.com/interviews/3512319/terror-deep-steve-altens-journey-getting-meg-big-screen-future-monsters

would therefore mean it would also be more expensive. That did not bode well.

Jan De Bont's maquette for New Line's *Meg*. © New Line

Meanwhile, De Bont "invested a substantial amount of money in artwork and mock-ups of how the shark would look like" according to one of the producers, Ken Atchity, as quoted in the *L.A. Times*.[198] As to the mock-up, Alten didn't like it. "It looked like a bonefish. It was horrible," Alten told Wired.com.[199] At this point, the estimated budget was said to be close to or above $200 million, a hefty sum for an as yet untested film franchise. Reportedly, to cut costs, De Bont and Salerno cut a few of the more ambitious scenes. These included the Meg being attacked by a pack of giant Humbolt squids, Meg attacking a helicopter, and Meg eating a surfer. As another cost-saving measure, De Bont thought that he could also shoot inside of 20th Century Fox's massive water tank in Rosarito Beach, where *Titanic* had been filmed.

---

[198] Morgan, "Meg To Get Made?" Cinema Blend (April 11, 2008) https://www.cinemablend.com/new/Meg-Get-Made-8471.html
[199] Raftery, "20-Year Journey of The Meg," Wired.com (August 9, 2018) https://www.wired.com/story/the-meg-movie/

The final nail in the coffin, according to Alten, was due to the fact that, "New Line's foreign rights guy undersold the foreign markets (who really wanted MEG) and, as a result, they couldn't get co-financing."[200]

In 2007, the rights reverted back to Alten, who spent the next ten years on the final road to getting his novel adapted. He did so with Belle Avery (*Before the Devil Knows You're Dead*), who co-wrote the new script with Alten and also helped to secure financing, a good chunk of which came from Gravity Pictures in China. Warner Bros was the final piece of the puzzle, and a version of *Meg* finally made its way onto theater screens in 2018. Not surprising to anyone who's read *The Meg*, it was a hit.

SHARK BITES: ELI ROTH'S *MEG*

ANOTHER STEP IN MEG'S DEVELOPMENT WAS THE HIRING OF ELI ROTH TO DIRECT BEFORE JON TURTELTAUB TOOK OVER. ROTH WANTED TO DO A BLOODIER, R-RATED VERSION OF *THE MEG*, AND SO EVENTUALLY DEPARTED THE PROJECT. AS R-RATED MOVIES TEND TO MAKE LESS MONEY, IT'S NO SURPRISE THAT THE PRODUCERS WANTED TO GO THE PG-13 ROUTE.

[200] https://bloody-disgusting.com/interviews/3512319/terror-deep-steve-altens-journey-getting-meg-big-screen-future-monsters

Direct-to-Video Debacle
JAWS: RISING

Developed: 2007

Screenplay by: John Lansing & Chris Morgan (alleged)
Proposed Cast/Characters: Mike Brody (Marine Biologist) **Proposed Creatures:** Giant Shark/sharks

COMMENTARY Despite *Jaws: The Revenge* being a critical and financial disappointment that was lampooned harder than *King Kong Lives* (1986), every few years, a rumor would arise that another sequel was in the works. While these did usually turn out to be just that—rumors—surely there was some truth to a few of them. After all, no matter how hard a sequel bombs, if the first few entries were mega-hits, the studios behind them will usually give them another try. The *Death Wish* films with Charles Bronson were a prime example of this. As with the *Jaws* series, the first three installments had been hits. But *Death Wish 4* and *5* were both critical and financial disappointments at the box office for Cannon Films. And yet, producer Menahem Golan still wanted to make a *Death Wish 6* to rekindle that old magic one more time.[201] You would be hard-pressed to convince me that at least a few Universal Executives didn't ponder a *Jaws 5* right away...even if we never heard about it.

To the best of my knowledge, concrete rumors of a *Jaws 5* didn't hit until twenty years after *Jaws: The Revenge* in February of 2007. Several different websites reported rumblings of a sequel, though the initial source was a now defunct website called Filmrot.com. Movieweb.com reported that,

> In the Filmrot.com story, which was given to them by a scooper/screenwriter who was apparently asked to pitch ideas for this new Jaws film, it seems that Universal is interested in doing the movie with a "CGI" shark. Also, Roy Scheider, who played Martin Brody in the first two Jaws films will not be coming back.[202]

In direct opposition to the last line, as the rumors continued to fly, Slash Film reported just the opposite, "According to the rumor, the film would completely negate everything that happened in JAWS 3 and JAWS 4 and again have Roy Scheider's character, Brody, returning to do battle."[203]

Ain't It Cool News spread some further interesting details, suggesting that if Scheider didn't come back, the only returning element from the series would be John William's iconic theme. Also, supposedly, Universal wanted *Jaws 5* to go direct to DVD to compete with Warner Bros direct-to-video *Deep Blue Sea 2*.

According to an editorial on Rotten Tomatoes by Scott Weinberg, the new story would not feature Martin Brody. Instead, Mike Brody would return once again as a marine biologist. Brody returns home to Amity Island at the same time that another killer Great White shark runs rampant. Along with Mike are his wife and

---

[201] It would've been called *Death Wish 6: The New Vigilante* and would not have starred Charles Bronson.
[202] Jacobs, "Jaws 5," Movieweb.com (February 8, 2007)
https://movieweb.com/jaws-5-and-van-helsing-2-going-straight-to-dvd/
[203] Sciretta, "Rumor Killer," Slashfilm.com(February 12, 2007)
https://www.slashfilm.com/rumor-killer-jaws-5-goes-direct-to-dvd/

SHARK BITES: KEVIN SMITH'S *JAWS 5*

IN 2014, KEVIN SMITH PITCHED HIS OWN *JAWS 5* IDEA TO MOVIEWEB: "YOU SET IT IN THE PRESENT, AND YOU USE A HURRICANE, AND YOU FLOOD [AMITY]. THEN THE SHARK IS IN THE TOWN. NOT JUST IN THE WATER. BECAUSE, AGAIN, ON THE LAND YOU'RE FINE. BUT ALL THAT IMAGERY FROM HURRICANE SANDY, OF HOUSES UNDERWATER - ADD A GREAT WHITE SHARK. THERE'S YOUR *JAWS*...BECAUSE THEN YOU GOTTA BE ON A ROOFTOP. A SHARK COULD COME INTO YOUR HOUSE, DUDE." I DON'T KNOW ABOUT EVERYONE ELSE, BUT IT SOUNDS LIKE A GOOD *JAWS* SEQUEL TO ME!
HTTPS://MOVIEWEB.COM/JAWS-MOVIE-SEQUEL-KEVIN-SMITH-STEVEN-SPIELBERG/

teenaged daughter. If this was meant to be Thea from *Jaws: The Revenge* is unknown, but if the continuity was correct she would be older than a teenager by 2007. Furthermore, as already stated, there was a desire to ignore the other Jaws sequels...even though Mike Brody would have had a similar job to what he had in *Jaws: The Revenge*!

The screenwriter for the new Jaws, called *Jaws: Rising*, was allegedly John Lansing, a writer-producer of the old Chuck Norris TV series *Walker, Texas Ranger* (1993-2001) among other things. Lansing's script was given to writer Chris Morgan (*Cellular; The Fast and the Furious: Tokyo Drift*). There was no announcement, or perhaps I should really say rumor, as to who would direct or when it would begin shooting.

The initial rumors hit the web on February 7th, and by the 12[th,] they had been debunked by a respected filmmaker in the form of Kevin Smith, who flat out asked a Universal Executive, David Linde, if the news was true.

Smith posted:

Allow me to debunk. I dropped an email to David Linde to ask if this was true, and he said folks are confused: there's an HD "Jaws" DVD on its way, but no "Jaws 5" straight-to-DVD. And if you can't believe Universal's top brass, who can you believe?[204]

---

[204] Ibid.

As it was, the news came amongst another slew of rumored direct to DVD movies, notably *Goonies 2* and *Gremlins 3*. Overall, some fans mourned and others rejoiced that there would be no "Jaws 5." Though this was debunked as a rumor, I personally still think there was some truth to it. Of all the major studios, Universal was one of the more successful ones whereas direct-to-DVD films were concerned. Notable examples included their *American Pie/Wedding* follow-ups and the *Tremors* sequels, all of which were straight to DVD. So, why wouldn't Universal have considered a direct-to-video Jaws movie?

Even after the 2007 direct-to-video debacle ended a rumor would float around about another iteration of *Jaws 5*. Jawsmovie.com, for instance, reported that they heard a rumor about a fifth film focusing on multiple sharks. Specifically, they said, "...there have been rumors of a JAWS 5 in development at Universal. One plot involves a school of great white sharks, with a story similar to Quint's tale about the USS Indianapolis."[205]

An appetite for a fifth Jaws seems to be out there, as evidenced by a number of fan-made trailers on YouTube. Most have a fanaticized concept of Hooper returning, and several use newer movie clips of Richard Dreyfuss to good effect. A few also inserted an older Roy Scheider. All in all, some of them are very well done and almost make one pine for the concept.

Having now been over thirty years since the release of *Jaws: The Revenge*, and with all the talk of remakes, I think it's safe to say that *Jaws 5* is dead in the water for good.

---

[205] http://jawsmovie.com/jaws-5/

Postscript
JAWS: THE REMAKE

Developed: 2010-Present

There comes a time in every franchise's life when studios quit talking about sequels and start talking about remakes or reboots. This usually occurs either because the last few sequels weren't regarded well, didn't make enough money, or even because the lead actors might be getting too old to play their parts. Nowadays, studios reboot franchises left and right (looking at you, Spiderman), but back in *Jaws'* day, that wasn't as common. Back then, you stuck to sequels (and, if you didn't like one of them, you just pretend it didn't happen as in the case of *Jaws: The Revenge* not following *Jaws 3-D*).

Rumblings of a *Jaws* remake began sometime after talk of a *Jaws 5* sequel finally died. The report that gained the most traction came about in the early months of 2010 when it was claimed that Universal was planning to remake *Jaws* in 3-D. This was not planned out of any affinity for 1983's *Jaws 3-D*, though. If you'll recall, this announcement came on the heels of *Avatar's* record-breaking release in December of 2009. Since the film's success was mainly attributed to its 3-D effects, studios began pondering what 3-D films they could produce. Universal immediately thought of *Jaws*.

And what other details surfaced about this alleged reboot? There really weren't any aside from one very intriguing casting rumor: that comedian Tracy Morgan (currently on NBC's *30 Rock*) would play Hooper. Cinema Blend reported the following:

> "A source of ours over at Universal Pictures says the studio is strongly considering a remake of the summer blockbuster in hopes of dazzling younger audiences with new special effects. Their claim is that people now expect more, visually, from their movie going experience. So, Hollywood studios are inclined to take some of their tried and true franchise names like Jaws and bring them into the 3D world. Our insider says Tracy Morgan was at one point being considered for the part of Matt Hooper, previously played by Richard Dreyfuss. While it's uncertain whether that's still the plan, it does indicate that they seem to be taking a more comedic direction with the part."[206]

Tracy Morgan was asked about the rumor by MTV at the premiere of *Cop Out*. "I would love to do a 'Jaws' movie. That was a great, great franchise," Morgan said but then added that he had not yet been asked about the project.

As of this writing, it's now been ten years since the reports of the 2010 3-D remake. If Universal was still quietly developing a *Jaws* remake over the last ten years is unknown, but by 2019 whispers of the Jaws remake began again. This certainly came as no surprise. While there had been a multitude of CGI direct-to-DVD shark movies for the past two decades, more recent theatrical releases like *The Shallows* (2016), *47 Meters Down* (2017), and *The Meg* (2018) proved that audience interest in sharks was still there.

---

[206] Zani, "3D Remake Of Jaws?" Cinema Blend (February 8, 2010) https://www.cinemablend.com/new/Universal-Planning-3D-Remake-Jaws-With-Tracy-Morgan-16954.html

SHARK BITES: *JAWS* SPECIAL CGI EDITION

DURING A 2018 INTERVIEW, RICHARD DREYFUSS MADE THE INTERESTING COMMENT REGARDING A JAWS SPECIAL EDITION. AND BY "SPECIAL EDITION," THEY MEANT OF THE 1997 STAR WARS VARIETY, WHEN THE FILM WAS RERELEASED TO THEATERS WITH NEW AND IMPROVED DIGITAL EFFECTS. DREYFUSS SAID, "I THINK THEY SHOULD DO IT, IT WOULD BE HUGE AND IT WOULD OPEN UP THE FILM TO YOUNGER PEOPLE. IS THAT BLASPHEMY? NO, NO, I DON'T THINK SO. THE TECHNOLOGY NOW COULD MAKE THE SHARK LOOK AS GOOD AS THE REST OF THE MOVIE."
HTTPS://MOVIEWEB.COM/JAWS-RERELEASE-CGI-SHARK-RICHARD-DREYFUSS-WISHES/

Some will cry cinematic blasphemy at the remaking of *Jaws*, but from a historical perspective, remakes don't necessarily tarnish the reputation of the original. The Dino De Laurentiis *King Kong* remake of 1976 received a great deal of vitriol from fans of the original, while many younger fans enjoyed it. It also lead to many of those younger fans deciding to check out the original and see just what it was about. It did not lead to anyone thinking less of the original. In fact, many people had an even greater appreciation for the original *King Kong* after the remake.

This is true with many remakes, reboots, and sequels that many purists claim to taint the original. So long as the original isn't a victim of revisionist history, and isn't forgotten, remakes can only help the films not to be forgotten. So, in summary, no, we do not need a remake of Jaws, but, yes, one day, we will likely see one. It's inevitable. And it most likely won't be as good as the original. But, whatever it is or it isn't, it will help a new generation of viewers discover *Jaws*. You can rest assured of that.

BIBLIOGRAPHY

Articles

Brosnan, John. "A Different Set of Jaws." *You Only Live Once* (2007). https://efanzines.com/YOLO/YouOnlyLiveOnce.pdf

Collis, Clark. "Fishy Business: The behind-the-scenes story of the 'Piranha' movies." *Entertainment Weekly* (August 18, 2010). https://ew.com/article/2010/08/18/cameron-piranha-3d-dante/

Gilliam, Brett. "Peter Benchley: The Father of Jaws and Other Tales of the Deep." PeterBenchley.com http://www.peterbenchley.com/articles/peter-benchley-the-father-jaws-and-other-tales-the-deep

Graham, Aaron W. "Little Shop of Genres: An interview with Charles B. Griffith." *Senses of Cinema* (April 15, 2005).

Jackson, Dave. "An interview with Jay Colligan, star of *Cruel Jaws*." Mondo Exploito. http://mondoexploito.com/?p=10922

Jacobs, Evan. "Jaws 5 and Van Helsing 2 Going Straight to DVD?" Movieweb.com (February 8, 2007). https://movieweb.com/jaws-5-and-van-helsing-2-going-straight-to-dvd/

Johnson, Steve. "Scariest Part of Benchley's 'Beast' May be the Concept." *Chicago Tribune* (April 26, 1996).

King, Susan. "That's One Mean Mollusk." *The Los Angeles Times* (April 28, 1996). https://www.latimes.com/archives/la-xpm-1996-04-28-tv-63810-story.html

Kleiner, Dick. "Writer Peter Benchley Finds 'Deep' Satisfaction." *Galesburg Register Mail* (August 9, 1977). https://newspaperarchive.com/galesburg-register-mail-aug-09-1977-p-5/

Lambie, Ryan. "*Jaws: The Revenge* – How The Sequel Went So Horribly Wrong." Den of Geek. (July 25, 2016). www.denofgeek.com/uk/movies/jaws-the-revenge/42396/jaws-the-revenge-how-the-sequel-went-so-horribly-wrong?

McClannahan, Sean. "[Interview] *'The Meg'* Author Steve Alten On the Long Road to Getting His Monster On the Big Screen." Bloody-Disgusting.com (August 10, 2018). https://bloody-disgusting.com/interviews/3512319/terror-deep-steve-altens-journey-getting-meg-big-screen-future-monsters/

Morgan, Jason. "Meg to Get Made?" Cinema Blend (April 11, 2008) https://www.cinemablend.com/new/Meg-Get-Made-8471.html

Naha, Ed. "Bert Gordon's Creature Features," *Starlog* #16 (September 1978).

------------ "Piranha." *Starlog* #18 (December 1978).

Pergament, Alan. "Attack of the Giant Squid." *The Buffalo News* (April 25, 1996). https://buffalo-news.com/1996/04/26/attack-of-the-giant-squid/

Pound, Roscoe. "New World's Monsters." *Famous Monsters* #160 (1980).

Raftery, Brian. "The 20-Year Journey of The Meg, the Movie the Internet Wouldn't Let Die." Wired.com (August 9, 2018). https://www.wired.com/story/the-meg-movie/

Rutkowski, Gary. "Joseph Sargent Interview." Archive of American Television. (March 9, 2006).

Sciretta, Peter. "Rumor Killer: Jaws 5 goes Direct to DVD." Slashfilm.com (February 12, 2007). https://www.slashfilm.com/rumor-killer-jaws-5-goes-direct-to-dvd/

Swires, Steve. "John Sayles: From Hoboken to Hollywood Part II." *Starlog* #94 (May 1985).

Tucker, Reed. "Clooney and a killer bear — the movie you may never see." *New York Post* (June 29, 2014) https://nypost.com/2014/06/29/the-star-studded-film-youll-probably-never-see/

Uncredited. "The Bite of the Devil Fish." *Starlog* #20 (March 1979).

Walker, Wes. "Nessie: The Loch Ness Monster Part Two." *Dark Terrors* #16 (1998).

BIBLIOGRAPHY

Wroclavsky, Damian. "Killer whales bring the hunt onto land." Science News (April 16, 2008). https://www.reuters.com/article/us-argentina-orcas-feature/killer-whales-bring-the-hunt-onto-land-idUSMAR71901420080417

Zani, Dave. "Universal Planning A 3D Remake Of Jaws With Tracy Morgan?" Cinema Blend (February 8, 2010) https://www.cinemablend.com/new/Universal-Planning-3D-Remake-Jaws-With-Tracy-Morgan-

Books

Clarke, Arthur C. *Greetings Carbon-Based Bipeds: Collected Essays, 1934-1998.* St. Martin's Griffin, 2001.

Danforth, Jim. *Dinosaurs, Dragons & Drama: The Odyssey of a Trickfilmmaker - Vol. 2* (CD-ROM). Archive Editions, 2015.

Jankiewicz, Patrick. *Just When You Thought It Was Safe: A Jaws Companion.* Bear Manor Media, 2015.

Koetting, Christopher T. *Mind Warp: The Fantastic True Story of Roger Corman's New World Pictures.* Midnight Marquee Press, Inc., 2018.

Loynd, Ray. *The Jaws 2 Log.* MCA Publishing, 1978.

McNeil, Dustin & J. Michael Roddy. *Adventures in Amity: Tales From The Jaws Ride.* (By the Authors, 2018).

Meikle, Denis. *A History of Horrors: The Rise and Fall of the House of Hammer.* Scarecrow Press, 2008.

Nashawaty, Chris. *Crab Monsters, Teenage Cavemen, and Candy Stripe Nurses: Roger Corman: King of the B Movie.* Harry N. Abrams, 2013.

Smith, Michael A. and Louis R. Pisano. *Jaws 2: The Making of a Hollywood Sequel.* Bear Manor Media, 2018.

Weaver, Tom. *Science Fiction Stars and Horror Heroes: Interviews With Actors, Directors, Producers, and Writers of the 1940s Through 1960s.* McFarland Publishing, 1991.

Websites

Defunctland. "The History of Jaws: The Ride." YouTube Video, 2017. www.youtube.com/watch?v=qO7dslkMbF0&t=311s

Gilbert Gottfried's Amazing Colossal Podcast! with Frank Santopadre. "Joe Dante." (February 8, 2016). https://www.gilbertpodcast.com/1494-2/

Yesterworld Entertainment. "The Jaws Ride You Never Got To Experience." YouTube Video, 2017. www.youtube.com/watch?v=yBsYVDlYkhs

www.grizzly2revenge.com

http://jawsmovie.com/jaws-5/

INDEX

INDEX

JAWS UNMADE

About the Author

Jaws Unmade is John LeMay's 20th book overall. He is the author of several lost film histories such as *Kong Unmade: The Lost Films of Skull Island*; *The Big Book of Japanese Giant Monster Movies: The Lost Films* and *Terror of the Lost Tokusatsu Films*. He is also the editor and publisher of *The Lost Films Fanzine*, published quarterly. LeMay also writes on the history of the Old West, with a focus on folklore. Some of these titles include *The Real Cowboys and Aliens* series with Noe Torres, *Tall Tales and Half Truths of Billy the Kid*, and *Cowboys & Saurians: Dinosaurs and Prehistoric Beasts as Seen by the Pioneers*. He is a frequent contributor to magazines such as *G-Fan*, *Mad Scientist*, *Xenorama*, *True West,* and *Cinema Retro*.

JOHN LEMAY

KONG UNMADE
THE LOST FILMS OF SKULL ISLAND

FOR MORE LOST FILMS CHECK OUT
THE LOST FILMS FANZINE (PUBLISHED QUARTERLY)

Printed in Great Britain
by Amazon